THE SUPERPOWERS
A NEW DETENTE

Opposing Viewpoints®

Other Books of Related Interest in the Opposing Viewpoints Series:

American Foreign Policy
Central America
China
Israel
Japan
Latin America and U.S. Foreign Policy
The Middle East
Nuclear War
Problems of Africa
The Soviet Union
Terrorism
The Third World
The Vietnam War

Additional Books in the Opposing Viewpoints Series:

Abortion
AIDS
American Government
American Values
America's Elections
America's Prisons
Animal Rights
Biomedical Ethics
Censorship
Chemical Dependency
Civil Liberties
Constructing a Life Philosophy
Crime and Criminals
Criminal Justice
Death and Dying
The Death Penalty
Drug Abuse
Economics in America
The Environmental Crisis
Euthanasia
The Health Crisis
Male/Female Roles
The Mass Media
The Political Spectrum
Poverty
Religion in America
Science & Religion
Sexual Values
Social Justice
Teenage Sexuality
War and Human Nature

THE SUPERPOWERS
A NEW DETENTE

Opposing Viewpoints ®

David L. Bender & Bruno Leone, *Series Editors*

Karin Swisher, *Book Editor*

OPPOSING VIEWPOINTS SERIES ®

Greenhaven Press, Inc.   PO Box 289009   San Diego, CA 92128-9009

Library of Congress Cataloging-in-Publication Data

The Superpowers : a new detente : opposing viewpoints / Karin Swisher, book editor.
    p.   cm. — (Opposing viewpoints series)
Includes bibliographical references.
Summary: Presents opposing viewpoints on the changes in the relationship between the United States and the Soviet Union in the era of Glasnost.
    ISBN 0-89908-418-4. — ISBN 0-89908-443-5 (lib. bdg.)
    1. United States—Foreign relations—Soviet Union. 2. Soviet Union—Foreign relations—United States. 3. Cold war. 4. Detente. 5. United States—Foreign relations—1989- 6. Soviet Union—Foreign relations—1985- [1. United States—Foreign relations—Soviet Union. 2. Soviet Union—Foreign relations—United States. 3. Cold war. 4. Detente.] I. Swisher, Karin, 1966-   . II. Series.
E183.8.S65S93   1989
327.73047—dc20   89-36525
                                                                      CIP
                                                                       AC

"Congress shall make no law . . . abridging the freedom of speech, or of the press."

First Amendment to the US Constitution

The basic foundation of our democracy is the first amendment guarantee of freedom of expression. The *Opposing Viewpoints Series* is dedicated to the concept of this basic freedom and the idea that it is more important to practice it than to enshrine it.

Contents

Chapter 5: Is Peace Between the Superpowers Possible?

Why Consider Opposing Viewpoints?

"It is better to debate a question without settling it than to settle a question without debating it."

Joseph Joubert (1754-1824)

The Importance of Examining Opposing Viewpoints

The purpose of the Opposing Viewpoints Series, and this book in particular, is to present balanced, and often difficult to find, opposing points of view on complex and sensitive issues.

Probably the best way to become informed is to analyze the positions of those who are regarded as experts and well studied on issues. It is important to consider every variety of opinion in an attempt to determine the truth. Opinions from the mainstream of society should be examined. But also important are opinions that are considered radical, reactionary, or minority as well as those stigmatized by some other uncomplimentary label. An important lesson of history is the eventual acceptance of many unpopular and even despised opinions. The ideas of Socrates, Jesus, and Galileo are good examples of this.

Readers will approach this book with their own opinions on the issues debated within it. However, to have a good grasp of one's own viewpoint, it is necessary to understand the arguments of those with whom one disagrees. It can be said that those who do not completely understand their adversary's point of view do not fully understand their own.

9

A persuasive case for considering opposing viewpoints has been presented by John Stuart Mill in his work *On Liberty*. When examining controversial issues it may be helpful to reflect on this suggestion:

> The only way in which a human being can make some approach to knowing the whole of a subject, is by hearing what can be said about it by persons of every variety of opinion, and studying all modes in which it can be looked at by every character of mind. No wise man ever acquired his wisdom in any mode but this.

Analyzing Sources of Information

The Opposing Viewpoints Series includes diverse materials taken from magazines, journals, books, and newspapers, as well as statements and position papers from a wide range of individuals, organizations and governments. This broad spectrum of sources helps to develop patterns of thinking which are open to the consideration of a variety of opinions.

Pitfalls To Avoid

A pitfall to avoid in considering opposing points of view is that of regarding one's own opinion as being common sense and the most rational stance and the point of view of others as being only opinion and naturally wrong. It may be that another's opinion is correct and one's own is in error.

Another pitfall to avoid is that of closing one's mind to the opinions of those with whom one disagrees. The best way to approach a dialogue is to make one's primary purpose that of understanding the mind and arguments of the other person and not that of enlightening him or her with one's own solutions. More can be learned by listening than speaking.

It is my hope that after reading this book the reader will have a deeper understanding of the issues debated and will appreciate the complexity of even seemingly simple issues on which good and honest people disagree. This awareness is particularly important in a democratic society such as ours where people enter into public debate to determine the common good. Those with whom one disagrees should not necessarily be regarded as enemies, but perhaps simply as people who suggest different paths to a common goal.

Developing Basic Reading and Thinking Skills

In this book, carefully edited opposing viewpoints are purposely placed back to back to create a running debate; each viewpoint is preceded by a short quotation that best expresses the author's main argument. This format instantly plunges the reader into the midst of a controversial issue and greatly aids that reader in mastering the basic skill of recognizing an author's point of view.

A number of basic skills for critical thinking are practiced in the activities that appear throughout the books in the series. Some of the skills are:

Evaluating Sources of Information   The ability to choose from among alternative sources the most reliable and accurate source in relation to a given subject.

Separating Fact from Opinion   The ability to make the basic distinction between factual statements (those that can be demonstrated or verified empirically) and statements of opinion (those that are beliefs or attitudes that cannot be proved).

Identifying Stereotypes   The ability to identify oversimplified, exaggerated descriptions (favorable or unfavorable) about people and insulting statements about racial, religious or national groups, based upon misinformation or lack of information.

Recognizing Ethnocentrism   The ability to recognize attitudes or opinions that express the view that one's own race, culture, or group is inherently superior, or those attitudes that judge another culture or group in terms of one's own.

It is important to consider opposing viewpoints and equally important to be able to critically analyze those viewpoints. The activities in this book are designed to help the reader master these thinking skills. Statements are taken from the book's viewpoints and the reader is asked to analyze them. This technique aids the reader in developing skills that not only can be applied to the viewpoints in this book, but also to situations where opinionated spokespersons comment on controversial issues. Although the activities are helpful to the solitary reader, they are most useful when the reader can benefit from the interaction of group discussion.

Using this book and others in the series should help readers develop basic reading and thinking skills. These skills should improve the reader's ability to understand what they read. Readers should be better able to separate fact from opinion, substance from rhetoric and become better consumers of information in our media-centered culture.

This volume of the Opposing Viewpoints Series does not advocate a particular point of view. Quite the contrary! The very nature of the book leaves it to the reader to formulate the opinions he or she finds most suitable. My purpose as publisher is to see that this is made possible by offering a wide range of viewpoints which are fairly presented.

David L. Bender
Publisher

11

Introduction

"Communism destroys democracy. Democracy can also destroy communism."

André Malraux, 1958.

Cold War and *detente* describe two opposing points on the spectrum of superpower relations. The term Cold War defines the adversarial relationship that encouraged the US and the USSR to amass the largest number of nuclear weapons in the world. Detente defines the brief periods of cooperation that have interrupted the Cold War and precipitated restraints in this military buildup. In 1985, Mikhail Gorbachev ushered in a new, and some say, the most significant period of detente when he became the general secretary of the Communist Party of the Soviet Union. Gorbachev has made extensive internal economic and political reforms including improving human rights conditions, withdrawing troops from Afghanistan, and proposing massive weapons cuts. In fact, many people argue that Gorbachev is actively wooing the West through these reforms. In a 1986 speech he said, "We can never be secure while the US feels insecure."

Many government officials and scholars believe Gorbachev's reforms signal an end to the Cold War. Author and superpower scholar Richard J. Barnet has said, "The principal conditions that more than forty years ago precipitated the deadly contest have fundamentally changed. The Soviet Union is not the secretive, paranoid, totalitarian state that it was in Stalin's time." Barnet and others believe that Gorbachev's reforms have fundamentally changed the Soviet Union. These supporters argue that the US should respond by increasing economic and political ties with the USSR. But others disagree.

Some policy experts regard the changes in the Soviet Union as superficial. Soviet expert Arnold Beichman, research fellow at the Hoover Institution at Stanford University in California, states, "The biggest task is to realize that what stands in the way of world peace and freedom is the Soviet political system." Beichman and others, including former president Richard Nixon and former secretary of state Henry Kissinger, think that Gorbachev's reforms are not being made to solicit peace, but because they are an economic and political necessity for the USSR. The US should not

13

be fooled, they believe, because as long as the USSR remains a communist state, the Cold War must continue. They hark back to the Communist Manifesto, which states that communism will eventually dominate the world. Because of this, the US should refuse new arms treaties or trade agreements with the USSR, these critics conclude.

While the question of whether the world is witnessing an end to the Cold War is debatable, the concept is a phenomenon that must be addressed. In 1983, Greenhaven Press published *The Arms Race* at a period of heightened superpower tension. *The Superpowers: A New Detente* reflects the radical change in the issues facing the US and USSR today. The topics included are Is the Cold War Over? Do the Superpowers Intervene in Other Countries? How Has the New Detente Affected Arms Control? Is More Economic Cooperation Between the Superpowers Possible? and Is Peace Between the Superpowers Possible? It remains to be seen whether the superpowers can achieve some kind of lasting peace or will continue to oppose each other philosophically, economically, and politically.

Is the Cold War Over?

Chapter Preface

With Ronald Reagan's election in 1980, US-Soviet relations distinctly chilled. During the campaign Reagan had emphasized the need to contain Soviet influence. One month before he took office, the Soviet Union invaded Afghanistan. Two years into his presidency, Reagan labeled the Soviet Union "an evil empire." Soviet leaders responded by calling Reagan a "warmonger."

By the end of the Reagan presidency, however, superpower relations had significantly improved. The US and the USSR had had four summit meetings and they had established a groundbreaking arms control treaty that allowed on-site verification. When George Bush took office in 1989, many observers believed his task was not to contain the Soviets but to match and effectively respond to Mikhail Gorachev's new calls for improved relations.

US-Soviet relations have dramatically changed from high tension in the early 1980s, to cooperation at the end of the decade. Does this signify the ending of the Cold War? The following chapter addresses this question.

"The Cold War is outdated."

The Cold War Is Over

George Kennan, interviewed by *New Perspectives Quarterly*

In 1947 George Kennan wrote what has been called the most in-fluential essay in the history of US foreign policy. Appearing in *Foreign Affairs,* and mysteriously identified as written by "Mr. X," Kennan's analysis outlined the Cold War frame of mind that has dominated American foreign policy toward the Soviet Union for forty years. Kennan reconsiders US-Soviet relations in the following viewpoint, excerpted from an interview conducted by the magazine *New Perspectives Quarterly.* Kennan contends that under Gorbachev, the USSR has become much less isolated and much more interested in genuine arms control and peaceful rela-tions with other countries. Kennan is a former diplomat and is now Professor Emeritus at the Institute for Advanced Study in Princeton, New Jersey.

As you read, consider the following questions:

1. Why does Kennan believe the Soviet threat to the world is an exaggeration?
2. According to Kennan, how does the US know the Cold War is over?
3. What relationship should the US and the USSR develop now that the Cold War is over, according to the author?

George Kennan interview, "Obituary for the Cold War," *New Perspectives Quarterly,* Summer 1988. Reprinted with permission.

N_{PQ}: Back in the late 1940s, you argued that two factors made the world a dangerous place: the end of the British and French empires which resulted in the polarization of power between the US and USSR and the "fanatic faith" of Soviet communism seeking to impose its authority globally. Hasn't all that changed? Hasn't the trend of history, the "correlation of forces," shifted decisively in favor of the West?

George Kennan: The trend has shifted to the West. But only in this sense: Compared with 1947, Western Europe has been stabilized, and Moscow's domination of the world Communist movement has been thoroughly shattered—primarily (but not entirely)—by the defections of Yugoslavia and Communist China.

Polarization of Power

The defection of Communist China in the late 1940s undermined the polarization of power. By the 1950s, the sharp bipolarity began to break down and has continued ever since. Some of us tried to draw attention to this more than 30 years ago, but had little success in overcoming Western stereotypes.

At any rate, the phrase "correlation of forces" is confusing because many people tend to give it a purely military connotation—as though this were all that mattered in relations among states. Military power is valuable only to the extent it can be translated into political realities. And this, as we and the Israelis and the Russians have all learned from recent experiences, is not always easy to accomplish.

NPQ: You have long been regarded as the key American figure who best understood the "nature" of the Soviet system.

Under Gorbachev, has the nature of the Soviet system changed in ways that no longer render it an inevitable threat to the West?

Kennan: What kind of a threat—military or political? It is important to distinguish.

I have never thought of the Soviet Union as a military threat to this country—except during the time of the Berlin blockade. Even then, Soviet motives were primarily defensive. Otherwise, since the Second World War, I have seen no evidence of Soviet desire or intention to attack us or our allies.

No Soviet Threat

The Soviet Union was a serious political threat only in the immediate aftermath of World War II, primarily because Western Europe was politically and economically unstable. Since Western Europe recovered (largely through the Marshall Plan), the Soviet Union has scarcely been a political threat to us.

A number of people in the entourages of both Presidents Carter and Reagan have seen a threat in Russia's developing closer military-political relations with a number of Third World countries. But, with the partial exception of Cuba, I don't agree with this view.

Since, for the last four decades, I have never seen the Soviet Union as a serious threat to us, it is hard for me to say whether the Gorbachev reforms have made it less of one. However, no Soviet leader has had less incentive than Gorbachev to muddy the international waters by threatening the United States.

The task of internal economic and political reform he has taken upon himself is gargantuan and extremely difficult. Accomplishing it will require every ounce of energy and attention he can give. No international complication or tension can fail to detract from the success of his effort, and hence be unwelcome to him.

Gorbachev's program, to be sure, does not envisage any fundamental change in the system (although it may, if he is not careful, unintentionally lead to something like that). But even if it did, it would not make the Soviet Union less of an "inevitable threat." That it has not been, and need not become.

NPQ: The strategy of containment sought to achieve several objectives "short of war:" to block the expansion of Soviet power; to expose the falsities of Soviet pretentions; to induce a retraction of Kremlin control and influence in the world; and to foster the seeds of destruction within the Soviet system so as to modify its behavior to conform with accepted international standards.

After the Cold War

The Cold War is over, but American leaders lack the imagination to turn this new reality into policies that serve our national interest. They seem unable to envisage a post-Cold War world.

The principal conditions that more than 40 years ago precipitated the deadly contest have fundamentally changed.

Richard J. Barnet, *Los Angeles Times*, June 6, 1988.

Have these objectives been achieved? If so, is their achievement primarily the result of the internal evolution of the Soviet system, or a result of US containment policy?

Kennan: As first conceived in the "X-article," the strategy of containment embraced the hope, and envisaged the possibility, that it would lead to a "mellowing" of the rigidities of Stalinist power, and to lead to a Russia which would be easier for us to deal with.

Stalin's Death

This is precisely what has occurred. The change began with Stalin's death. It has been slow, but it has never been insignificant. And today, under Gorbachev's influence, it is advancing

19

faster than ever.

These changes are primarily the result of forces operating within Soviet society: the general dislike of the Stalinist system (even within the Party); the change of the generations; the influence of the non-Russian nationalities within the Soviet empire—including the Jews; and the gradual recognition on the part of many people (outstandingly Gorbachev himself) that the remaining Stalinist rigidities were seriously undermining the Soviet system and making it uncompetitive with the advanced countries of Asia and Europe.

To the extent that we have tended to over-militarize our relationship with the Soviet Union, we have been more of a hindrance than a help to this "mellowing" process. It was my view, in writing the "X-article," that not only would this process of change have to occur as a response to indigenous impulses from within Soviet society, but that this was the only way it could come if it was to be healthy and lasting.

Stalin's Rigidities

NPQ: What do you mean by "Stalin's rigidities?"

Kennan: I'm referring to the terrorism which affected the people closest to power even more than the mass of the population. The Party itself abhorred Stalin's terror. The people around Stalin were immensely relieved when he died. If he hadn't died when he did, they would have surely tried to pull themselves together and remove him. Everybody hated government by terror.

This feature of the Soviet system is gone. There is simply no comparison between the Gorbachev era and the Stalin years.

NPQ: As long as the one-party system remains, can the nature of the Soviet system truly change?

Kennan: The Soviet system will remain an authoritarian system with one-party rule. Nobody is considering changing that.

But, within that framework, things have changed a great deal and are continuing to change.

NPQ: Is the Soviet system beyond reverting to Stalinism?

Kennan: I don't think it could possibly revert to Stalinism.

Soviet Bureaucracy

Brezhnev's death marked the end of the period of Stalinist influence. There are very few remnants in the Soviet bureaucracy that remain loyal to Stalinist principles. Very few.

There are some people who would like to return to Brezhnevism, but every serious person in the senior ranks of the Party realizes that even this is impossible. Even Mr. Ligachev, the man considered to be Mr. Gorbachev's chief opponent, realizes that there is no returning to what existed in 1978. He's committed to *perestroika*. After all, the whole country had gone downhill by the end of Brezhnev.

NPQ: In 1948, you were concerned that a devastated economy and the rising power of communists in Japan would enable the Soviet and Chinese revolutionaries to exploit the power vacuum which would result from the departure of US occupation forces. . . .

You wrote then that Japan's economic potential should once again be permitted to become an important political and economic force in the area, conducive to peace and stability. You even criticized MacArthur's breakup of the *zaibatsu* as a policy "eminently agreeable to anyone interested in the future communization of Japan."

The Cold War

Not only is the Cold War over, but it's been over for much longer than anyone acknowledges. And we've won it. That's the easy part.

John Steinbrunner, quoted in *Los Angeles Times*, December 10, 1988.

Well, those who want to break up the *zaibatsu* today are more concerned with the future of America's ability to compete than the rise of communism in Japan.

Does this irony suggest that our policy of containment worked so well that we created a new set of problems for ourselves?

A Political-Economic Balance

Kennan: In 1947, I and others saw that it was necessary to strengthen the economies of Japan and Western Europe in order to create a proper political-economic balance with the Soviet Union. Now, we are at a point where this is creating serious problems of a different nature.

But these problems are serious only to the degree of failure of our own competitive economic power posture. Even at their worst, present problems of economic competition are not as serious as the problems which confronted us in the immediate aftermath of World War II. If we had been able to foresee the current situation in 1947, I think we would have still felt it necessary to do what we did at that time.

NPQ: Is the INF [Intermediate-Range Nuclear Forces] Treaty, the prospect of a 50% reduction in strategic nuclear arsenals, and the withdrawal from Afghanistan primarily a result of Reagan's buildup and negotiation from strength, or Gorbachev's bold initiatives?

Kennan: The Soviet acceptance of the INF Agreement and the withdrawal from Afghanistan were overwhelmingly the result of decisions that Gorbachev and those around him made. Changes in the American military posture that occurred over these last years had very little to do with those decisions. In the case of Afghanistan, I would say nothing at all.

NPQ: How should the US relate to a Soviet Union that has mellowed? Should we keep up the pressure of a "containment" type of policy? Or should we accommodate *perestroika* by loosening up trade and technology restrictions?

Kennan: In 1947, containment was devised against the political threat of international communism under Stalin's control, especially the communist parties in France and Italy. Those parties are in no sense a danger today.

In short, the notion of containment is today irrelevant.

Accommodating Perestroika

NPQ: Would you venture to put a new name on what our strategy toward the Soviet Union should be today?

Kennan: We should regard our relations with the Soviet Union today as being relations with a normal great power which is the heir to the congenital problems of the Russian empire. The communist aspect of it all has very little to do with the Soviet Union today.

The Marxist-Leninist ideology is a stale and sterile ritual to which lip service must be given because it is the only ostensible source of legitimacy for the Communist Party in Russia. Beyond that, nobody takes it seriously.

Mr. Gorbachev and his chief ally in the Politburo, Aleksandr Yakovlev, believe in socialism but not in communism in its world revolutionary sense. That is clear. The whole rhetoric of communism that existed from Stalin to Brezhnev has now been abandoned.

NPQ: Should we encourage the flow of capital and technology?

Limit Sensitive Technology

Kennan: Yes. Of course we must limit the flow of technology that has sensitive military aspects to the Soviet Union or to any great power that is not an ally of this country.

But beyond that we shouldn't attempt to influence the course of events in Russia very much. I don't think we can be successful in that, and I don't see why we should try to make things more difficult for Mr. Gorbachev.

It is completely in our interest that Mr. Gorbachev succeed in his program of liberalization.

NPQ: Can US public opinion and the politicians let go of the Soviet bogeyman as the defining point of our world view?

Kennan: That is a very good question. I am skeptical about that possibility.

A large segment of the American population has the need to cultivate the theory of American innocence and virtue—which must have an opposite pole of evil.

Doonesbury

BY GARRY TRUDEAU

NPQ: When will the Cold War be over?

Kennan: I feel very strongly that the extreme military anxieties and rivalries that have marked the high points of the Cold War have increasingly lost their rationale. Now, they are predominantly matters of the past. The Cold War is outdated.

Of far greater importance are areas which demand collaboration between the Soviet Union and the United States.

Of these, I would cite global environmental deterioration; the need to control the revolution in electronic communication; North-South economic relationships; and the situations in the Near and Middle East. Compared with the dangers these situations present, the perceptions of danger that inspired the Cold War pale into insignificance.

NPQ: Aleksandr Yakovlev said similar things . . . in Moscow: "The world has become multi-polar. It has become interwoven and interdependent with the revolution in electronics. With nuclear weapons, war has become impossible. Ecologically, the world is interdependent."

Are men like Yakovlev and Gorbachev sincere?

Kennan: They are sincere. In adapting to the new global realities—especially the fact that military competition is less and less important in the affairs of great powers—they are more serious than people in high positions in this country.

We have a community of interests with the Soviets. The Soviet leaders today see this.

New Realities

NPQ: Have the Soviet leaders succeeded better than our own leaders in stepping out of the Cold War frame of mind and adapting to new realities?

Kennan: Yes. They don't have to deal with a public opinion which can only be changed very, very slowly.

What worries me more than whether Gorbachev has changed the Soviet Union for the better is the American media's persistent dramatization of Cold War myths and stereotypes. The Soviets dropped the Cold War mentality. Now, it's up to us to do the same thing.

"The causes of the cold war—Moscow's domination of Eastern Europe and aggressive foreign policies around the world—still endure."

The Cold War Is Not Over

Richard Nixon

Richard Nixon was the nation's vice president from 1953 to 1960 at the height of the Cold War. He was president of the US from 1969 to 1974. He is the author of seven books; the latest, *1999*, was published in 1988. In the following viewpoint, Nixon asserts that the Soviets have designed the reform program, perestroika, to enhance their national security and advance their global influence. The Soviet threat to the world remains, but is more subtle, argues Nixon. Thus, the Cold War continues.

As you read, consider the following questions:

1. What problems in the Soviet Union prompted Gorbachev to initiate a system of reforms, according to Nixon?
2. According to the author, what does Gorbachev hope to achieve with his reform program and how should the US respond?
3. How do the reforms broaden Soviet influence around the world, according to Nixon?

Richard Nixon, "American Foreign Policy: The Bush Agenda," *Foreign Affairs*, Winter 1988/1989. Copyright © Richard Nixon.

After almost half a century, the communist world's leader, President Mikhail Gorbachev, has undertaken dramatic changes within the Soviet bloc that give the free world's leader, President George Bush, another historic opportunity to enhance the West's security and to effect a sea change in the U.S.-Soviet relationship. Gorbachev's policies of glasnost and perestroika have been hailed, even by some hard-line Western leaders, as heralding the end of the cold war. While his reforms give reason for a reappraisal of the West's policy toward the Soviet Union, we must bear in mind that the causes of the cold war—Moscow's domination of Eastern Europe and aggressive foreign policies around the world—still endure. Those who urge the West to "help Gorbachev" with low-interest loans and subsidized credits fail to realize that such actions are not in our interest until he makes an irrevocable break with the Kremlin's past policies.

An opportunity now exists to make genuine progress toward a more stable peace. President Bush can exploit this opportunity if he takes a hard-headed look at the Soviet Union under Gorbachev and devises a policy that presents the Kremlin leaders with intractable strategic choices. We must make Gorbachev choose between a less confrontational relationship with the West and the retention of his imperial control over Eastern Europe, between a continuing race in arms technology and arms control agreements that could create a stable strategic *and* conventional balance, and between access to Western technology and credits and continuing Soviet adventurism in the Third World. . . .

Gorbachev's Reforms

Gorbachev has launched his reforms and pursued a more conciliatory approach to the West because the communist economic system failed at home and the Soviet Union's foreign policy became counterproductive abroad. The centrally planned economy of the Brezhnev era has become a monument to corruption and inefficiency. Brezhnev's militarism and expansionism not only mobilized the West to strengthen its armed forces but also gave the Soviet Union a severe case of imperial indigestion after it gobbled up Third World countries. By the early 1980s, Moscow's clients in Afghanistan, Cuba, Nicaragua, Vietnam, Angola and Ethiopia cost the Kremlin at least $20 billion a year to keep in power. It is a mistake to think that only Gorbachev would have initiated a reform program, for these realities would have forced whoever came to power into rethinking Soviet domestic and foreign policy.

Unlike his predecessors, Gorbachev sees the world without ideological blinders. He has realistically assessed the Soviet Union's enormous economic, political, imperial and geopolitical problems. First, he recognizes openly that the Soviet economy has stagnated, with negligible or even negative growth rates since the late 1970s. Without economic reform and access to Western technology and capital, the Soviet Union will fall hopelessly behind the United States, Western Europe, Japan and—perhaps as early as the middle of the next century—China.

Second, Gorbachev initiated his economic reforms—perestroika—because he knows that the Soviet people can no longer be motivated with political slogans. The increased East-West contacts of the détente era and the revolution in mass communications have rendered futile the Stalinist strategy of isolation and ideological indoctrination. Today, the Soviet people are aware that their standard of living—cramped housing, endless food lines and empty store shelves—compares unfavorably not only with that of the West but also with those of the newly industrializing countries of the Third World. Gorbachev knows that only material incentives, not ideological exhortations, will induce the people to work harder. They will produce more only if they can actually purchase decent consumer goods with the additional rubles they earn.

The Cold War Continues

The Cold War is not yet over, and the U.S. would be foolish in the extreme to let its guard down one single centimeter.

Allan H. Ryskind, *Human Events*, May 6, 1989.

Third, Gorbachev knows that economic failure and political repression have created seething unrest throughout the Soviet empire that could erupt at the slightest provocation. Time bombs lie just below the surface ready to explode, not only in virtually all his East European satellites but also in many of the non-Russian republics of the Soviet Union itself. Through glasnost, he has tried to create a safety valve to defuse this pent-up frustration, but by venting these angers he may have let the genie out of the bottle. He will find that demands for pluralism in Eastern Europe and greater national autonomy for the non-Russian peoples are difficult to control. Ironically, Soviet leaders used appeals to nationalism to expand their empire into the Third World. Now nationalism threatens to tear that empire apart.

Fourth, as Gorbachev surveys the global political scene, he must be struck by the fact that instead of improving the Soviet Union's position in the world, the Kremlin's foreign policy has managed to unite all the world's major powers against Moscow. The United States, Canada, Western Europe, Japan and China—which together account for over 60 percent of the world economy and which pose the threat of a two-front engagement in any world conflict—have cooperated actively for more than 15 years in opposing Moscow's traditional expansionist ambition. Moscow's old thinking led to a dead end, so Gorbachev has launched his "new thinking" in foreign affairs to loosen the bonds of, or break up, that anti-Soviet bloc.

Fifth, Gorbachev, as a communist, instinctively believes in the importance of the battle of ideas, but as a realist, he knows that the Soviet Union has lost that battle. Around the world—not only within the Soviet bloc but also in Africa, Asia and Latin America—Soviet socialism is perceived as the road to stagnation, not prosperity. It still appeals to those who want to seize and hold power but not to those who want to build a better life for their people. Through his reforms, Gorbachev seeks to create a new model and image for socialism and to give the communist ideology a second wind.

Reinvigorating Communism

Gorbachev's goal is to reinvigorate his country's communist system, to make the Soviet Union a superpower not just in military but also in economic and political terms. Without sweeping reforms, he will not be able to afford the costs of the Soviet military establishment and of Soviet client-states, to provide the Soviet people with a better life, to create a model that can be competitive in the global ideological battle and to keep the Soviet Union in the front rank of world powers. . . .

Gorbachev faces a profound philosophical dilemma: he can choose ideology or progress. If he chooses communism, he cannot have progress; if he chooses progress, he cannot have communism. Only by abandoning the ideology that is the bedrock of his power can he produce progress that will match that of the West. . . .

We must keep Gorbachev's reforms in perspective. He does not want to overturn the Soviet system; he wants to strengthen it. To paraphrase Churchill from another context, Gorbachev did not become general secretary to preside over the demise of the Communist Party. We have an interest in the success of his reforms only to the extent that they change the system to make it less threatening to our security and interests. We should applaud glasnost and perestroika but not pay for them, for if his reforms do not irrevocably alter Soviet foreign policy we will be subsidizing the threat of our own destruction.

No End to the Cold War

Those who parrot today a fashionable slogan—"the cold war is over"—trivialize the problems of Western security. Gorbachev's public relations experts have made many Western policymakers forget that a more benign Soviet image does not mean a more benign Soviet foreign policy. As a result, the race to Moscow is already on. Western leaders have jetted off to the Kremlin with planeloads of eager bankers and industrialists in tow, and Soviet leaders have gleefully lined up more than $10 billion in easy credit. Unless the West steps back and designs a coherent strategy, we will squander our leverage and lose the historic opportunity presented by events in the Soviet Union. . . .

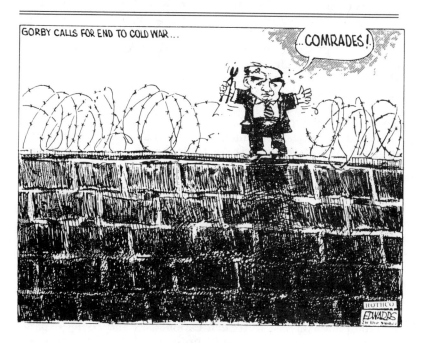

© Edwards/Rothco

We should design a common approach to the problem of Eastern Europe. The cold war began in Eastern Europe, and it will not end until Moscow's satellites receive their independence. In the past, it has always been in the West's interest, but not in Moscow's, to address the issue of Eastern Europe. Today, since Gorbachev needs East-West economic links and reduced tensions for perestroika to succeed, a new settlement is in the Kremlin's interest as well.

We have to recognize that the situation we face now is infinitely more complex than the one we faced at the outset of the cold war forty years ago. At that time, the threat was as clear as Stalin's Iron Curtain and his belligerent rhetoric about the inevitability of war, all of which enabled President Truman to prevent a return to isolationism, adopt a policy of containment and win bipartisan support for entry into NATO [North Atlantic Treaty Organization] and unprecedented levels of peacetime defense spending.

Gorbachev has brilliantly changed the game. In Europe, he has discarded the traditional Soviet tactics of diplomatic bluster and military threat and has mastered those of deceptive propaganda and political maneuver. He has substituted the wiles of diplomacy for the threat of force as his chosen instrument for foreign policy conquests. As a result, at a time when Soviet superiority in conventional military forces and in accurate landbased intercontinental ballistic missiles [ICBMs] is larger than ever before, he has made more progress toward the traditional Soviet objective of dividing the NATO alliance than any of his predecessors. We cannot counter his "peace offensive" simply by loudly warning about the military threat of Moscow's Red Army. Instead, we must launch our own political offensive to achieve our strategic and geopolitical objectives. . . .

Without a political settlement in Eastern Europe, no stable, enduring improvement in East-West relations is possible. Post-war history is the story of continual attempts by the East Europeans to wrest their freedom from Moscow. The workers' uprising in East Germany in 1953, the popular rebellion in Hungary in 1956, the Prague Spring in 1968, the Solidarity movement in Poland in 1980, and the scores of other smaller incidents of open opposition all testify to the popular determination to be free. All these outbursts had to be suppressed directly or indirectly by Soviet arms, and all those interventions destroyed the prospects for an immediate improvement in East-West relations.

That pattern could soon recur. Eastern Europe has become an economic and political powder keg waiting to blow up. Today, the tectonic plates of East European nationalism and Soviet expansionism have built up enormous pressure as they have pushed against each other. We have seen the first tremors in the rise of East European dissident and reform movements. But a political earthquake is inevitable in the 1990s. If Moscow responds with military force, it will mean a return to sharper tensions in East-West relations and an abortion of Gorbachev's reforms. . . .

Gorbachev's Aspirations

In the short run, we can sympathize with the thrust behind many of Gorbachev's aspirations. We both want to reduce military competition and the danger of nuclear war. We certainly should applaud those of Gorbachev's reforms that reduce, even marginally, the repression and poverty which plague the people of the Soviet Union. At the same time, we must keep in mind that in the long run the goals of the two sides diverge diametrically. Gorbachev wants reform because he wants a stronger Soviet Union and an expanding Soviet empire. We should support those reforms in the hope of making the Soviet Union less repressive at home and less aggressive abroad.

"As the Soviet Union opens to the outside world after centuries of self-imposed insularity, the United States' policy should be to encourage that opening."

US-Soviet Cooperation Should Increase

Thomas M. Magstadt

The Soviet reforms, known as perestroika, can provide new political and economic opportunities for the United States, according to Thomas M. Magstadt. Magstadt argues in the following viewpoint that these reforms are unlike any others in the history of the Soviet Union. He asserts that the US should increase trade with the USSR, encourage Soviet involvement in the resolution of regional conflicts, and encourage new arms control initiatives. Magstadt is chairperson of the political science department at Kearney State College in Kearney, Nebraska.

As you read, consider the following questions:

1. According to the author, what changes should the US pressure the USSR to make?
2. What advantages do the Soviet economic reforms hold for the US, according to Magstadt?
3. What link does Magstadt see between the Soviet economy and its military? How does that link affect the US?

Thomas M. Magstadt, "Gorbachev and Glasnost—A New Soviet Order?" Cato Institute's *Policy Analysis*, March 20, 1989. Reprinted with permission.

As the Soviet Union opens to the outside world after centuries of self-imposed insularity, the United States' policy should be to encourage that opening, in part by redoubling efforts to expand cultural and scientific exchanges, student exchanges, and economic and commercial ties. The Soviet Union should be pressured to open areas presently off limits to U.S. tourists (in return for similar concessions by the United States), to accept more U.S. students into Soviet universities (on a reciprocal basis), and to lift existing restrictions on Soviet travel abroad. If Gorbachev means what he says about "openness"—if the Kremlin has nothing to hide from the outside world and no longer wants to hide the outside world from its own citizens—why should easy travel back and forth between Moscow and Paris or Leningrad and New York (for their citizens as well as for ours) not be possible?

Gorbachev should also be pressured to tear down the longstanding barriers to Western ideas, fashions, films, music, books, magazines, and newspapers. As two keen observers of the Soviet reform movement, Henry S. Rowen and John B. Dunlop, have suggested, "The United States should make full use of Radio Liberty and the Voice of America and other communications."

At the same time, the Soviet Union should be encouraged to export the products of its own diverse cultures. Competition in the cultural arena would benefit East and West alike. The publication of an English language edition of the *Moscow News* is a start. Soviet films, documentaries, tapes, records, and the like should be available to Western consumers as well. The Soviet Union encompasses more than a hundred ethnic groups. As a consequence, no other country displays a more impressive and colorful mosaic of indigenous cultures. American culture is avidly "consumed" in the USSR; conversely, there is no obvious reason why the products of Soviet cultures would not appeal to consumers in the West.

Emigration Restrictions

The U.S. government should encourage and facilitate private efforts to petition the Soviet Union on behalf of religious groups, national minorities, political prisoners, refuseniks, and others. Many Soviet national minorities, especially Latvians, Lithuanians, Estonians, Ukrainians, and Armenians, have vocal émigré support groups here in the United States. The same holds true for religious denominations such as Russian Orthodox, Roman Catholic, Baptist, and Pentecostal. In this regard, the cooperation between the State Department and the Jewish community in urging Moscow to lift restrictions on Jewish emigration could serve as a model.

Similarly, careful attention should be given to ways the United States can support the efforts of other Western nations to focus on continuing human-rights violations in the Soviet Union and Eastern Europe. Thus, for example, the United States should make known its support for Vatican efforts to focus attention on the plight of Ukrainian Catholics, for Israeli efforts on behalf of Soviet Jews, for West German efforts to negotiate greater freedom of movement for East Germans, or even for Hungarian efforts to bring the persecution of Hungarians in Romania to light.

The Romanian case is instructive concerning the effectiveness of possible U.S. tactics to encourage reform. The United States granted Romania most-favored-nation (MFN) treatment in 1975, largely to reward Bucharest for pursuing a foreign policy independent of Moscow. Romania's human-rights record, however, has been among the most deplorable in Eastern Europe (most observers agree that it has actually gotten worse since 1976). In 1988, a measure to withdraw Romania's MFN status was introduced in Congress; in Feburary 1988 the Romanian government, faced with growing pressure from the White House as well as the Congress, preempted the issue by renouncing its right to MFN treatment before the United States could withdraw it. As a result, the United States now has less influence with the Romanian government than it once had. What did the United States gain by withholding MFN treatment for over two decades, then granting it for more than a decade, then threatening to withdraw it? Are Romania's ill-treated evangelical Christians better off now that Romania's exports to the United States—which totaled a paltry $775 million in 1988—will be reduced by a third or so?

Gorbachev's Initiatives

Mr. Gorbachev's initiatives mean the United States can end its single-minded obsession with the Soviet Union as a target or a partner. An assertive and dynamically pragmatic foreign policy might well serve America best in the 1990's.

Dimitri K. Simes, *The New York Times*, December 27, 1988.

On the contrary, it seems likely that if there is any connection between trade and human rights—and the connection is tenuous at best—it works the other way. The more East-West trade, the more influence the United States and the West European nations are likely to be able to exert through both public and private diplomatic channels.

The West should look more broadly at the whole range of commercial and financial ties. If the Soviet Union and its Warsaw Pact allies want to do business with Western corporations (if they want to attract Western capital and technology), the way to do it is to decentralize their economies and democratize their political

33

systems. The best insurance policy Western firms can have against arbitrary changes in rules affecting ways of conducting business in Soviet bloc countries is a diffusion of political power. Restructuring economies of those countries is a necessary step. But as long as the levers of power remain in the hands of an oligarchic party, Western assets can be seized at any time without warning, due process, or just compensation (an enduring lesson of the October Revolution and its offspring).

In the absence of fundamental political reforms in the Soviet Union and Eastern Europe, the U.S. government should urge the business and banking community to proceed cautiously. The government should also make it clear that companies investing in politically unregenerate Communist countries will do so at their own risk.

In other areas of mutual interest to the superpowers—including regional conflicts, arms control, and European security—the Gorbachev thaw presents new opportunities and possibilities. The Soviet withdrawal from Afghanistan is one indication of movement away from previous expansionist positions. But Afghanistan may not be the only place where Gorbachev seeks conflict resolution and is willing to make concessions to get it. In Central America, for example, Moscow's ardor for Nicaragua's Ortega regime appears to be cooling. In the Middle East, it is worth exploring whether Gorbachev is willing to play a constructive role—perhaps by urging Syria and the Palestine Liberation Organization (among others) to recognize Israel as part of a larger regional peace plan.

The festering Indo-Pakistani conflict is another area in which progress toward peace is possible with superpower collaboration. Gorbachev's visit to India in November 1988 underscores the continuing friendship between Moscow and New Delhi. In Pakistan, the electoral victory of Benazir Bhutto, coupled with the traditionally close ties between Islamabad and Washington, presents new opportunities for the United States to exert a positive influence. South Asia is a region especially ripe for a joint superpower effort aimed at fostering negotiations to bring about regional peace. Moreover, success in one region might set a precedent and provide the momentum needed for successes in other regions.

Client States

There is mounting evidence that Moscow is applying pressure on client states, from southern Africa to Southeast Asia, to end costly conflicts that impose an undesirable burden on the Soviet treasury. The apparent success of a U.S.-mediated peace plan in Angola and Namibia may serve as a model for settlements elsewhere. Cuba has agreed to withdraw its 50,000 troops from Angola; South Africa has reportedly proposed giving the Soviet

Union a role in the verification process for troop withdrawal. The Soviet Union was no doubt instrumental in urging both Cuba and Angola to accept the plan, just as the United States is prevailing upon South Africa to do so.

Western Reaction

The fate of Gorbachev's reforms depends on the reaction of the West to a greater extent than is generally realized. The Western powers, particularly the United States, are now facing the first promising opportunity in forty years to reconsider their strategic objectives and the division of postwar Europe itself. So far, they have been unable to arrive at a unified policy. . . . If the Western countries have the courage and imagination to engage in a similarly deep rethinking of their own strategic goals, the prospect could open up of a world order based not on superpower rivalry but on international cooperation.

George Soros, *The New York Review of Books*, June 1, 1989.

In Indochina, Vietnam has recently displayed a new flexibility concerning Cambodia, where Hanoi has maintained a puppet government for nearly a decade. Soviet support for Hanoi's hegemonic policies in Indochina has been the major stumbling block to improved Sino-Soviet relations, as well as an irritant in U.S.-Soviet relations. The guerrilla war, which has smoldered in Cambodia since Vietnam crushed the blood-thirsty Pol Pot regime in 1978-79, will very likely not end unless Hanoi agrees to give up control in Cambodia. Having subsidized Vietnam heavily for more than two decades, Moscow now appears to be exhorting Hanoi to reduce its external liabilities and get its economic house in order: precisely the formula Gorbachev himself is following.

Arms control presents still another set of opportunities and possibilities. The Intermediate-Range Nuclear Forces [INF] Treaty signed in November 1987 was a sign of Moscow's need to reduce superpower tensions and decelerate the arms race. The connection between *perestroika* and strategic arms reduction is suspected in the West but until recently unconfirmed by the government. The connection underscores the fact that breakneck military spending is sharply at odds with Gorbachev's number one policy priority: economic revitalization. Thus, a reasonable supposition is that not only might Moscow now be willing to negotiate a sharp reduction in existing strategic nuclear arsenals, but Gorbachev might be amenable to measures leading to future cuts in military spending. These measures are not necessarily confined to sophisticated nuclear-weapon delivery systems: significant reductions in conventional forces—still the most expensive for both sides—should also be given high priority by the administration.

Gorbachev's December 7, 1988 offer to make unilateral cuts in Soviet conventional forces (including 500,000 troops and 10,000 tanks) was a step in the right direction, albeit a small one. Apart from the recent Soviet move, there has been no restructuring of Soviet conventional forces in Europe since Gorbachev came to power in 1985; moreover, the Soviet Union continues to act like a nation addicted to the arms race, despite soothing assurances to the contrary.

Conventional Weapons

According to General John Galvin, the Soviet Union is producing 700 combat aircraft, 10 nuclear submarines, and 3,400 advanced T-80 tanks per year. (The Warsaw Pact currently has 30,000 more tanks than NATO [North Atlantic Treaty Organization].) If these figures are accurate, Gorbachev has been smiling at the West with iron teeth. Accordingly, any future conventional arms control talks must focus on the need for sharp cutbacks in the *production* of new battlefield weapons as well as in the reduction of existing weapons. (Any plan should also include the huge Soviet stocks of ammunition in East Germany and Czechoslovakia.)

Such concerns underscore the continuing importance of European security issues to peace and prosperity on both sides of the ideological divide—all the more reason for the Bush administration to undertake new initiatives in this area. Mutual and balanced force reductions (MBFR), as well as a variety of confidence-building measures, may now be possible. While it would be foolish to think that every diplomatic *demarche* directed at Moscow will succeed, it would be even more foolish to forgo the possibility of success by assuming failure.

The signing of a new human rights accord at the beginning of 1989 paves the way for conventional arms talks in Europe. . . . The accord is evidence that winds of change are indeed stirring in the Soviet Union, and clearly the initiative came from Moscow. The leaders of East Germany, Czechoslovakia, Romania, and Bulgaria want economic concessions from the West; they still defer to Moscow in foreign policy, but they are hardly eager to expand human rights. The police breakup of a demonstration in Prague only one hour after Czechoslovakia had signed the new agreement was as a reminder that old habits die hard, as was Romania's brazen disclaimer, which served notice that its signature was not to be taken seriously. . . .

Diplomatic Means

How can the United States keep the pressure on Gorbachev to continue restructuring the Soviet economic and political system? Above all, Washington can work assiduously *by means of diplomacy* to enhance security interests of the West. Proposing that the NATO alliance be *gradually* dismantled while insisting that the Soviet Union reciprocate by dismantling the Warsaw Pact would allow the United States to take the diplomatic high ground at a time when arms control is at or near the top of both superpowers' agendas. The reciprocal dismantling would also allow the Bush administration to seize the initiative in promoting superpower military disengagement from Central Europe.

Dissolving Alliances

Gorbachev might view such an initiative as an opportunity to disengage from Eastern Europe in an orderly and honorable way. The possibility—indeed the likelihood—that pressures for democratization in Poland and Hungary (and perhaps in Czechoslovakia) will sooner or later threaten Communist rule in those countries is no doubt a matter of grave concern to Gorbachev. A new American proposal to dissolve the two alliances in Europe would probably add fuel to the fires of reform in the East bloc countries. But a simultaneous disbanding of NATO and the Warsaw Pact would give Gorbachev a face-saving way out. He could formally disavow the Brezhnev Doctrine (which justified Soviet military intervention on grounds of "socialist internationalism"). In so doing, he could stress that the Soviet Union is now practicing what it preaches—namely, noninterference in the internal affairs of other countries. This gesture would not only appear magnanimous but would also greatly enhance Gorbachev's international image as a new kind of Soviet leader.

Moving forward with a new approach to European security might, in time, obviate the need for both superpowers to continue spending more and more money on new, expensive, conventional weapons systems. Success in this enterprise is not a matter of military capabilities so much as a matter of politics and diplomacy. If the United States has an Achilles' heel, it is certainly not our armed might. It is our post-World War II tendency to rely on "nuclear diplomacy"—surely an oxymoron if ever there was one.

The Soviet reforms are incomplete to be sure. But a close examination points to the conclusion that they are quite promising—more so than any other reforms since the Bolshevik Revolution. In these new circumstances, old nostrums will not do. The United States' posture should be one of caution combined with creative diplomacy. Policymakers must avoid the tendency to believe that the limits of diplomacy associated with the Cold War are immutable laws of nature. The INF Treaty, the withdrawal from Afghanistan, and Gorbachev's highly publicized diplomatic meetings with every major Western leader in the closing months of 1988 all suggest that Moscow is in a mood to negotiate.

VIEWPOINT

4

"U.S. policy toward the Evil Empire should be a total boycott—no aid, trade, 'cultural exchanges,' or any kind of assistance."

US-Soviet Cooperation Should End

James J. Drummey

In the following viewpoint, James J. Drummey argues that the Soviet Union and the United States should remain enemies despite Soviet reforms. He argues that aiding or encouraging perestroika would be counterproductive and dangerous for the US. Drummey is senior editor of *The New American*, a conservative weekly newsmagazine.

As you read, consider the following questions:

1. What, if any, indication has the Soviet Union given that its reform program is genuine or long-lasting, according to Drummey?
2. What stance does the author take on the subject of increased trade with the USSR?
3. Why does the author believe increased relations will endanger US security?

James J. Drummey, "Building the Evil Empire," *The New American*, July 20, 1987. Reprinted with permission.

For 70 years, the U.S. government, under Republican and Democratic Presidents, has financed the economic and military development of the Soviet empire. We have created and sustained a Communist monster that has already gobbled up nearly half the world, that has made plain by words and actions that it intends to consume the rest of the globe, and that has forced the American taxpayer to come up with $300 billion a year supposedly to defend ourselves against this ravenous creature.

But isn't it a contradiction and an absurdity to spend this huge amount of money on defense when at the same time our political-industrial-financial complex is providing equipment, technology, food, and loans to build up the enemy whose global designs require this vast expenditure? We have for decades been in the bizarre position of helping both sides in what ought to be as clearly defined a conflict between good and evil as has ever existed in human history. American political leaders have at times used rhetoric that seemed to indicate a cogent understanding of the Communist enemy, but their policies have seldom lived up to their words.

As a result of years of aid to and trade with the Communists, we are now confronted with what Antony Sutton has called "the best enemy money can buy." Mr. Sutton has meticulously researched and written five books detailing Free World assistance to Soviet dictators from Lenin to Gorbachev. It is a shocking story and one that is not well known by many Americans. The purpose of this article is not to review the history of the past seven decades—Sutton and others have done that very competently—but to describe the situation today.

Communist Countries

While much of the information about exports to Communist countries, as well as the names of the companies and business executives involved, is either classified or virtually impossible to get, there has been enough information in the media over the past few years to identify the principal aiders and traders who are leading America into national suicide. They may have enriched themselves by putting profits ahead of patriotism, but they have gravely endangered the free society that enabled them to become successful businessmen. Their manipulations and machinations need to be exposed and halted before the darkness of totalitarianism blankets the entire world.

At a news conference nine days after he entered the White House in 1981, President Reagan was asked whether he thought the Soviet Union was still "bent on world domination" or whether "under other circumstances détente is possible." Here is Mr. Reagan's reply:

Well, so far détente's been a one-way street that the Soviet

Union has used to pursue its own aims. I don't have to think of an answer as to what I think their intentions are. They have repeated it. I know of no leader of the Soviet Union since the revolution and including the present leadership that has not more than once repeated in various Communist congresses they hold, their determination that their goal must be the promotion of world revolution and a one-world socialist or Communist state, whichever word you want to use.

Now, as long as they do that and as long as they at the same time have openly and publicly declared that the only morality they recognize is what will further their cause, meaning they reserve unto themselves the right to commit any crime, to lie, to cheat, in order to attain that . . . I think when you do business with them, even as a détente, you keep that in mind. . . .

Steve Kelley. Reprinted with permission.

If the words are true—and 70 years of history demonstrate conclusively that they are true—then the actions are either foolish or, worse, sinister. America's political leaders know and understand the criminal nature of the enemy, and they support the annual expenditure of $300 billion to defend their country against the enemy. Why then do they also support building up the enemy? As Senator William Armstrong (R-CO) has pointed out: ''America's budgetary woes would not be nearly so severe if our economy were not groaning under the stress of financing two military budgets: our own and a significant portion of the Soviet Union's."

In the same speech from which the previous quote was taken, Senator Armstrong told his colleagues on April 13, 1982 that "in the last 10 years alone, the United States and other Western nations have sold to the Soviet Union and its satellites more than $50 billion worth of sophisticated technical equipment the Communists could not produce themselves." He said that "this equipment has been used to produce nuclear missiles, tanks, and armored cars, military command and control systems, spy satellites, and air defense radars. In addition, the Soviets have been able to purchase entire factories, designed and built by Western engineers and financed in large part by American and Western European banks. Much of the production of these factories is devoted to the manufacture of military transport, ammunition, and other logistical items for the Soviet war machine."

Two of the most outrageous examples cited by Senator Armstrong were authorized by the Nixon Administration in the early Seventies. One was the sale to the Soviet Union of 164 precision ball-bearing grinders manufactured by the Bryant Chucking Grinder Corporation of Vermont. These machines, 45 of which had been approved for sale to the Reds a decade earlier by the Kennedy Administration, enabled the Soviets to put multiple warheads on their giant missiles and to improve their accuracy tenfold. This strategic aid to the enemy may have exposed the United States to the danger of what Armstrong called "a nuclear Pearl Harbor." . . .

Technology Transfer

Although technology transfer to the enemy flourished under the Nixon, Ford, and Carter Administrations, things were supposed to change with the election of Ronald Reagan. The 1980 GOP Platform said that "Republicans pledge to stop the flow of technology to the Soviet Union." There were some improvements in coordinating interagency efforts to block the export of critical technology to the Reds, thanks in part to men like Larry Brady in the Commerce Department and Richard Perle in the Defense Department, both of whom are no longer in government. Perle frequently called attention to the scope of the problem, pointing out in 1985, for example, that "there would be no significant Soviet microelectronic capability today without acquisition of U.S. technology." He said that the National Aeronautics and Space Administration (NASA) "has an extremely liberal publication policy, to the point where NASA has published information that has led directly to improvements in Soviet weapons systems." . . .

In 1985 and 1986, at least $11 million worth of highly

41

sophisticated U.S.-made computers, high-capacity disk drives, and software were diverted through Western Europe to the Soviet bloc. Some 40 state-of-the-art engineering work stations, made by Tektronix Inc. of Beaverton, Oregon, went to the Soviet bloc via West Germany, Belgium, Austria, and Turkey. Tektronix representatives said they thought that a West German company was going to get the stations, which are vital in the design of advanced memory chips and microprocessors, military aircraft and missiles, and components of space-based weapons systems.

In June 1987, the *New York Times* reported on the sale to the USSR by Japanese and Norwegian companies of four giant milling machines, worth more than $17 million and used to make quieter submarine propellers. The Soviets first requested the machines in 1980, possibly at the prompting of their secret agent John Walker, but were turned down under the rules of the Coordinating Committee on Multilateral Export Controls (CoCom), which is made up of the NATO [North Atlantic Treaty Organization] countries and Japan. There is evidence that the machines are already making it easier for the Soviet sub fleet to avoid detection with the quieter propellers, and the U.S. Navy estimates that it might have to spend $1 billion or more to improve its noise-detecting capabilities and undo the damage caused by the Japanese-Norwegian sale.

Internal Social Change

If the Soviet Union is ever going to change, it is going to require something much more traumatic than piecemeal evolution. To force this type of internal social change, the capitalist West must tighten the economic screws, not loosen them.

This *is* a historic opportunity. By increasing economic aid and trade, the West would prevent the Communists from paying the social and political price for their folly. Jean-François Revel is right: We must let "the sickness . . . run its course."

Mark D. Isaacs, *The New American*, March 27, 1989.

If the problem of *illegal* transfers to the Soviet bloc remains a very serious one, the situation regarding *legal* exports is also growing steadily worse, not only in the quantity and quality of the goods and technology sent behind the Iron Curtain but also in the enthusiastic support for this suicidal policy by high-ranking members of the Reagan Administration. The aiders and traders had the President's ear during his first term as they persuaded him to continue helping the Communist regimes in Romania, Yugoslavia, and Hungary; to lift sanctions against U.S. and foreign companies supplying equipment for the Soviet gas pipeline; to approve the sale of 200 pipelayers, worth $90 million, to the USSR; and to sign a new five-year grain agreement with the Kremlin. . . .

There have been many arguments advanced over the years to justify aid to and trade with the Communist enemy. One argument is that aid and trade will mellow our "potential adversaries," the latest euphemism for avowed enemies. Seven decades of Communist aggression, terrorism, and slaughter of tens of millions have disproved that theory over and over again. Another contention is that, if we don't sell goods and technology to the Reds, someone else will. Senator William Armstrong provides the answer:

> This argument is, of course, morally flawed. Just because there are dope peddlers who sell dope to small children does not mean we have to install vending machines in the school cafeteria to dispense marijuana, cocaine, and amphetamines. But this argument is also practically flawed. In a number of highly critical areas, computers and microprocessors in particular, the United States has technology which is unavailable anywhere else. And in many areas where hardware as capable as our own can be obtained elsewhere, the software that makes the hardware go cannot be.
>
> Finally, what makes a great nation different from simply a large nation is its ability to lead. All the nations with technology comparable to ours in the West trade much more with us than they do with the Soviet Union, and rely on us rather than the Soviet Union for their protection. Through a combination of the carrots and sticks at our disposal, we ought to be able to persuade these nations—most of which are allied to us—to tighten up their own technology export policies.

There are those who say restrictions on trade with the Communists wil hurt American businesses. But should American firms make profits selling goods and technology to an enemy that has used and will continue to use both to kill Americans? How plausible would this argument be if we substituted Nazis for Communists and Hitler for Gorbachev? The Communists have killed ten times the number of people the Nazis killed, so why are they considered by some to be less of a threat to our survival than Hitler's hordes were? Lysander Spooner, a 19th century writer, put it well when he said that "the men who loan money to governments, so called, for the purpose of enabling the latter to rob, enslave, and murder their people, are among the greatest villains that the world has ever seen."

Defense Feedback

Even those who think that exporting food to the USSR is a good idea are wrong. Not only does American grain never get to those most in need of a better diet, but it frees up domestic resources that can then be used to produce more tanks, planes, and missiles. This in turn imposes a "defense feedback" cost on the United States, which must spend more money to counter the increase in

Soviet military hardware that would not have been possible if the Reds had to incur the cost of agricultural production. Aren't we concerned about the huge grain surpluses piled up by American farmers? Sure we are, but the solution is not selling wheat to the enemy, which it won't even buy at subsidized prices some of the time. The answer is to get the federal government out of agriculture and let supply and demand determine how much grain should be planted and what its selling price ought to be.

Soviet Lies

One of the things we know is that the Soviet Union lies. It lies habitually, deliberately, and massively. . . . The dozens of treaties and agreements that America has with the Soviet Union can only benefit the Communists and hurt the Americans. The West is facing an enemy that is as methodical as it is evil.

Abdul Shams, *In Cold Blood*, 1987.

As for the argument that offering trade and other inducements to the Soviet Union will lead to human-rights concessions and release of dissidents, experience indicates otherwise. Soviet Jews have become a bargaining chip because the Reds know they can be exchanged at a profit. Such a policy only encourages the Communists to take, torture, and trade other prisoners in the future. Bribing the Soviets for decent behavior not only enriches them, but it leads to *more* human-rights violations, said Melvyn Krauss in the *Wall Street Journal* on June 24, 1986. For every dissident released, the Reds will arrest someone else to take his place.

U.S. policy toward the Evil Empire should be a total boycott— no aid, trade, "cultural exchanges," or any kind of assistance that would help the Communists achieve their goal of world domination. The Free World has sustained its most dangerous enemy for 70 years. We had better reverse that process before it is too late. "The Soviets are depending on us to continue to supply them with 'the rope' until they have enough to hang us," said Senator Armstrong. "But there is still time to yank the rope away."

"The United States is prepared to join the Soviet Union in an expanded process of negotiations to end the cold war."

Superpower Relations Can Improve

Stephen F. Cohen

Stephen Cohen is a professor of politics and director of Russian Studies at Princeton University in New Jersey. In the following viewpoint, Cohen asserts that Mikhail Gorbachev's reform program is genuine. The reforms offer the US a historic opportunity to end the cold war, according to Cohen. He believes the two superpowers should overcome past hostilities and deepen economic and political ties.

As you read, consider the following questions:

1. According to the author, how should the US respond to the Soviet program of reforms?
2. According to Cohen, what initiative should the US take to improve relations with the USSR?
3. How can Cohen's ten steps improve superpower relations?

Stephen F. Cohen, "The Next President's Historic Opportunity: Will We End the Cold War?" *The Nation*, October 10, 1988. Reprinted by permission of *The Nation* magazine/The Nation Company, Inc. Copyright © 1988.

The cold war, with the U.S.-Soviet arms race as its most characteristic expression, has become the greatest threat to America's national interests in two profound ways. Above all, it threatens our national survival. As Carl Sagan has aptly said, since 1945 "the United States and the Soviet Union have booby-trapped the planet with almost 60,000 nuclear weapons," far more than enough to destroy every city on earth and "probably enough to destroy the global civilization." The United States exists today only because no one in Moscow, and no accident anywhere, has sprung the trap. Nor is there any infallible system, computerized or otherwise, to protect us against such a mishap. That is the lesson of Korean Air Lines Flight 007, Challenger, Chernobyl and Iran Air Flight 655, disasters resulting from human and "high-tech" fallibility and auguring much worse.

A Drain on the Economy

The cold war is also sapping America's economic health, which is as important for real national security as are weapons. In present-day dollars, according to Sagan's calculations, the United States has spent roughly $10 trillion on the cold war during the past four decades. Imagine all the economic, educational, medical, cultural and scientific sacrifices that has meant. Today, as U.S. defense spending approaches $300 billion a year, most of it directed against a perceived Soviet threat, the problem has become starkly evident in the decline of many of our nonmilitary industries, the largest budget and trade deficits in our history and the number of our fellow citizens who live in poverty.

Nor is the cold war over, contrary to euphoric reports in the media inspired by four Reagan-Gorbachev summit meetings since 1985. The nuclear and conventional arms race goes on, its fast-paced technology speeding far ahead of the political half-measures taken to constrain it. The ratified intermediate-range nuclear forces (I.N.F.) treaty, which promises to remove and destroy American and Soviet medium-range missiles in Europe, is important as a first symbolic act of nuclear abolitionism. But the two sides have given themselves three full years to abolish missiles capable of carrying, at most, only 4 percent of their stockpiled nuclear warheads. Discussions now focus on a so-called START [Strategic Arms Reduction Talks] agreement that would eliminate 30 to 50 percent of the strategic arsenals. By the time it is negotiated, ratified, verified and fully implemented, technological geniuses on both sides are likely to have invented new nuclear weapons that formally comply with the treaty but are even more deadly than those to be abolished. Meanwhile, both sides contemplate a "modernization" of conventional weapons, and a full range of underlying cold war conflicts—ideological, political, and regional—continue to rage around the world.

In reality, three years of mostly inconclusive negotiations and media atmospherics could not possibly end a historical phenomenon of the magnitude of the cold war, whose ideological origins date back seventy years to the Bolshevik Revolution; whose modern-day embodiment in the arms race has been under way since 1945; and whose dynamics are sustained on both sides by a powerful array of institutions, elites and popular attitudes formed over those decades. Despite episodes of détente going back to the 1930s, and even a U.S.-Soviet military alliance during World War II, virtually all of us—American and Soviet citizens alike—are children of the twentieth century's cold war. Not surprisingly, many officials and citizens have come to accept it as the only possible relationship, even as a virtuous one.

Western Values

Now we are living in a time when Western values are in the ascendancy, when our allies have become strong and, for the most part, prosperous. This changing world has challenged the Soviet Union. It is a challenge that the Soviet Union, acting in its own interests, has tried to meet through *perestroika*. Yes, we have heard claims of new thinking, and we have seen some of it translated into action. And we are saying to the Soviet Union: Let us continue. Free people can work together peacefully, linked by a common destiny. Let us deal, therefore, with the new problems of a different era guided by a vision of a free and peaceful world.

James A. Baker III, speech before the Center for Strategic and International Studies, May 4, 1989.

To go beyond this mountainous legacy of cold war to a valley of safer U.S.-Soviet relations will require a long march and bold leadership on both sides. Events since 1985 tell us that the journey is now possible if the American President meets Gorbachev half way. President Reagan, to his lasting credit, went farther in that direction than most people thought possible. But it has not been nearly enough, and not only because the cold war goes dangerously, needlessly on. Even the modest progress in arms control achieved since 1985 has been due largely to a long series of concessions by Gorbachev. No national leader can safely persist in such one-sided compromises to a foreign adversary, least of all Gorbachev, who is deeply embattled in a struggle with powerful opposition to his far-reaching domestic reforms, or *perestroika*, and to his conciliatory policies toward the West. It is time for comparable U.S. initiatives and compromises. After all, it was the Soviet leadership, not democratic America, that responded to the growing perils of cold war with "new thinking," boldness and flexibility. To do no less is the real challenge, and historic opportunity, that awaits the President. . . .

And yet, a great many influential Americans in both major political parties are sternly warning against any such policy. Some of them are theological cold warriors for whom there can never be an alternative U.S.-Soviet relationship, no matter how great the necessity or possibility. But the majority of these influential advisers belongs to the self-described "bipartisan center"—a large company that includes many of yesterday's officials and policy intellectuals whose worn concepts obscure today's historic changes and opportunities. They speak of policy toward Gorbachev's Soviet Union in abstract jargon and empty clichés about "toughness" and "negotiating from strength," as though everyone else advocates dealing from weakness. In effect, by insisting that U.S. policy never deviate from "bipartisanship" and the center, they reflexively oppose the new anti-cold war thinking and measures that America so urgently needs. . . .

A Dependent Fate

While there are significant differences between our wild-eyed cold warriors and statesmanlike centrists, they are united by their opposition to a fundamentally new course in U.S.-Soviet relations. Their recommendations vary, from a policy of escalated cold war and arms race to one of indifference or business as usual toward Gorbachev's leadership. Given the influence they exercise in policy circles, their essential arguments need to be examined. . . .

Though the struggle is essentially an internal Soviet one, it is both untrue and irresponsible to deny that the United States will play an important role in its outcome, for better or worse. Gorbachev has wagered much of his personal authority on the hope that eventually the United States will meet him halfway in new thinking and bilateral compromises. If it does not, his position as leader in both foreign and domestic policy will be greatly weakened. More generally, if we rudely rebuff or simply remain aloof from his calls to reduce cold war tensions and end the arms race, Gorbachev will never be able to persuade recalcitrant Soviet elites to reallocate large resources from the military to the civilian economy, or to undertake the risks inherent in his program to decentralize and liberalize the political system. We may not hold Gorbachev's fate in our hands, and yet it is hardly independent of what we do.

But do we want him to succeed? Should we fear a reformed Soviet system as a greater threat to the United States? Such a perspective offends common sense and America's professed ideals. Gorbachev's advisers frankly admit that their large-scale reforms will take several decades. During that long historical period, America also will have a chance to become stronger by turning inward to its own economic problems and neglected citizens.

Moreover, where is the potential danger if Gorbachev's reforms transfer huge quantities of rubles and scarce technology from the Soviet military-industrial complex to consumer goods, services and welfare; give citizens more freedom, a larger role in decision-making and more access to the West; and persuade this and subsequent generations of Soviet officials to seek their legitimate destiny in reform at home rather than in expanded power abroad? Let us heed Andrei Sakharov, who struggled and suffered for the changes finally under way: "The West and the entire world also have an interest in the success of reforms in the U.S.S.R." . . .

Necessary Steps

The President need only speak candidly to the people. He must say that Gorbachev's proposals represent a long-awaited possibility, though not yet a certainty, of ending the cold war, and that he is determined, for the sake of America's best interests, to begin his presidency by testing Gorbachev's sincerity rather than new weapons. He should emphasize that the long journey to a post-cold war relationship is certain to include temporary setbacks and disappointments, and that the realistic destination is not likely to be a U.S.-Soviet friendship or alliance. Very different historical experiences, dissimilar political systems and real conflicts have made our two nations natural rivals for the foreseeable future.

Eliminating Tension

It ought now to be our purpose to eliminate as soon as possible, by amicable negotiation, the elements of abnormal military tension that have recently dominated Soviet-American relations, and to turn our attention to the development of the positive possibilities of this relationship, which are far from insignificant.

George Kennan, *The New York Times*, April 9, 1989.

The President must explain that the joint quest, based on a U.S.-Soviet partnership in survival, is for a relationship in which cooperation and tolerance displace the most dangerous conflicts, and in which the residual rivalry can be expressed primarily in nonmilitary ways. If the United States and the Soviet Union must compete, let us do so not in an arms race that threatens everyone and benefits no one but in a compassion race to improve the lives of our respective peoples and those of less developed countries. Let us compete to demonstrate in deeds, rather than in provocative ideological assertions, which is the more caring system, American democratic capitalism or the Soviet socialism with a human face of which Gorbachev speaks. And let that competition go on indefinitely.

As the leader of this discussion, the President should introduce two important principles. First, while Americans dislike many aspects of its behavior, the Soviet Union is a legitimate great power with rightful interests in world affairs. Recognizing this principle of political parity, the United States is prepared to join the Soviet Union in an expanded process of negotiations to end the cold war through mutual concessions that safeguard the reasonable interests of both countries. (The President might add that it no longer matters which nation bears the greater responsibility for the history of the cold war, only that both sides agree it must stop.) Clinging to a specious analogy, cold warriors will cry "Appeasement!" but the President will reply that there is no one-way street to mutual security or to the end of the cold war.

Demilitarization

Second, the President must take the leading role in demilitarizing American thinking about the Soviet Union by fully rehabilitating the principles and practices of political diplomacy and accord. All of our underlying conflicts with the Soviet Union are political ones. This does not mean that the United States should disarm unilaterally or be militarily weak. It does mean that it must stop seeking solutions to political conflicts by inventing new weapons systems, as both sides have done for so many years. The goal is to replace that overwhelmingly military relationship with a diplomatic one. It also means that no arms control agreements will ever be stable without larger political accords to protect them against the underlying conflicts, as we learned with SALT II [Strategic Arms Limitation Talks] and the A.B.M. [Anti-ballistic Missile] treaty and as will be true of I.N.F., START and any other treaties to come.

If the President wants to provide such anti-cold war leadership, he will have to translate it very quickly into bold U.S. actions and proposals. The pace of the arms race, growing conflicts around the world and Gorbachev's embattled position at home leave no time for the prolonged ritual of muscle-flexing. Ten steps are particularly important.

1. The President should . . . assure Gorbachev that the United States is now ready for open-minded and good-faith negotiations on every disputed U.S.-Soviet issue, without exception. To initiate this expanded process of negotiations as quickly as possible, he should send one or two of his closest personal associates to Moscow to convey his own preferred agenda of discussions and to learn Gorbachev's.

2. The President also should accept Gorbachev's longstanding offer of an immediate U.S.-Soviet moratorium on the testing of all nuclear weapons and devices, including space-based antimissile systems. Such a moratorium, which can be reliably verified, is

crucial. It will stop the ongoing nuclear arms race, because weapons that cannot be tested will not be deployed, and thus are unlikely to be funded. It will thereby give the snail's pace process of arms limitations talks much-needed time to catch up with the torrid pace of weapons technology. And it will be a dramatic indication of U.S.-Soviet determination to end the nuclear arms race forever.

3. No less important, the President must not compensate by rushing into a buildup (or "modernization," as it is euphemistically called) of conventional weapons. These armaments and the requisite troops account for almost 80 percent of U.S. defense spending. If they continue to grow, no substantial budgetary funds will ever be liberated for nonmilitary purposes, and another dimension of the cold war will go on, perhaps even intensify. Instead, the President should explore fully Gorbachev's extraordinary offer to reduce Soviet and U.S. conventional forces in Europe in "asymmetrical" ways that will eliminate the perceived Soviet superiority in various categories. Having always wished for fewer Soviet troops in central and Eastern Europe, how can we not prefer this alternative to yet another costly buildup?

4. What may be the Soviet Union's changing role in both Eastern and Western Europe also requires a farsighted response by the President. The Brezhnev doctrine, formulated to justify the Soviet invasion of Czechoslovakia in 1968, seems to have been officially repudiated under Gorbachev. According to the recently declared "Gorbachev doctrine," as a Soviet newspaper termed it, Moscow now acknowledges that every ruling Communist Party in Eastern Europe is "fully autonomous in its actions" and thus no longer subject to the threat of Soviet military intervention. If so, the President should respond positively to this development by fully normalizing U.S. political and economic relations with all of those governments. He also should encourage growing political and economic relations between our Western European allies and Moscow. Since the Soviet Union is in significant respects a European nation, such relations ought to be viewed as part of a healthy normalization of European politics, not as a threat to U.S. interests. If the Atlantic alliance is really based on the shared democratic values of its members, why the constant alarm that Moscow may somehow deceive or "decouple" America's NATO [North Atlantic Treaty Organization] allies?

End of the Arms Race

5. Aware that even the most determined measures to end the arms race will fail without equal efforts to diminish U.S.-Soviet political conflicts everywhere, the President should propose substantive and symbolic acts of cooperation in the Third World, the scene of so many present and potential superpower collisions. Above all, as the largest suppliers of arms to those regions, which

51

serve only to increase the murderous nature of indigenous civil wars, the United States and the Soviet Union must agree to replace military aid with economic assistance. They must also negotiate a code of mutual restraint banning direct or covert use of superpower forces, proxies and even military advisers in those regional conflicts. In addition, as a potent symbol of a post-cold war era of cooperation, the President could propose the creation of an American-Soviet Youth Corps that will send to Third World countries not weapons and soldiers but young doctors, teachers, agronomists and engineers, who together can heal, teach, cultivate and build. When they return home, these young people may become future leaders of a post-cold war world.

6. In the same spirit, the President should propose the formation of a special U.S.-Soviet task force, composed of visionary thinkers from both countries, to design other forms of cooperation; for example, strengthening the United Nation's peacekeeping capabilities, halting nuclear proliferation, devising antiterrorism measures, fighting worldwide diseases and hunger, seeking safe sources of energy, protecting the earth's environment, exploring outer space and resolving regional conflicts already under way. The task force would not replace foreign policy bureaucracies in either country, but it must be far more creative than they have proved to be over the years.

Improvements Under Gorbachev

7. One exceedingly dangerous regional conflict requires the President's urgent attention. Acknowledging that both superpowers have vested interests in the Middle East and that no lasting peace settlement there is possible without the support of both, he must ask the Sovet Union to rejoin multilateral negotiations, from which it has been excluded since 1978. In return, the President will expect the Soviet Union to restore full diplomatic relations with Israel, which it broke off in 1967, and to persuade Syria and the Palestine Liberation Organization to recognize irrevocably Israel's right to a secure existence.

8. In addition the President should respond positively to some promising improvements under Gorbachev affecting Soviet Jews who wish to emigrate and those who do not. The Jackson-Vanik and Stevenson amendments, passed by Congress in 1974, severely limited U.S.-Soviet trade by linking it to Jewish emigration from the Soviet Union. In light of recent developments, the President should promise to seek ways to expand the economic relationship between the two countries.

9. It is also important for the President to acknowledge publicly that the Soviet Union, like the United States, is understandably alarmed by perceived threats in neighboring countries. In particular, perhaps as much as 15 to 18 percent of Soviet defense

spending, and a quarter of the country's troops, are directed against China, with whom it shares a 4,500-mile border. With this in mind, the President should renounce any intention of a Washington-Beijing alliance against Moscow, the so-called China card, and announce that his Administration will not supply any kind of weapons to China. The United States seeks a flourishing political and economic relationship with Beijing, not a military one. Indeed, the President could add that he applauds the growing signs of a détente in Sino-Soviet relations.

10. Finally, so that all these initiatives can be pursued vigorously and consistently, and without the internecine conflicts that characterized previous U.S. Administrations, the President should appoint to all the relevant foreign policy positions only people deeply committed to his anti-cold war effort.

When Gorbachev's radical proposals to solve his country's problems were opposed by his own centrists, he replied defiantly, "If not now, when? If not us, who?"

"The Cold War is far from over. And Soviet strategic deception still serves as a useful concealment of Soviet offensive programs."

Superpower Relations Cannot Improve

H. Joachim Maitre

The USSR has sought to spread communism throughout the world since the Communist Revolution in 1917, according to the author of the following viewpoint, H. Joachim Maitre. The USSR has always offered internal political and military reforms as evidence of its peaceful intentions, argues Maitre, but these reform programs have been false. Maitre argues that the US should mistrust Soviet reform initiatives and should keep relations with the USSR minimal. Maitre is dean of the School of Communications at Boston University in Massachusetts.

As you read, consider the following questions:

1. According to Maitre, what aid does Gorbachev hope to receive from the West?
2. What does Maitre predict would happen if the US responded positively to the Soviet reforms?
3. How does Maitre believe the West should respond to Gorbachev's reforms?

H. Joachim Maitre, "A Strategy of Deception." This article appeared in the March 1988 issue and is reprinted with permission of *The World & I*, a publication of The Washington Times Corporation. Copyright © 1988.

Glasnost, the alleged Soviet "new openness," is an ideal disguise for the regime's ongoing predicament: The Soviet Union is in desperate need of Western credit, Western trade, and Western scientific and technological know-how. Glasnost is intended as the new Potemkin Village to attract needed aid, in the tradition of Lenin's New Economic Policy of the 1920s.

Western credit for the Soviet Union, to be sure, is already massive. The West and Japan have supplied the Soviet Union with roughly $48 billion, and its indebtedness is rapidly increasing. In 1986, the Soviets and their satellites borrowed at the rate of $2 billion a month. At least 80 percent of the money—according to William E. Simon, former U.S. secretary of the treasury—was handed to the East bloc with no strings attached.

Soviet Policy

Western governments are now faced with an urgent question— What to do? Clearly, our policy toward the Soviet Union must proceed from a sober appreciation of the fundamental differences between the two systems, from a realistic assessment of Soviet policy as it is, not as we wish it to be. Glasnost, and its cousin perestroika, in their foreign versions for Western consumption, are attempting to convince us that admitted former differences are vanishing, and the gullible are rushing to the Soviets' support. Writes one innocent and syndicated columnist: Soviet leader Mikhail Gorbachev "wants Russia to become a 'normalized' country. He wants Russia to be part of Western civilization. What he really wants is respectability in the world, which can come only through Western recognition of the Soviet Union as a normal country."

The same writer, enchanted with the Soviet "withdrawal" from Afghanistan, embraces the basis for an alleged new Soviet foreign policy: "The Russians now want to be accepted as a respected and respectable international partner of the big countries. They are bored, angered and fed up with the hopeless little countries such as Cuba." And with equally hopeless Ethiopia, Mozambique, São Tomé, and the Cape Verdes, one hopes. But why, then, is the Soviet Union still pumping billions into Cuba and Nicaragua?

Certainly not for the first time, the West is being asked to take the East's rhetoric at face value. The Soviet Union "wishes to live in peace with all countries including the United States," and it "does not nurture aggressive plans, does not impose the arms race on anyone, does not impose its social order on anyone." The Soviet Union "will continue to do everything possible to uphold peace on earth." These words were spoken by Yuri Andropov in 1983, four years after the invasion of Afghanistan, but the Soviet leadership's propensity for the truth, as they see it, does not change with the party's chairmanship. On behalf of the entire Soviet leadership, Gorbachev asserted on New Year's Eve 1986 that "when working out our policy in matters of war and peace, we are as honest with the American people as with our own people."

Apparently, no irony was intended, and none was detected when Gorbachev's assertions were repeated in America's prestige media. Not a single commentator or columnist suggested the truth—that no Soviet government trusts its citizens, that few Soviet citizens trust their government, that risks are involved anywhere in placing trust in Soviet propaganda speeches. Glasnost had found its first victims, in the United States.

Barely two years later, on December 7, 1988, before the United Nations, Gorbachev's rhetoric reached extreme heights of audacity: "Freedom of choice is a universal principle that should allow for no exceptions; no genuine progress is possible at the expense of the rights and freedoms of individuals and nations." He added, incredibly: "The use or threat of force can no longer and must no longer be an instrument of foreign policy." Gorbachev's speech climaxed with an announcement of unilateral Soviet troop and weapons cuts in Europe.

The Soviet leader followed up with a dramatic statement on the state of the Soviet economy before top leaders of the Communist Party (January 7, 1989): "We can cut defense spending without lowering the level of security and the country's ability to defend itself."

Soviet Grip Remains

All over America and throughout the remainder of the West, talk proceeds about supposedly marvelous transformations in the Kremlin and how world peace is now possible. But the peoples of the once-free Baltic states know otherwise. So, too, do others who live under Moscow's tyrannical rule.

For decades, Soviet-inspired national liberation campaigns all over the globe have succeeded in placing Communists and Communist-sympathizers atop scores of nations. But when a legitimate striving for freedom occurs in a Soviet-dominated area, the Soviets crush it.

Communism not only has not changed; it cannot change. What *should* change is the West's support for it.

John F. McManus, *The New American*, December 19, 1988.

More than 2,000 years ago, the Chinese philosopher and strategist Sun Tzu judged deception to be the basis of all warfare. Today, Soviet deception specialists have become an integral part of the Soviet foreign policy machine. "Deception is a relatively easy game," writes former Czech intelligence officer Ladislav Bittman, "particularly against anyone willing to be deceived."

The average citizen in the West is such an easy target. What is he to think of the Soviet offer to host a major international conference in Moscow with the sole aim of discussing "worldwide humanitarian issues"? On the agenda would be the issue of human rights in its entirety, including the free flow of information and ideas—all topics dealt with in the Helsinki Accords of 1975 and taken up again in Bern in 1985, when Moscow was convicted verbally of having broken every single one of its previous pledges of compliance. Moreover, what is the average citizen in the West to think of Washington's willingness to let Moscow host this conference?

With its customary contempt for the West's resolve to enforce vital rules, such as those of free trade, the Soviet Union now seeks entry into the World Bank and the International Monetary Fund. The West is being asked, in effect, to provide credit for the maintenance and further buildup of the Soviet empire. Washington and its Western allies would be well advised to block these Soviet bids. But can they afford to do so in the face of disinformed public opinion at home?

When viewing contemporary glasnost and the state of U.S.-Soviet relations after the Reagan years, it is essential to recognize the development of the politico-military correlation of forces over the past decades.

Aggressive and Expansionist

When NATO [North Atlantic Treaty Organization] was founded in 1949 in response to the aggressive and expansionist foreign policy of the Soviet Union, the United States was not only the undisputed leader of the West, but was also uncontested as a world power. Its might was based on three solid foundations: military hegemony rooted in a monopoly of nuclear weapons, economic supremacy, and unrivaled financial power.

By 1950, the Soviet Union had exploded its first atomic bomb and it continued with determination on the road to superpower status. Meanwhile, the remaining foundations of American global might also began to erode. A decisive shift in America's military supremacy was triggered by the 1962 Cuban Missile Crisis, when the United States, by forcing the Soviet Union to withdraw its newly landed missiles from Cuba, seemingly administered a serious setback to Soviet superpower ambitions. Yet, in a conciliatory gesture toward its humiliated adversary, the United States withdrew all of its 100 Thor and Jupiter intermediate-range, land-based missiles from Turkey, Italy, and Great Britain, while the Soviet Union kept its 450 SS-4s (1,900-kilometer range) and SS-5s (4,000-kilometer range) in its Western military districts.

The geostrategic East-West balance in the mid-1960s, at the onset of the Brezhnev era, can be summed up as follows: (1) the Warsaw Pact was significantly superior to NATO in conventional forces and nuclear intermediate-range missiles; (2) this Warsaw Pact superiority was matched by NATO's lead in battlefield nuclear weapons plus U.S. strength in nuclear strategic forces; and (3) the West was still ahead globally, mainly in naval forces and strategic nuclear arms, but the Soviet Union was no longer just a formidable conventional power. Under Brezhnev, the Soviet Union's military buildup resulted in undisputed superpower status.

Achieving Military Superiority

By 1981 the USSR was close to achieving break-through superiority in Central Europe; NATO would have to use nuclear weapons to stop a conventional assault. Furthermore, the Soviets had built up a lead in tactical nuclear weapons, thus limiting Western options; had expanded their fleet of strategic transport aircraft and surface ships, enabling them to land troops more quickly in Asia and Africa than could the West; and had punctured the American nuclear umbrella by achieving parity in long-range nuclear delivery systems.

The Barbaric Record

If we review once more the barbaric record of the Communists in this century—the deliberate and calculated slaughter of more than 100 million human beings; the social, religious, and political persecution that has driven other tens of millions out of their native lands; and the monstrous cruelty that is being inflicted on so many fellow humans in so many parts of the world today—it will shake us out of our apathy. Perhaps then we will demand that the President and the Congress stop providing military, economic, and moral assistance to the rulers of the Evil Empire. And perhaps then the suffering people of the Captive Nations will come to enjoy the blessings of freedom that we take for granted.

James J. Drummey, *The New American*, July 18, 1988.

With Jimmy Carter's defeat in November 1980, the decade of détente ended, a strange and one-sided relaxation of tension during which Western nations had attempted to build cooperation and understanding with Soviet bloc states by means of cheap credit and advanced technology, while the Kremlin expanded its influence and military might at the expense of Western interests.

By the end of the Carter administration, the Soviet Union had established a decisive lead over the United States as a military power, having surpassed the United States in all measures of nuclear armaments, except numbers of warheads. After more than a decade of efforts by Washington to achieve an effective agreement on strategic arms control, Moscow had upgraded and enlarged its nuclear arsenal from a position of inferiority to one of superiority. By 1980, the Soviet Union possessed roughly 40 percent more strategic missiles than the United States. Since then, the lead has widened in both numbers and throw-weights (payloads). The Soviet SS-18 intercontinental ballistic missile (ICBM) has a throw-weight 10 times that of the U.S. Minuteman ICBM. The SS-18's 25-megaton warhead has 2,000 times the destructive power of the Hiroshima bomb. Today, the Soviet Union could destroy 90 percent of American ICBMs in a first-strike strategic assault with only one-fifth to one-third of its own ICBMs.

Strategic Forces

The Soviet buildup of land-based strategic forces during the 1960s and 1970s was complemented by similar achievements in sea-based strategic forces and nuclear and conventional naval forces. By the early 1980s, the United States had lost its traditional superiority in naval power over the Soviet Union, which by 1984 had the world's largest and most modern surface navy, the largest fleet of attack submarines, and the largest fleet of strategic submarines equipped with ballistic missiles. For the first time in naval history, the Red Navy is deploying aircraft carriers in two oceans, thus demonstrating the capacity necessary for projecting Soviet naval power globally.

During the crucial years of Soviet naval buildup from 1968 to 1980, the U.S. Navy was forced to halve its number of ships, from roughly 1,000 to 453. "The Soviets built, we mothballed," said former U.S. arms negotiator Paul Nitze.

Yet the Soviet buildup most directly affecting U.S. ties to Western Europe occurred in intermediate-range nuclear weapons and short-range (battlefield) nuclear forces. By 1983, the Soviet Union had in service 351 SS-20 reloadable launchers and 39 rocket regiments. The Soviet Union's new SS-21, SS-22, and SS-23 short-range missiles add to the massive threat facing NATO in Central Europe.

A Coherent Defense

A realistic assessment of Moscow's arms policies is the first step toward organizing a coherent defense, but we must realize from the beginning that the buildup of arms and arms doctrines is a consequence, and not a cause, of particular state policies. The nature of the state and the ambitions of its rulers determine the direction and pace of armament, the kinds and numbers of weapons, and military tactics. The Soviet Union is no exception to this rule.

Ronald Reagan is rightly credited with successfully rebuilding U.S. armed forces. A congressional backlash, however, became effective at the end of his first term, and yet another build-down commenced. In 1984, Congress cut the president's fiscal 1985 defense request by 6.4 percent. In 1985, the cut rose to 11.3 percent. In 1986, the president's request, already reduced, was cut by 9.6 percent.

Meanwhile, the Soviets continued their military buildup. Over the last decade, they have produced 25,300 main battle tanks, against 7,600 tanks built in the United States over the same 10 years. Over the last decade, the Soviets procured 27,300 artillery pieces, the United States 3,200. As regards fighter aircraft, the numbers are 7,700 (USSR) versus 3,600 (U.S.). In nuclear-capable artillery and rocket launchers, the number ratio is 17 to 1 against us. We can no longer claim "qualitative superiority." The Soviets long ago lifted themselves out of their former technological backwardness. The equipment coming off Soviet production lines equals our best; often it is superior to ours. As of 1984, new generations of strategic bombers, submarines, and sea- and air-launched cruise missiles have augmented Soviet strategic options. New fighter-aircraft squadrons equipped with high-tech Sukhoi SU-27 Flankers and Mikoyan/Gurevich MiG-29 Fulcrums today provide the Warsaw Pact with air superiority over Europe. Despite grave economic problems, the Soviet Union has continued to allocate an estimated 15 to 20 percent of its GNP [gross national product] to the military. How can President Bush respond?

Soviet World Domination

Bear in mind that Gorbachev has never changed the objectives set by his predecessors: eventual Soviet world domination and that includes the United States.

Henry Mohr, *Conservative Chronicle*, May 24, 1989.

Gorbachev's "blueprint for world peace" (as his UN speech was described in the *Manchester Guardian*) will make it impossible for Bush to obtain congressional support to increase defense spending, even for the purpose of matching inflation. The INF [Intermediate-Range Nuclear Forces] Treaty of 1988, which "eliminates" all U.S. and Soviet land-based intermediate-range nuclear missiles—but not a single nuclear warhead or guidance system—had already eliminated any prospect for a dramatic spending increase, such as would be needed for a genuine Strategic Defense Initiative. Neither Congress nor the president is going to add large amounts to the defense budget while negotiating new arms reductions with the Soviets.

American pressure on Western Europe to shoulder a greater share of the NATO defense burden is bound to increase. Yet Western European governments are reluctant to maintain present defense expenditures, let alone boost them.

Gorbachev's announcement of sweeping troop, artillery, and armor cuts "will stir neutralist tendencies in Europe, pull at the ties that bind NATO and incline many Americans to conclude it's safe to pull out of Europe and cut the American defense budget," the *Washington Post* commented.

Defense Debate

For years, the defense debate in NATO has been preoccupied with the hypothetical threat of tens of thousands of Soviet T-64, T-72, and T-80 tanks pouring across the West German border and reaching the Rhine within a few days. This imagined "worst-case" scenario is, in reality, a best-case scenario, one that ignores the fact that Soviet psychological intimidation—through the ever-present threat of excessive armed force—serves as a means for "peaceful" political conquest of desirable territory.

Reagan had it right when, commenting on the Soviet arms buildup in June 1977, he said:

> The Soviet Union does not want to fight a war if it can be avoided. Instead, the Soviet buildup seems to be designed primarily for political leverage—to achieve their aims indirectly. . . . They want to accomplish the gradual encirclement of the West and reduction of its strategic and economic influence.

Ever since World War II, the dominant aim of Soviet foreign policy has been the removal of the American military presence from Western Europe and the subsequent establishment of Soviet hegemony over all of Europe—without firing a single shot.

The Soviet Union—by establishing itself as a superpower, challenging the United States worldwide, and thus forcing reevaluation of traditional commitments and priorities in NATO/Europe and in the United States—inched closer to reaching that objective during the Reagan years. . . .

Glasnost and Perestroika

More than just caution is advisable toward glasnost and perestroika. Soviet military power will not be weakened by the troop and weapons cuts announced by Gorbachev. Soviet military power and the threat it represents are not abstract notions. The Soviets' willingness to use military force to exact compliance through threats or armed aggression, as they did in Budapest and Prague, then in Afghanistan, is not deniable. The Cold War is far from over. And Soviet strategic deception still serves as a useful concealment of Soviet offensive programs.

a critical thinking activity

Recognizing Deceptive Arguments

People who feel strongly about an issue use many techniques to persuade others to agree with them. Some of these techniques appeal to the intellect, some to the emotions. Many of them distract the reader or listener from the real issues.

A few common examples of argumentation tactics are listed below. Most of them can be used either to advance an argument in an honest, reasonable way or to deceive or distract from the real issues. It is important for a critical reader to recognize these tactics in order to rationally evaluate an author's ideas.

a. *scare tactics*—the threat that if you don't do or don't believe this, something terrible will happen

b. *personal attack*—criticizing an opponent *personally* instead of rationally debating his or her ideas

c. *categorical statements*—stating something in a way that implies there can be no argument

d. *strawperson*—distorting or exaggerating an opponent's ideas to make one's own seem stronger

e. *slanters*—trying to persuade through inflammatory and exaggerated language instead of through reason

f. *testimonial*—quoting or paraphrasing an authority to support one's own viewpoint

The following activity can help you sharpen your skills in recognizing deceptive reasoning. The statements below are derived from the viewpoints in this chapter. *Beside each one, mark the letter of the type of deceptive appeal being used. More than one type of tactic may be applicable. If you believe the statement is not any of the listed appeals, write N.*

1. The US should stand resolutely against communism, a monster that has gobbled up nearly half the world and intends to consume the rest of the globe.

2. Americans who support and/or conduct trade with the Soviet Union are traitors who have enriched themselves by putting profits ahead of patriotism.

3. The United States should end its insane obsession with the Soviet Union and pursue a peace-loving foreign policy.

4. The original architect of the Cold War, George Kennan, now believes that the Cold War is outdated. The US should take Kennan's advice and seek better relations with the USSR.

5. Just because Gorbachev has said a few nice words on world peace, American liberals believe the Soviet Union is no longer a threat.

6. The Cold War will never be over. The US would be extremely foolish to let its guard down.

7. Those who oppose ending the Cold War simply have a subconscious need for an enemy to fight against, and don't want to admit that the Soviet Union has changed.

8. If we review the barbaric record and the monstrous cruelty of the communists, perhaps then we will demand the US stop assistance to the Evil Empire.

9. The US and the Soviet Union should strive for peace because the Cold War has left the world booby-trapped with sixty thousand nuclear weapons. It is only luck which has kept the world from being destroyed up to now.

10. Cold War militarists think Gorbachev is no different from Josef Stalin. They believe the Soviet Union has not changed at all in forty years.

11. The Cold War is over, so we should stop pursuing Cold War policies.

12. The day the Cold War ends is the day the US will be taken over by communism.

13. If the US does not support Gorbachev, he will be overthrown by hardline military leaders who will make matters much worse.

Periodical Bibliography

The following articles have been selected to supplement the diverse views presented in this chapter.

Georgi Arbatov	"Is America No Longer Exceptional?" *New Perspectives Quarterly*, Summer 1988.
John Barry, Margaret Garrard Warner, and Evan Thomas	"After the Cold War," *Newsweek*, May 15, 1989.
Lev Bezymensky	"Entering the 1990s," *New Times*, no. 1, January 1989.
Zbigniew Brzezinski	"A Proposition the Soviets Should Refuse," *The New York Times*, March 13, 1989.
Frank Carlucci	"No Time To Change US Defense Policy," *The New York Times*, January 27, 1989.
Walter Isaacson	"The Gorbachev Challenge," *Time*, December 19, 1988.
George F. Kennan	"After the Cold War," *The New York Times Magazine*, February 5, 1989.
Charles Krauthammer	"Beyond the Cold War," *The New Republic*, December 19, 1989.
Charles Krauthammer	"No, the Cold War Isn't Really Over," *Time*, September 5, 1988.
Anthony Lewis	"Cold War Comfort," *The New York Times*, April 27, 1989.
Vladimir Lobov	"The Armed Forces," *New Times*, no. 8, February 1988.
Michael Mandelbaum	"Ending the Cold War," *Foreign Affairs*, Spring 1989.
Horst Schmitt	"Anti-Communism Hit by Perestroika," *World Marxist Review*, October 1987.
Galina Sidorova and Alexander Pumpyansky	"The Fourth Step," *New Times*, no. 23, June 1988.
The Wall Street Journal	"Cold War Facts," April 14, 1989.
Ivan Yefremov	"Progress or Progression?" *New Times*, no. 43, August 1988.

CHAPTER

2

Do the Superpowers Intervene in Other Countries?

Chapter Preface

On the surface, both the US and the USSR appear to be interven-
ing less in other countries' affairs than they did in the past. In
1989, the Soviet Union withdrew its troops from Afghanistan, and
the US ended military aid to the Nicaraguan contras. The Soviet-
backed Cubans are leaving Angola, and the US is considering
removing its military bases from the Philippines. These well-
publicized events suggest an end to superpower meddling.

But other evidence hints that the two superpowers have simply
changed their tactics, not their involvement. The US continues
to send military aid to rebel forces in Afghanistan. It also continues to send Central America humanitarian aid that many fear
is diverted and used for military purposes. The Soviets send
military aid to the pro-Soviet army in Afghanistan. The Soviets
also continue to support Cuba's Marxist government.

Are the US and the USSR truly decreasing their level of intervention? The following chapter debates this question.

"What does it mean that our nation is gearing up to make war on the Third World?"

The US Intervenes in the Third World

Michael T. Klare

The author of the following viewpoint, Michael T. Klare, defines low-intensity conflict (LIC) as non-nuclear confrontation ranging from terrorism and counterinsurgency to full-scale conventional war. According to Klare, the US military has replaced nuclear tactics with LIC. He believes that LIC in the Third World is aggressive, unnecessary, and destructive. Klare is the director of the Five College Program in peace and world security studies based at Hampshire College in Amherst, Massachusetts.

As you read, consider the following questions:

1. According to the author, how does the US justify involvement in the Third World?
2. How does Klare differentiate between nuclear conflict and low-intensity conflict?
3. What are the Great Fear and the Soviet Scare and what point does the author make with these two phrases?

Michael T. Klare, "Stopping the War Against the Third World," *The Progressive*, January 1988. Reprinted by permission from *The Progressive*, 409 East Main Street, Madison, WI 53703. Copyright © 1988, The Progressive, Inc.

For many years now, the peace movement has been preoccupied with one overwhelming threat: the risk of an Armageddon, an all-out nuclear conflict between the United States and the
Soviet Union that virtually annihilates human society. In focusing on this threat, we have generated a number of terrifying images
that have haunted our dreams and clouded our visions of the
future – leading those of us in the movement to devote many of
our evenings and weekends to the struggle to prevent a nuclear
catastrophe. . . .

No one can measure these things with certainty, of course, but
I would argue that the improvement in relations between
Washington and Moscow and the resumption of serious arms- control talks has significantly reduced the likelihood of a nuclear confrontation between the superpowers. For this, we should be
grateful, and we should take pride in the role we played in mobilizing public concern over the nuclear peril. . . .

What I see for our nation in the years ahead is not nuclear
Armageddon but something almost as hideous: the slow decay and
contamination of our nation's moral foundation, of its basic human
decency.

What is the cause of this moral poisoning, and why do I fear
it now? The answers lie, in my view, in an analysis of the changes
that have taken place in U.S. military strategy over the past few
years.

Cold War Rhetoric

Because of President Reagan's virulent Cold War rhetoric and
our own worries about nuclear conflict, we have tended to
perceive all international conflict issues in East-West terms – in
reference, that is, to the military competition between the United
States and the Soviet Union. But the tempo of that competition
has subsided and will, in all likelihood, continue to do so in the
future. This is not the result of a change of heart by American
officials, who remain as anticommunist as always. Rather, it is
a product of the changing international economic environment.

While our political system does incorporate some suicidal
tendencies, most top leaders of this country have come to understand the basic economic picture spelled out by such analysts as
Paul Kennedy of Yale University, whose book, *The Rise and Fall
of the Great Powers*, was an overnight sensation in 1988. Kennedy
warns that hegemonic systems inevitably decline when their
military expenditures exceed the carrying capacity of their
economies. Most American leaders now acknowledge that we
must diminish our investment in military spending to be able to
devote additional resources to economic renewal. And because
the U.S.-Soviet arms race is by far the most costly component of
the military budget, that is where the cuts have to be made, and

are being made.

So far, so good. But there is a dark side to all of this: Having established a permanent peacetime security establishment to manage the Cold War, we are now saddled with a powerful military-industrial infrastructure that is not about to disband itself voluntarily. One way to get at this problem is through economic conversion, which would provide incentives for industry and labor to switch from military to peacetime production. That will work— so long as we are talking about engineers and welders and machine-tool operators. But what do you do with people whose profession is systematic slaughter? How do you convert a tank gunner or an artilleryman or a bomber pilot?

Victory in Counterrevolution

Before Vietnam, with exceptions such as the Bay of Pigs invasion, Washington had a long record of victory in counterrevolution, with and without U.S. combat troops—from the early wars against Native Americans and frequent interventions in Central America and the Caribbean to post-World War II Greece, the Philippines, Iran, Guatemala, Lebanon, Haiti, Ecuador, the Congo, Brazil, Dominican Republic, Indonesia, Ghana, Uruguay, Chile, and Bolivia. Since the Vietnam War, Washington has propped up the Mobutu dictatorship in Zaire, derailed the first Manley government in Jamaica, and occupied Grenada....

The war on Nicaragua is official administration policy, and deception is used to confuse and cover up. That's standard operating procedure.

Holly Sklar, *Zeta Magazine*, March 1989.

I'm not sure that I have the answer. But, in any case, the military establishment has come up with its own answer: what is innocuously called "low-intensity conflict," or, in practice, war against the hungry and angry and frustrated peoples of the Third World.

Low-Intensity Conflict

By now, many people have heard the term "low-intensity conflict." I doubt, however, that many know what it really entails. Low-intensity conflict, or LIC, is both a military strategy and a state of mind.

As a strategy, LIC affirms that American forces must be retrained and reconfigured to fight in the underdeveloped Southern Hemisphere against rebellious peasants and Soviet- or Cuban-backed guerrilla armies, instead of in the East, against Warsaw Pact forces. In practice, this means the "revitalization" of America's Special Operations Forces, the creation of four new "light infantry divisions" specifically configured for combat in the Third World, a one-third increase in the Navy's amphibious assault forces, a 100 per cent increase in long-range airlift and sealift capabilities, and the creation of two new carrier battle groups and four surface action groups built around refurbished World War II-vintage battleships.

The total cost of this buildup, which has continued apace throughout the entire Reagan period, *far exceeds* total spending on "Star Wars" and other exotic nuclear programs. This effort has been accompanied, moreover, by stepped-up U.S. military exercises and deployments in Third World conflict areas, especially the Persian Gulf, the Mediterranean, the Indian Ocean, and the Caribbean.

But LIC also represents a reorientation of the military mindset. In essence, this outlook holds that the real threat to long term American security lies not in the East, across the Fulda Gap in East Germany, but in the South, across the Rio Grande, the Caribbean, the Mediterranean, the Indian Ocean. There, in the troubled and disordered regions of the Third World, America faces billions of disadvantaged people who seek a fairer share of the world's wealth. They produce much of the food and raw materials consumed in the North, and they no longer will settle for dismal poverty. . . .

The Great Fear

Of course, it is easy to submerge the Great Fear – the fear of rebellious Third World peoples – into the Soviet Scare and to portray them as one and the same, calling all Third World unrest a product of communist subversion. This propaganda tactic has been standard operating procedure during the Cold War. What is happening now, however, is a separation of the two fears into their component elements, with the Great Fear taking precedence over the Soviet Scare.

The primacy of LIC began to emerge in the 1970s, among military strategists who attempted to assess the "lessons" of Vietnam. Of particular importance was an influential 1977 Rand Corporation study, *Military Implications of a Possible World Order Crisis in the 1980s.* This study suggested that "mankind is entering a period of increased social instability and faces the possibility of a breakdown of the global order as a result of a sharpening confrontation between the Third World and the industrial democracies." Because of the growing gap between rich and poor, "the North-South conflict . . . could get out of hand in ways comparable to the peasant rebellions that in past centuries engulfed large parts of Europe or Asia, spreading like uncontrollable prairie fires." And because only the United States has the capacity to fight these conflagrations, it will "be expected to use its military force to prevent the total collapse of the world order."

General Maxwell D. Taylor, former Chairman of the Joint Chiefs of Staff and architect of U.S. intervention in Vietnam, echoed the warning. "As the leading affluent 'have' power," he wrote in *Foreign Affairs*, "we may expect to have to fight to protect our national valuables against envious 'have-nots.' "

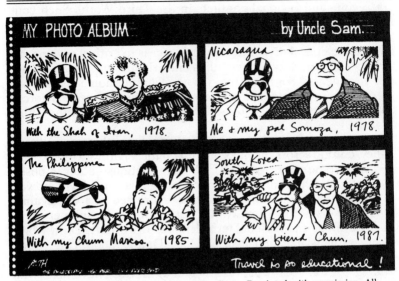

In the early 1980s, the Reagan Administration obscured this change in outlook by dwelling on nuclear-weapons development and the Soviet threat in Europe. However, the new perspective surfaced again in the mid-1980s, when many younger military officers began to argue that the European-oriented buildup of the early 1980s had diverted U.S. policymakers' attention from the mounting threat in the Third World. In 1985, for instance, Colonel James B. Motley of the Army wrote in *Military Review* that "the United States should reorient its forces and traditional policies from an almost exclusive concentration on NATO [North Atlantic Treaty Organization] to better influence politico-military outcomes in the resource-rich and strategically located Third World areas."

A Third World Orientation

Advocating a Third World orientation would have been considered heretical by most American policymakers only recently, but now it is becoming the conventional wisdom. With input from Henry Kissinger and Zbigniew Brzezinski, the U.S. Commission on Integrated Long-Term Strategy published a report entitled *Discriminate Deterrence* which sketches out the new strategy. The report argues that an "excessive focus" on "apocalyptic showdowns between the United States and the Soviet Union" has led to "tunnel vision among defense planners," diverting them "from trying to deal with many important and far more plausible [conflict] situations." The "more plausible situations" envisioned by the Commission are revolts and regional conflicts in the Third World. Such conflicts, the report notes, "are obviously less threatening than any Soviet-American war would be, yet they have had and will have an adverse cumulative effect on U.S. access to critical regions, on American credibility among allies and friends, and on American self-confidence." For these reasons, the Commission calls on Congress to approve a massive buildup of U.S. "power-projection" forces and to support a more activist U.S. military posture in the Third World.

This view represents the core of elite U.S. thinking on military policy, cutting across the lines of both political parties. Unless overtaken by some new crisis in U.S.-Soviet relations – a not impossible (but in my view unlikely) contingency – this outlook will prevail in the 1990s. It will not, however, be expressed as a war against the have-nots of the Third World. Rather, it will be submerged in rhetoric about international terrorism, the drug trade, Third World disorder, the Islamic upheaval, and illegal immigration. Thus, when U.S. leaders speak of the threat posed by terrorism and drug trafficking, they are really expressing fear of "envious have-nots" who seek to confiscate our "national valuables."

If we look around us we can, I think, see many signs of this Great Fear. I see it in the prominence accorded to the Pledge of Allegiance issue in the Presidential campaign, in the popular idolization of Oliver North, in the success of "Rambo-type" movies, in the rage for war toys and camouflage gear among American youngsters, in efforts to seal off the U.S. border to Hispanic immigrants, in the approval given to President Reagan's April 1986 attack on Colonel Muammar Qaddafi's living quarters in Tripoli, and in the glee expressed by many Americans about the shootdown of an Iranian civilian airliner with 300 people aboard.

The Peace Movement

These impulses are strong, they are growing, and, so far as I can tell, they are not being actively resisted by the American peace movement. We talk about nuclear holocaust and military waste while ordinary Americans talk about Qaddafi and Khomeini, about terrorists and drug pushers.

The American people *support* efforts by the U.S. military to realign itself from an anti-Soviet to an anti-Third World force. . . .

What does it mean that our nation is gearing up to make war on the Third World? It means, for the most part, fighting to protect entrenched oligarchies against the mass of the population. And it seems to me that you cannot preserve democracy and freedom and justice at home when you are fighting to preserve tyranny and exploitation and inequality abroad....

Is this inevitable? No, not necessarily, but it surely is much more likely than a nuclear war. Indeed, if we ever *do* suffer a nuclear war, it will probably occur because of U.S. intervention in a small war, a low-intensity conflict, that escalates into a big war and drags the two superpowers into an unexpected confrontation leading to the initial use of nuclear weapons.

Counterinsurgency

The resurgence of low-intensity conflict – and of counterinsurgency, its most important element – is the result of a US desire to keep or regain control of the Third World in a very complicated international situation and after a period of waning influence. In this sense, low-intensity conflict has the function of confronting the Soviet Union, or what US decisionmakers like to perceive as Soviet proxies, in the Third World. It weakens or destroys liberation movements or progressive governments in Latin America, the Middle East, Africa, and Asia.

Jochen Hippler, *Middle East Report*, January/February 1987.

How do we resist the moral corrosion of our society? The first step obviously must be to examine these trends, and to make a commitment to engage them head on. Second, we must look into xenophobic and racist dimensions of the American psyche and search for methods to isolate and eradicate them. Until we begin to resist the tendency to view the world's have-nots as America's enemies, we will not be able to stem the revival of interventionism and, with it, the risk of another Vietnam-like quagmire.

"If Gorbachev is serious about the political resolution of disputes, non-interference, and human rights, he could withdraw. . .forces from an extended, decrepit empire."

The USSR Intervenes in the Third World

John W. Coffey

John W. Coffey is associate professor of political science at Rockford College in Rockford, Illinois. He served in the Office of the Secretary of Defense from 1986 to 1988. In the following viewpoint, Coffey argues that Soviet arms control agreements are insincere and further the Soviet plan for world domination. He believes that the USSR will take advantage of these agreements to continue military and economic support to Third World clients like Cuba and South Yemen. In addition, he writes, the Soviets are adding allies among noncommunist countries like Peru.

As you read, consider the following questions:

1. What methods does Coffey believe the Soviet Union has used to intervene in Third World countries?
2. According to the author, how does the USSR justify its intervention in the Third World?
3. How does Soviet intervention in the Third World affect the United States, according to the author?

John W. Coffey, "New Thinking or New Tactics in Soviet Foreign Policy?" *Global Affairs,* Winter 1989. Reprinted with permission.

Soviet leader Mikhail Gorbachev has waged a vigorous peace offensive, persuading some Westerners that radically "new thinking" about world politics is brewing in the Kremlin. Gorbachev's public relations flair, however, may conceal both less and more than meet the eye.

In a September 1987 *Pravda* article, Gorbachev reiterated his concept of a "comprehensive system of international security" broached at the 1986 27th Party Congress. This new system would operate within an enlarged U.N. [United Nations] framework. Among other things, Gorbachev called for: strict observance of the U.N. Charter; non-interference in nations' internal affairs (except for the struggle against apartheid); a multilateral center to reduce the danger of war and verify compliance with international agreements; a guarantee of regional security by U.N. Security Council permanent members; a global information network to erase stereotypes and the "enemy image" of peoples; and a consultative council of the world's intellectual elite. He urged progress toward a "new world economic order" to ensure security for all states and a global environmental protection program. Asserting that human rights are incompatible with placing "the chandeliers of exotic weapons" in space, Gorbachev affirmed the human (particularly economic) rights of all peoples.

The Greatest Evil

Describing nuclear weapons as "the greatest evil," Gorbachev advocated their abolition along with all other means of mass destruction. Peace must be maintained, he said, with drastically reduced and balanced levels of conventional arms. Gorbachev stressed the new Soviet doctrine of "military sufficiency," that is, a level of forces adequate to repel aggression but unable to conduct offensive operations. He proposed moving toward a new security regime by withdrawing nuclear and other offensive weapons from borders and creating demilitarized zones; eventually military blocs would dissolve, and all troops stationed abroad would return home. Gorbachev claimed his system of international security would herald a "new organization of life in our common planetary home." . . .

Political Resolution

If Gorbachev is serious about the political resolution of disputes, non-interference, and human rights, he could withdraw his own and his proxy forces from an extended, decrepit empire. To take a few examples, while the U.S. Congress haggled over whether to send token military support or Band-Aids (or nothing) to the Nicaraguan Contras, in 1986 Managua received $500 million in economic aid from the East bloc and $600 million in military equipment, over five times the amount for all of 1985. Since 1960,

Cuba has received about $9 billion in military aid, and during the 1980s the USSR gave Cuba over $4 billion per year in economic aid and subsidies. In return for use of the largest naval base outside the USSR at Cam Ranh Bay, since 1978 Hanoi has received almost $9 billion in military and $8 billion in economic assistance. In 1986 the Marxist government of Angola received $1 billion in military aid, marking a 50 percent increase over the previous year and bringing total Soviet military assistance to $4 billion in the past decade. UNITA's [Union for the Total Liberation of Angola] 63,000 troops face 140,000 government troops backed by 36,000 Cuban military surrogates together with Soviet and East bloc advisers. By contrast, in 1986 UNITA received $15 million in U.S. military aid. In sub-Saharan Africa, over $4 billion in military hardware along with substantial logistics support and 1,700 Soviet military advisers have given Ethiopia the largest army in the region. Since 1979, Soviet aid to Ethiopia has been ten times greater than that provided by the United States to the neighboring nations of Kenya, Sudan, Somalia and Djibouti.

The March of Communism

Communism, the God that failed, still continues its march today—the list is long: Angola, South Yemen, Ethiopia, Mozambique, Nicaragua, and, likely next, South Africa. And, today, 2 billion people, 40 percent of the globe, already live under communism.

Nicholas Patterson, *Vital Speeches of the Day,* December 1, 1988.

Due in large measure to U.S. support for the *mujahideen,* Moscow has withdrawn its troops from Afghanistan, but in view of the fact that the United States spends less than $1 billion a year in support for all anti-communist resistance movements, for a modestly enhanced investment the United States could encourage Gorbachev to follow suit elsewhere. A low-cost, low-risk strategy for the West could assist Gorbachev in divesting the USSR of its imperial burden in other places such as Angola, Ethiopia, Mozambique, South Yemen, Kampuchea, Laos, and Nicaragua. Gorbachev could also demonstrate his "new thinking" by abolishing the Soviet forced labor system and releasing his Helsinki and psychiatric watch groups from prison and psychiatric hospitals, allowing Solidarity to organize in Poland, and freeing his captive East European population. But if Gorbachev's utopian plan to attain mankind's "immortality" through lasting peace on earth is implausible, we must take its strategic aims seriously. . . .

A strategic aim behind Gorbachev's "new thinking" derives from the Kremlin's long-standing arms control objective of denuclearizing the West and its overriding post-1945 goal of disengaging the

United States from Europe. The abiding Soviet goal of global hegemony can be achieved by uncoupling the Atlantic alliance and outflanking the United States in the Third World; without its trans-Atlantic mooring Europe would inevitably fall under Moscow's sway, and Japan and China would then soon come to terms with the new correlation of forces. Gorbachev realizes that Leonid Brezhnev's tactics in the 1970s, nuclear intimidation and military adventurism, finally alarmed the West and provoked it to react. Gorbachev, therefore, has replaced crude coercion with a more subtle tactic of seduction.

To its traditional military muscle in Asia, Moscow has added diplomatic and economic initiatives, although it has not abandoned the instrument of military force. Moscow's fifty-five divisions deployed in the Far East double the number of forces it had there twenty years ago. Its airpower has quadrupled since 1978, and today one-third of its naval aviation is located in the region. The largest of its four fleets, the Soviet Pacific fleet, has grown 80 percent in size since the mid-1960s and today possesses a modern submarine force of 120 submarines in the Pacific. The ratio of Soviet to U.S. forces in the region is 20 to 1 in ground forces, 1.5 to 1 in air forces, 2 to 1 in submarines, and 4 to 1 in total naval forces. The U.S. commander in the Pacific, Adm. Ronald Hays, has stated that the Soviets are building a four-million-gallon fuel storage facility at Cam Rahn Bay in Vietnam to support naval and air forces operating out of that base, and the completion of a seventh pier at the installation increases dock space by 20 percent. A continuing Soviet military buildup, therefore, has not been replaced but rather supplemented by politico-economic overtures.

New Asian Policy

Affirming that "the Soviet Union is also an Asian and Pacific country," Gorbachev launched his "new Asian policy" in a speech at Vladivostok in July 1986, advocating closer political and economic ties with Pacific-Asian countries, particularly Japan and China. Since Vladivostok, Moscow has sought improved relations with both nations together with Thailand, Indonesia, and Australia and would like to gain membership in the Asian Development Bank. In March 1988 the newly created Soviet National Committee for Asia-Pacific Economic Cooperation was placed under the leadership of Yevgeniy Primakov, director of the Institute of World Economics and International Affairs at the USSR Academy of Sciences.

Gorbachev amplified his "new Asian policy" in a September 1988 speech in the Siberian city of Krasnoyarsk. In addition to offering to place the Krasnoyarsk radar complex under international control for space exploration, he proposed: a withdrawal of Soviet naval forces from Cam Rahn Bay in exchange for U.S. relinquishment of its Philippine bases; establishment of a regional security forum and multilateral talks to reduce tensions; normalization of relations with Japan; development of economic relations with South Korea; negotiations to limit naval activities in the Pacific and a "zone of peace" in the Indian Ocean; and a freeze on the number of Soviet nuclear weapons in the region....

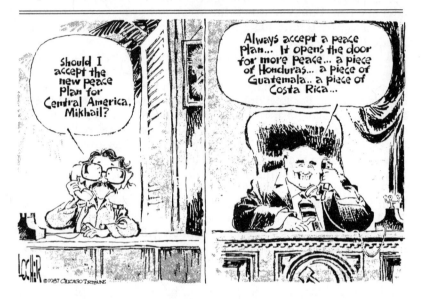

Dick Locher. Reprinted by permission: Tribune Media Services.

In the Third World Gorbachev has courted major, non-socialist nations instead of fomenting new national liberation movements. The Soviets have not acquired costly, new dependencies lately, but as the figures attest, they have not cut support to former clients. This continuity of policy is further illustrated in the Middle East, where Moscow has sent new weapons to Libya and Syria, including SA-5 missiles and MiG-25 fighters. The new diplomatic tack, however, can be seen in Latin America, where Moscow has endeavored to broaden commercial and diplomatic relations. In Peru the Soviets have offered to buy fishing and commercial vessels along with personal computers. Cultural and economic accords have been signed with Brazil and Uruguay, and in 1986 the USSR concluded its first major fishing agreement with Argentina. Moscow has offered to sell Brazil a launching vehicle to boost a Brazilian satellite into space and has agreed to a joint venture to produce ferromanganese along with cooperation in other areas such as energy and fishing. The Soviets have also negotiated to buy optical fibers from Brazil and have shown keen interest in computers and computer software.

In the West, Gorbachev has conducted a charm offensive and has manipulated arms control to use anti-nuclear and neutralist sentiment to drive a wedge in the Western alliance. It would be folly to believe, however, that Gorbachev intends to forfeit Soviet military, especially nuclear, might, which alone makes the USSR a superpower; without that power the level of its economy and society would place the Soviet Union in the ranks of Third World countries. Gorbachev has put to effective use Lenin's advice to Foreign Minister Chicherin before the 1922 Genoa Conference: "Both you and I have fought against pacifism as a program for a revolutionary proletarian party. This is obvious. But where, when and who denied utilization of pacifists by this party in order to demoralize the enemy, the bourgeoisie?

"The Soviet Union, the world's most formidable imperialistic power, is clearly on the march."

The USSR Is Expansionist

William Kintner

William Kintner is the author of *Soviet Global Strategy*. Kintner argues in the following viewpoint that the Soviets have no intention of abandoning their plan to eventually take over the world. The USSR continues to actively encourage other countries to adopt communism, according to Kintner.

As you read, consider the following questions:

1. Why does the USSR undermine other countries' political systems, according to the author?
2. How does the author describe the changes Gorbachev has made in Soviet foreign policy?
3. According to Kintner, how does world opinion affect Soviet foreign policy?

William Kintner, *Soviet Global Strategy*. Fairfax, VA: Hero Books, 1987. Reprinted with permission of Hero Books.

Within its overall strategy, the Soviets appear to be pursuing three related goals: (1) resource strangulation of Western Europe, Japan, and the United States; (2) isolation of the United States from its Western European, Middle Eastern, and Asian allies; and, (3) the neutralization of China. The primary Soviet strategic goal is to confine the United States within the Western Hemisphere.

The Soviet Union has a flexible timetable and a variety of methods to pursue its long-range strategic goals. Soviet aggression uses a wide range of methods—changing the fields of battle, military weapons, and the nonmilitary instruments of subversion, propaganda, and sustained pressure. Soviet political warfare is quite pragmatic. Within the political spectrum, groups are probed for both vulnerability and utility. The Soviet Union's strategy is not at all concerned with the concepts of "left" or "right" as they are defined in the West. Soviet support of Argentina during the 1982 Falkland War is a case in point. They will support groups identified as either or both if they can gain incremental victories in this way.

Soviet analysts perceive that the world situation is unfolding satisfactorily according to their strategic design. The Soviet Union, the world's most formidable imperialistic power, is clearly on the march. Moscow's spokesmen have written "a radical restructuring of international relations" in favor of the Soviet Union. Attempts to restructure international politics so that the Soviet Union attains world leadership are intrinsically offensive, and thus the Soviet global strategy is an offensive one, admirably suited to advance a restructuring of the international system.

Soviet Intentions

Official Soviet announcements since the beginning of the USSR have stressed the unremitting conflict between communism and capitalism, and the inevitable doom of the latter. Even during the height of détente, ideological warfare and supporting "wars of national liberation" were a feature of Soviet statements and propaganda.

In an insightful article, "Gorbachev's Great Push and the Reluctant Public" (December 18, 1986), veteran *New York Times* correspondent Serge Schmemann told how "restructuring" to check the economic stagnation, the political corruption, and the blight of drunkenness had had little impact. Unless the overall situation improves, Gorbachev may decide that the best way to cope with massive internal problems is to launch new adventures outside Soviet borders.

George Feifer, who has written many articles and books about the country, wrote [in *Harper's*] a devastating account of the fundamental and irreversible flaws in the Soviet System. Yet, according to Feifer, Soviet domestic media distorts world news so effectively that the Soviet leaders can count on the blind obedience of the masses. Although the Soviet people realize how badly they have been treated they accept their dismal fate. Feifer concludes, "even with this realization, they'll shoot whom they're told to."

A History of Conquest

The Soviets have an uninterrupted history of conquest under the banner of liberation, and control under the banner of independence. Communist wars of liberation have succeeded in the postwar era because the United States, the only Western power that could have played a leadership role, ignored the plight of the Third World.

Doan Van Toai, *The World & I,* February 1988.

Soviet leaders frequently speak and act as if they were already at war with the U.S., their principal imperialist enemy. Hence, Soviet capabilities reflect intentions which rule out accommodation and which stress unrelenting conflict until one of the powers is vanquished.

Ideological Imperatives

When the Bolsheviks captured Russia, Vladimir Lenin's work *Imperialism: The Highest Stage of Capitalism,* provided the ideological rationale for an unrelenting campaign to destroy the Western democratic, industrial system. While the Soviet intelligentsia is indeed cynical about Soviet ideology, it does provide a rationale for Soviet leaders to undermine and destroy the West.

Ideologically, antagonism between the Soviet Union and the noncommunist world will continue as long as the Soviets adhere to Marxism-Leninism as a basis for policy. Milovan Djilas, a defiant and knowledgeable confidant of both Joseph Stalin and Josip Tito, holds that, "Communism is ideologically and structurally incapable of transforming itself into a democratic, parliamentary, pluralistic polity. . . ."

While Soviet strategy and tactics vary as the correlation of forces between the superpowers changes, the ideological commitment to eliminate all but Marxist-Leninist political systems remains. Soviet leadership devotes vast resources to propagating this ideology, which bestows the harsh Soviet system with some legitimacy.

Most Western analysts see little evidence that the Kremlin shares real interest with Western democracies in the development of a peaceful and cooperative world community. Nor is there any evidence that the ultimate objective of Soviet foreign policy is to establish Soviet-American accord.

The Soviets operate on the fundamental principle of the irreversibility of the socialist revolution. Soviet strategy probes take advantage of Western weaknesses and exploit sociopolitical conflicts in unstable countries to change the global correlation of forces in their favor. Their objective appears to be Soviet hegemony. The Soviet record over the past 20 years supports this conclusion.

This pessimistic conclusion is reinforced by the prolonged Soviet military buildup that far exceeds the requirements of a prudent defensive posture. Secondly, Soviet, or Soviet-Cuban, or Soviet-Vietnamese intrusions since 1975 into Afghanistan, Angola, South Yemen, Ethiopia, Nicaragua, Kampuchea, and Syria have all been supported indirectly by Soviet arms and, directly or indirectly by Soviet soldiers. Finally, the increasing brazenness with which the Soviets and their surrogates conduct their operations reflects self-confidence and disdain for their opponents.

Some general conclusions can be drawn.

The Soviet Union is willing to pay heavily for strategic gains – its big investments in North Korea, Indonesia, Cuba, Egypt, India, Vietnam, Somalia, Angola, Ethiopia, People's Democratic Republic of Yemen, Turkey, and Afghanistan, are proof of that. It focuses on strategic target countries, and does not spread its resources randomly.

The Soviets have utilized internal conflicts in other countries to penetrate into Western-dominated regions, perpetuate local disputes to prolong dependence on Soviet arms, and control local conflicts to prevent all-out wars, which could escalate and necessitate Soviet military forces.

Stand-By Countries

The Soviets promote relations with "stand-by" countries regardless of the state of existing ties, recognizing that many Third World governments are unstable and unpredictable. This tactic minimizes the impact of changes in political factions and has enabled the Soviet Union to cut its losses and shift to another near-by target country. This flexible approach operated in conflicts between Turkey and Greece following the 1974 Cyprus crisis, Syria and Egypt after the 1973 Yom Kippur War, India and China following the 1962 border war, both Yemens, Ethiopia and Somalia in 1977-1978, and Vietnam and Indonesia after the 1965 coup.

The Soviets intrude into the power structure of a strategically valuable Third World country with diplomatic and/or economic penetration, spearheaded by adroit political warfare, followed by military support. At the very least, military paraphernalia provides the Soviets with opportunities for increasing their influence.

The Soviets generally give full support to countries whose policies serve their own aims – Soviet support of Cuba and Vietnam vis-a-vis the United States, and Vietnam vis-a-vis Kampuchea and China, are striking examples of this principle. . . .

The Soviets have become increasingly adept at using proxies for combat which advances their interests. The Cuban legionnaires are the most notable force employed by the Soviets, but North Koreans and, in some situations, the Vietnamese may assume this role.

Messianic Ideology

The USSR will invariably seek ways of increasing its influence in international affairs. At the same time, it will continue to underwrite efforts throughout the world to diminish the clout of the United States. . . .

The Soviets, because of their messianic Marxist-Leninist ideology and long history of foreign invasions, tend to conceptualize foreign relations in terms of systemic conflict and geographical power politics. True to the tenets of geopolitical theory, the Soviet Union – the quintessential world-island land power – will continue to place control of the rimlands of Europe and Asia after national survival on its list of priorities.

Bruce D. Slawter, *Global Affairs*, Winter 1989.

The Soviets disdain world public opinion on issues of strategic importance. They will defend, preserve, or expand their interests regardless of international opinion. To put it differently, they prefer to be respected and even feared rather than liked – the Soviet invasion of Czechoslovakia, their support of Neto in Angola and the Vietnamese in Kampuchea, the use of their own troops in Afghanistan, illustrate this principle.

Soviet strategy tends to avoid unnecessary risks. But when the Soviets do move, they move massively, as in Ethiopia and Afghanistan. Their strategy of incremental gains is well-suited to the nuclear age, particularly in the post-Vietnam period. They have become increasingly adept at interpreting the mood in Washington. They took full advantage of American passivity during most of the 1970s, while avoiding measures that might have aroused the United States to act.

In summary: patience and persistence characterize Soviet strategy. Would the Soviets attempt cooperation at the expense of giving up active influence in areas of vital interest to industrialized democracies? This is not likely. Instead, the expanding military power of the Soviet Union will continue to support an activist Soviet policy.

"The Soviet leadership has decided to substantially cut its commitment of resources abroad."

The USSR Is Not Expansionist

Seweryn Bialer

Seweryn Bialer is a professor of international relations at Columbia University in New York City. He is also the director of the Research Institute on International Change at Columbia. In the following viewpoint, he argues that the Soviets have reduced their commitment to Third World client states like Afghanistan. Bialer writes that the Soviets are no longer expansionist for two reasons: first, because intervention costs money which could be better used to bolster the Soviet economy, and second, because the Soviets seek better relations with the West.

As you read, consider the following questions:

1. What changes in Soviet foreign policy does Bialer describe?
2. According to Bialer, how will the changes affect the USSR's Third World client states?
3. According to the author, how will an end to expansionism affect the Soviet Union's position in the world?

Reprinted by permission of Westview Press from *Gorbachev's Russia and American Foreign Policy*, edited by Seweryn Bialer and Michael Mandelbaum. Copyright 1988 Westview Press, Boulder, Colorado.

Seventy years after the establishment of the Soviet state, forty years after its victory in World War II, and more than thirty years after the death of Stalin, the tyrant who believed in Soviet economic and political autarchy, the Soviet Union for all its international activism found itself isolated internationally. The universe in which Gorbachev took the reins of the Soviet Union was one in which his country had no major friends, and was strapped with an unruly and economically and politically sick "alliance" of satellites and semi-satellites. America was resurgent and the capitalist countries in Europe and Asia were in the throes of a new technological revolution. The evaluation of the existing situation by the new leadership led to the beginning of major revisions in Soviet thought and action with regard to their security and foreign policies.

Gorbachev's leadership and the internal change in the Soviet Union that he has set in motion are of primary interest to the West because of their potential impact on Soviet international behavior. Gorbachev and his colleagues are well aware that foreign and security policies begin at home, and that their international aspirations depend on the availability of a variety of domestic resources to back them up. The efforts of the new leadership to make the Soviet Union a modern nation are dictated as much by its domestic needs as by its international goals. The situation at home, including the change of leadership, cannot but influence Soviet international behavior and its security policies. Because he believes that domestic vitality is necessary for foreign success, Gorbachev's domestic program is his most important foreign policy statement.

Domestic Strength

This new leadership understands the decisive influence of domestic strength on foreign policy. Khrushchev was a gambler who tried to achieve success in foreign policy on the cheap. Brezhnev was cautious and conservative: although he presided over the attainment of strategic parity with the United States, he let his country's domestic power deteriorate to the point that it became insufficient to support the Soviet Union's global ambition. . . .

Gorbachev's Foreign Policy

The distinction between Soviet security policy and foreign policy is to a large extent artificial. What influences security policy also influences the foreign policy of the Soviet Union. . . . This does not mean that all aspects of Soviet security policy are in harmony with Soviet foreign policy goals, nor that all elements of Soviet foreign policy contribute to Soviet security. As a matter of fact, there was and continues to be a tension between these two dimensions of Soviet international behavior. This tension, unintended by the policy-makers, reflects the distinction between these areas of policy and their relative independence of each other.

The primary goal of any country's security policy is to prevent an attack on its own territory or on that of its allies or vassals, and to assure victory in case of war. The primary goals of foreign policies are given to less clear and definitive descriptions because they are more diffuse. Moreover, at different periods in a country's history the relations between its security policy and its foreign policy may be quite different. In the Soviet case, for most of its history foreign policy was subordinated to national security goals – as was the case with the international Communist movement when it was under firm Soviet control. The foremost goal of Soviet foreign policy and the activity of the international Communist movement were intended to prevent the formation of military alliances against the Soviet Union and an attack on the Soviet Union.

Redefining National Security

The Soviets are redefining national security to emphasize its mutual, interdependent character and to place less emphasis upon military power and territorial control, more upon long-term political adjustment.

These new perspectives are reflected in encouragement of change in Eastern Europe and in action to resolve third-world conflicts; in a new stress upon multilateralism and international institutions; in an effort to redefine the Soviet military posture under the conceptual rubrics of "reasonable sufficiency" and "defensive [non-offensive] defense"; and in a very serious Soviet approach to arms control.

Robert H. Johnson, *The Christian Science Monitor*, April 12, 1989.

Under Stalin, this subordination was absolute. Khrushchev weakened it by seeking power and influence in the Third World. His adventures in the Third World reflected his revolutionary hopes and his zeal in exploiting the dissolution of old empires. They had little to do with Soviet security *per se*, or with the defense of the Soviet homeland. In the Brezhnev era, when strategic parity with the United States was achieved, the largely expansionist aims and practices of Soviet foreign policy, which were clearly unrelated to Soviet security goals, began to grow. They went so far as to become harmful to Soviet security by overextending Soviet resources, contributing to the domestic economic crisis and encouraging the military build-up of Russia's adversaries. One may also look at this process from another perspective and conclude that the Soviet concept of national security had broadened. Under Stalin, it was the security of "socialism in one country" that was assigned the highest priority. During the post-World War II period of Stalin's rule and under Khrushchev it was the security of "socialism in one empire" that became all-important. Under Brezhnev, the concept of national security began to include the growing Soviet position as a global power.

The relation of the goals of Soviet national security policy to those of foreign policy between Stalin's death and the end of Brezhnev's rule had come full circle: from the unquestioned subordination of Soviet foreign policy to the security of the Soviet state to Soviet national security being a base for increasingly ambitious Soviet foreign policy. The Soviet leadership during the Brezhnev era viewed the attainment of strategic parity with the United States as a license to seek expansion by military means in the international arena. Their insistence, which started at the beginning of the 1970s, that they were the "equals" of the United States meant that they had the unquestioned right to expand beyond Europe without a challenge from the United States. At this early stage of Gorbachev's leadership, firm conclusions about the relationship between Soviet security and foreign policy as he sees them would be premature. There is mounting evidence, however, that once again the basic tendency is to subordinate Soviet foreign policy to the security of the Soviet state.

The changes in Soviet security policy under Gorbachev are more far-reaching and explicit than are the changes in Soviet foreign policy. While the connection between Soviet domestic conditions and Gorbachev's foreign policy is strong, for a number of reasons, it seems to have had a more limited effect on Gorbachev's foreign policy.

Superpower Concerns

In foreign policy, the balance between overlapping superpower concerns on the one hand, and their conflicting interests on the other, is much less favorable to Soviet-American reconciliation than in security matters, where the area of overlapping interests is large. The long-range Soviet-American conflict is real, after all, and not simply the product of misperception. Even if the superpowers were to move away from their status as mortal enemies, they will most certainly remain global rivals even for the long-range foreseeable future.

Realistically, the changes in the Soviet Union and in the United States do not have the potential of doing away with the conflict, but rather of tempering its virulence, of moderating "the rules of the game," of increasing their prudence in international behavior and of moving the two powers away from situations of direct confrontation. If all of these goals can be achieved, we will have arrived at a major turning point in Soviet-American relations. Without the modifications of Soviet and American foreign policies, however, such an achievement will be impossible.

Gorbachev is hampered by the foreign policy blunders and entanglements he inherited from Brezhnev. Starkly described, his dilemma is how to prevent any further decline in Soviet great power status, how to save face and preserve credibility both domestically and internationally, while at the same time bringing to a swift conclusion some of Brezhnev's costly or foolish foreign policies. . . .

The Security Dilemma

Moscow's "new thinking" comes to terms with the security dilemma: unilateral measures to improve one's position stimulate countermeasures, making the initial move self-defeating. In contrast, Soviet military thinking traditionally emphasized relative advantage. But according to Alan B. Sherr, Gorbachev understands that "if Soviet military procurements make the United States and NATO less secure, the security of the Soviet Union itself is diminished."

Joseph Lepgold, *Bulletin of the Atomic Scientists,* May 1989.

This limits the changes that Gorbachev can make in Soviet foreign policy. Yet, it would be a mistake to assume that his general program of change has found no expression in Soviet foreign policy on either a conceptual or practical level. The pattern of Soviet international activity and foreign policy plans is discernibly connected with Gorbachev's evaluations of the domestic situation and his plans for reform. Gorbachev alluded to this connection in an interview with the editors of *Time* magazine: "You know our domestic plans, draw your own conclusions about what kind of a foreign policy this plan requires." Gorbachev's foreign policy is still evolving; the most important and difficult decisions have yet to be made by the Politburo. It is nonetheless fair to say that the present course of Soviet foreign policy is marked by the following characteristics:

• Soviet foreign policy is becoming subordinated, more that at any time in the post-Stalin era, to exigencies at home; Mikhail Gorbachev seems to be turning inward, toward galvanizing a moribund economy and mobilizing an apathetic public.

• The Soviet leadership wants to insulate both the future of the ongoing succession process and the difficult implementation of radical reforms from international challenges, roadblocks and negative interventions.

• The Soviet leadership has decided to substantially cut its commitment of resources abroad. Some of those cuts, (e.g., to the "frontline" black nations in Southern Africa) are politically easy; others, such as those to the East European vassal states, are difficult and may even become dangerous.

• Gorbachev seems determined to integrate Soviet and East European economies more closely – a goal that eluded his post-Stalin predecessors – and to insist that Eastern Europe contribute more to the process of Soviet economic development.

• Soviet policy-makers seem determined to avoid new military adventures abroad even if opportunities present themselves. In such marginal ventures as support for the Sandinistas in Nicaragua, their position is that they will provide enough military and economic support to prevent a victory of the "Contras," but limit their own involvement to avoid a confrontation with the United States, and to stop short of as major a commitment as that to Cuba. . . .

• To facilitate their program of domestic reconstruction and renewal, the Soviets are increasing their flexibility in dealing with all capitalist countries and trying to minimize the existing political points of contention without yet making major concessions, *e.g.*, on the Pacific islands they occupy that are claimed by Japan.

• The Soviet strategy in dealing with capitalist countries is to make radical arms control initiatives the centerpiece of their policies, thus creating public pressure in those countries for better relations with them.

A Global Power

• Gorbachev's policies show no sign that he is willing to give up the Soviets' hard-won international status as a global power and the increased international influence that goes with it. Soviet international activity is directed at preventing any decline in this status. Examples of such policies are the undiminished commitment to Ethiopia, the only genuine Marxist-Leninist government in Africa; the continued commitment to Angola, a strategic country in any future revolutionary war in South Africa; the commitment to participate in the Middle Eastern affairs and the increasingly strong desire to be part of Arab-Israeli negotiations.

Neither the domestic Soviet situation nor the international environment is conducive to the forcible expansion of Soviet influence. It is therefore not surprising that Soviet foreign policy under Gorbachev is defensive. At the same time, however, the current international environment does not pose a major threat to Soviet security.

"The goals we seek are the goals which the people of Central America yearn for: democracy, security, and peace."

US Intervention in Central America Is Just

George Bush and the Bipartisan Accord on Central America

In 1987, the presidents of El Salvador, Guatemala, Honduras, Nicaragua, and Costa Rica signed the Central American Peace Plan, Esquipulas II. The US responded to Esquipulas II on May 24, 1989, with an agreement between the Congress, the Secretary of State, and the President, called the Bipartisan Accord on Central America. Part I of the following viewpoint is by George Bush who was vice-president of the US from 1980 to 1988 and then became President in 1989. Part II is the full text of the Bipartisan Accord on Central America. According to Bush, the Accord complements regional efforts for peace and promotes democracy in Nicaragua.

As you read, consider the following questions:

1. According to Bush what are the goals of the Bipartisan Accord on Central America?
2. Why should the US be involved in Central America, according to Bush?
3. What is the purpose of the Bipartisan Accord, as stated in its text?

George Bush, "US Support for Democracy and Peace in Central America" statement on March 24, 1989. Bipartisan Accord on Central America, March 24, 1989. United States Department of State, Bureau of Public Affairs, Selected Documents No. 36.

I

We have signed today together a Bipartisan Accord on Central America. It sets out the broad outlines of U.S. policy toward that troubled region and commits both the executive branch and Congress to work together to achieve it.

The goals we seek are the goals which the people of Central America yearn for: democracy, security, and peace. Those are the pledges made by the Central American Presidents in the Esquipulas II accord. That agreement is an integrated whole: all of its provisions must move forward together if any of them is to be fulfilled. Our challenge now is to turn those promises into concrete realities.

Democratic Leaders

The only way we can meet that challenge is if Latin democratic leaders and the United States work together, with the support of our European friends and allies, as true partners with candor and mutual respect. I believe Latin leaders are asking for that kind of relationship as we confront together the many challenges facing our hemisphere. As President, I pledge the United States is ready to respond.

Under this Central America agreement, insurgent forces have the right to reintegrate into their homeland under safe, democratic conditions with full civil and political rights. That is the desire of the Nicaraguan Resistance. It is what they are fighting for. We hope and believe it can be achieved through a concerted diplomatic effort to enforce this regional agreement.

To achieve these goals the bipartisan leadership of Congress has agreed to support my request for continued humanitarian assistance to the Nicaraguan Resistance through the elections scheduled in Nicaragua.

There will be extensive consultations and review with respect to these funds, by the bipartisan leadership and relevant committees. However, I have been assured that the leadership in both Houses supports the extension of this assistance through the Nicaraguan elections, barring unforeseen circumstances.

No Shortcut to Democracy

There is no shortcut to democracy; no quick fix. The next weeks and months will demand patience and perseverance by the democratic community and the hard, technical work of ensuring compliance with the Esquipulas accord. The United States will work in good faith to support that kind of diplomatic effort, but we will not support a paper agreement that sells out the Nicaraguan people's right to be free.

We do not claim the right to order the politics of that country.

This is for the people of Nicaragua to decide. We support what the Esquipulas accord requires: free, open, political processes in which all groups can fairly and safely compete for political leadership. That means the playing field must be level; all, including the current government, must respect the majority's decision in the end, and the losers must also retain the political rights to operate as a legal opposition and contest again for political authority in the next recurring election contest.

A Communist Base

The presence of a communist base in Central America threatens neighboring nations, including the United States, and jeopardizes U.S. supply lanes to its allies elsewhere. . . . The long-term objective must be the replacement of Sandinista rule by a democratic system.

W. Bruce Weinrod, *The World & I,* January 1989.

The burden of proof is on the Sandinista government to do something it has steadfastly refused to do from 1979 to 1989: to keep its promises to the Nicaraguan people to permit real democracy; keep its promises to its neighbors not to support subversion in Central America; and keep its obligation to this hemisphere not to permit the establishment of Soviet-bloc bases in Central America. If those promises are kept, we have an opportunity to start a new day in Central America; but if those pledges continue to be violated, we hope and expect that other nations will find ways to join us to condemn those actions and reverse those processes.

The Soviet Obligation

The Soviet Union also has an obligation and an opportunity: to demonstrate that its proclaimed commitment to "new thinking" is more than a tactical response to temporary setbacks but represents instead a new principled approach to foreign policy.

In other regional conflicts around the world, the Soviet Union has adopted a welcome new approach that has helped resolve longstanding problems in constructive ways. In Central America what we have seen from the Soviet Union and Cuba can only be described as "old thinking."

The Soviet bloc since 1979 has poured at least $50 billion in aid into Cuba and Nicaragua. Soviet and Cuban aid is building in Nicaragua a military machine larger than all the armies of the other Central American nations combined and continues to finance violence, revolution, and destruction against the democratically elected government of El Salvador. Indeed, Soviet-bloc military support for the Marxist guerrillas [in El Salvador] has increased

93

since the United States ended military support for the Nicaraguan Resistance, and Soviet military aid to the Government of Nicaragua continues at levels wholly uncalled for by any legitimate defensive needs. The continuation of these levels of Soviet-bloc aid into Central America raises serious questions about Soviet attitudes and intentions toward the United States.

No Security Interest

The Soviet Union has no legitimate security interest in Central America, and the United States has many. We reject any doctrine of equivalence of interest in this region as a basis for negotiations. Instead, the Soviet Union and Cuba have an obligation to the leaders of Central America to stop violating the provisions of the Esquipulas accord, which the Soviet Union and Cuba both pledged to uphold. The time to begin is now.

In signing the Esquipulas accord, President Oscar Arias of Costa Rica said: "Without democracy, there can be no peace in Central America." He is right. But with democracy and peace in Central America can come new hope for economic development in which all of the people of the region can share. One can look at the terrible violence ravaging Central America and despair, but I have a different vision of its future.

I can see a democratic Central America in which all of the nations of the region live in peace with each other; where the citizens of the region are safe from the violence of the state or from revolutionary guerrillas; where resources now devoted to military defense could be channeled to build hospitals, homes, and schools. That is not a dream if all the people and nations of the Americas will it to be true. I hope the Esquipulas accord and perhaps, also, the Bipartisan Accord, will someday be seen as the first step toward its fulfillment.

II

The executive branch and the Congress are united today in support of democracy, peace, and security in Central America. The United States supports the peace and democratization process and the goals of the Central American Presidents emobdied in the Esquipulas accord. The United States is committed to working in good faith with the democratic leaders of Central America and Latin America to translate the bright promises of Esquipulas II into concrete realities.

Democratizing Nicaragua

With regard to Nicaragua, the United States is united in its goals; democratization; an end to subversion and destabilization of its neighbors; an end to Soviet-bloc military ties that threaten U.S. and regional security. Today the executive branch and the Congress are united on a policy to achieve those goals.

To be successful the Central American peace process cannot be based on promises alone. It must be based on credible standards of compliance, strict timetables for enforcement, and effective, ongoing means to verify both the democratic and security requirements of those agreements. We support the use of incentives and disincentives to achieve these U.S. policy objectives.

We also endorse an open, consultative process, with bipartisanship as the watchword for the development and success of a unified policy toward Central America. The Congress recognizes the need for consistency and continuity in policy and the responsibility of the executive to administer and carry out that policy, the programs based upon it, and to conduct American diplomacy in the region. The executive will consult regularly and report to the Congress on progress in meeting the goals of the peace and democratization process, including the use of assistance as outlined in this accord.

Promises of Democracy

We want the people of Nicaragua, as well as all others in Central America, to be able to participate freely and fully in democracy. And now, together, the executive branch and the Congress will work to ensure that the promises of democracy in Nicaragua become democracy in fact.

James A. Baker III, Statement on March 24, 1989.

Under Esquipulas II and the El Salvador accord, insurgent forces are supposed to voluntarily reintegrate into their homeland under safe, democratic conditions. The United States shall encourage the Government of Nicaragua and the Nicaraguan Resistance to continue the cessation of hostilities currently in effect.

Humanitarian Assistance

To implement our purposes, the executive will propose – and the bipartisan leadership of the Congress will act promptly to extend – humanitarian assistance at current levels to the Resistance noting that the Government of Nicaragua has agreed to hold new elections under international supervision. Those funds shall also be available to support voluntary reintegration or voluntary regional relocation by the Nicaraguan Resistance. Such voluntary reintegration or voluntary regional relocation assistance shall be provided in a manner supportive of the goals of the Central American nations, as expressed in the Esquipulas II agreement and the El Salvador accord, including the goal of democratization within Nicaragua and the reintegration plan to be developed pursuant to those accords.

We believe that democratization should continue throughout

Central America in those nations in which it is not yet complete, with progress toward strengthening of civilian leadership, the defense of human rights, the rule of law and functioning judicial systems, and consolidation of free, open, and safe political processes in which all groups and individuals can fairly compete for political leadership. We believe that democracy and peace in Central America can create the conditions for economic integration and development that can benefit all the people of the region and pledge ourselves to examine new ideas to further those worthy goals.

Soviet Violations

While the Soviet Union and Cuba both publicly endorsed the Esquipulas agreement, their continued aid and support of violence and subversion in Central America is in direct violation of that regional agreement. The United States believes that President Gorbachev's visit to Cuba represents an important opportunity for both the Soviet Union and Cuba to end all aid that supports subversion and destabilization in Central America, as President Arias has requested, and as the Central American peace process demands.

The U.S. Government retains ultimate responsibility to define its national interests and foreign policy, and nothing in this accord shall be interpreted to infringe on that responsibility. The United States need not spell out in advance the nature or type of action that would be undertaken in response to threats to U.S. national security interests. Rather it should be sufficient to simply make clear that such threats will be met by any appropriate constitutional means. The spirit of trust, bipartisanship, and common purpose expressed in this accord between the executive and the Congress shall continue to be the foundation for its full implementation and the achievement of democracy, security, and peace in Central America.

"The bipartisan accord upholds the self-ordained U.S. right to intervene."

US Intervention in Central America Is Unjust

Holly Sklar

In the following viewpoint, Holly Sklar asserts that the Bipartisan Accord on Central America permits further US intervention in Central America. The Accord calls for continued humanitarian aid to Nicaragua, but Sklar believes the aid is money to support the Contra military opposition. Sklar argues that US intervention does not promote democracy, but instead violates Central Americans' right to determine their own governments and futures. Sklar contributes to *Zeta Magazine*, an independent political magazine. She is also the author of several books on US intervention in Central America.

As you read, consider the following questions:

1. According to Sklar, what is the true purpose of the Bipartisan Accord?
2. What should US policy be toward Central America, according to the author?
3. What steps does Sklar believe the US should take to implement that policy?

Holly Sklar, "Bipartisan Thrust toward Nicaragua," *Zeta*, June 1989. Reprinted with the author's permission.

In reprinting the text of the March 24, 1989 Nicaragua accord between Congress and the Bush administration, the *New York Times* made an appropriate typo in the conclusion: "The spirit of *thrust*, bipartisanship, and common purpose expressed in this Accord between the Executive and the Congress shall continue to be the foundation for its full implementation and the achievement of democracy, security, and peace in Central America." Democrats and Republicans alike trust in Washington's right to thrust.

Central America's Destiny

As an undersecretary of state put it in a confidential memorandum: "We do control the destinies of Central America, and we do so for the simple reason that the national interest absolutely dictates such a course. . . . Until now, Central America has always understood that governments which we recognize and support stay in power, while those which we do not recognize and support fall. Nicaragua has become a test case." The year was 1927; U.S. Marines fought Sandino's guerrillas in a counterrevolutionary war unpopular at home. A decade after Sandino's heirs overthrew the U.S.-supported Somoza dictatorship, Washington is still trying to make the Sandinista-led government fall.

In their bipartisan accord against Nicaragua, President George Bush, House Speaker Jim Wright, Senate Majority Leader George Mitchell, House Majority Leader Tom Foley, Senate Minority Leader Bob Dole, and House Minority Leader Bob Michel declared: "The United States is committed to working in good faith with the democratic leaders of Central America and Latin America to translate the bright promises of Esquipulas II into concrete realities on the ground.

"With regard to Nicaragua, the United States is united in its goals: democratization; an end to subversion and destabilization of its neighbors; an end to Soviet bloc military ties that threaten U.S. and regional security. . . .

"The United States Govermment retains ultimate responsibility to define its national interests and foreign policy, and nothing in this Accord shall be interpreted to infringe on that responsibility. The United States need not spell out in advance the nature or type of action that would be undertaken in response to threats to U.S. national security interests. . . ."

In other words, the bipartisan accord upholds the self-ordained U.S. right to intervene. The administration and congressional leadership are united in the goals of transferring power to pro-U.S. forces, subverting and destabilizing Nicaragua and unilaterally ending the Soviet military assistance which, given the U.S. blockade of Western military aid to Nicaragua, has enabled Nicaragua to thwart the U.S.-made contra invasion.

98

Washington sabotaged the Contadora treaty which would have banned foreign military advisers and bases (the bases are all U.S. bases), restricted military maneuvers, prohibited assistance to insurgent forces, and limited troops and weapons in the Central America region.

Foreign Policy Deceptions

We can appreciate the immense deceptions that underlie US foreign policy. While professing a dedication to peaceful, nonviolent change, US policymakers have committed themselves to a defense of the status quo throughout the world that regularly relies on violence. They sometimes seize upon the revolutionary ferment that might exist in impoverished lands as an excuse for *not* making economic changes. Not until the situation in this or that country has been sufficiently stabilized, they say, can we venture upon reforms. Until then, we must rely on the police and military to restore order. But once "order" and "stability" are reimposed, that is, once the democratic agitation has been crushed or subdued, there is no longer any felt pressure for *economic* reform.

Michael Parenti, *The Sword and the Dollar*, 1989.

Washington refuses to be subject to Central American sovereignty and observe the same conditions applied to the Soviet Union or any foreign power. As Nicaraguan Foreign Minister Miguel D'Escoto told me, the United States "considers it a terrible affront to be regarded as a foreigner in its own 'backyard.' Meanwhile, the U.S. government rounds up Latin American refugees in detention camps and separates them into legal and illegal "aliens." A recent headline read, "79 Aliens Seized on Jet." Those so-called "aliens" weren't from Mars – the headline was in the *New York Times*, not the *National Enquirer*.

Washington has been translating the "bright promises" of Esquipulas II into concrete contra realities on the ground. With little attention in the United States, contras inside Nicaragua continue to kidnap and kill Nicaraguan civilians. To take recent attacks documented by the Washington-based Witness for Peace, contras killed 3 civilians and wounded 5 near Matagalpa on April 15, 1989. On March 10, 1989, contras attacked a cooperative near Rama killing two adults and wounding three children. Another group of contras, first attempting to pose as Sandinista soldiers, kidnapped 7 men from a cooperative near Matiguas. They tortured and killed 2 of them, slitting their throats, cutting their tongues off and shooting them in the head.

In April, 1989, Congress approved the latest in a series of multi-million-dollar contra aid installments since the Iran-contra coverup hearings. The contra aid package provides for $66.6 million in funding, including nearly $50 million in "humanitarian aid," nearly $13 million for administrative and transport expenses, and a hypocritical $4 million in medical assistance for civilian war victims.

"Humanitarian Aid"

"Humanitarian aid," a bipartisan euphemism for contra war support since 1985, debases a term well established in international law. Under the Geneva Conventions, humanitarian aid must be provided impartially by neutral agencies on the basis of need to civilians and noncombatants. U.S. contra aid mocks all these criteria.

Whatever it's called, contra aid violates the August 1987 Central America Peace Accord (Esquipulas II) and the February 1989 Central America Accord to disband the contras signed in El Salvador. As stated in the 1987 accord: "The Governments of the five Central American countries (Costa Rica, El Salvador, Guatemala, Honduras, Nicaragua) shall request the Governments in and outside the region that openly or covertly provide military, logistic, financial, propaganda, manpower, armament, ammunition and equipment assistance to irregular forces or insurrectional movements to cease such assistance as an essential element for achieving a stable and durable peace in the region." The accord stipulated, "Not included in the foregoing is assistance for repatriation, or where that is not possible, relocation. . . ."

In the February 1989 accord, "The Central American Presidents firmly repeated the request contained in. . .the Esquipulas II Accord that regional and extra-regional Governments which either openly or secretly supply aid to irregular forces or insurrectional movements in the area immediately halt such aid, with the exception of the humanitarian aid that contributes to the goals of this document," i.e., aid for the purpose of repatriation or resettlement.

In 1989, as in 1987, the U.S. mass media follow the administration lead in treating the contra aid prohibition as if it were written in invisible ink. Meanwhile Washington invests unilateral requirements for Nicaragua for whom it professes to be judge, jury, and executioner. Once again, Honduras and Costa Rica are buckling under U.S. pressure to reinterpret the accord as requiring Nicaraguan "democratization" (i.e. ceding power to pro-U.S. forces) before contra demobilization.

The Bush administration opted for "humanitarian aid" because it could not count on enough congressional votes for direct military aid given continued public opposition and the obvious failure of contra strategy. As Secretary of State James Baker, known as the "Velvet Hammer," put it in an interview with *Time* magazine (February 13, 1989): "You will have to continue to support (the contras) through humanitarian assistance. . . . We need to at least leave open the prospect they could be re-established as a fighting force if Oretega continues to thumb his nose at his neighbors."

Democracy in Nicaragua

The reality is that no U.S. policy is going to guarantee democratization in Nicaragua, especially if the "litmus test" is American-style democracy or abdication by the Sandinistas.

Morris Blachman and Kenneth Sharpe, *Tikkun*, May/June 1988.

While the new aid installment may prove to be "mustering out pay," as rightwingers fear and liberal Democrats hope, the administration wants the option to say, "We tried negotiations, but Ortega 'thumbed his nose,' so it's time for more contra military aid." This option assumes the contras won't disintegrate past the point of no return through desertion to Miami, infighting over the shrinking spoils of war, and repatriation with amnesty in Nicaragua.

Whatever the future contra role in the continued U.S. effort to destabilize the Nicaraguan government, Washington is placing increased emphasis on the internal front. U.S. efforts to build a viable internal front go back to the Carter administration's overt and covert attempts to forge an anti-Sandinista alternative to Somoza. U.S. aid to the conservative Nicaraguan business organization COSEP [Higher Council of Private Enterprise], *La Prensa*, and other conservative forces has continued since the Sandinista victory in 1979. The CIA (Central Intelligence Agency) has tried and failed to mold a unified internal front throughout the contra war.

During a 1984 MADRE [a women's health care organization in Central America] delegation to Nicaragua, Health Minister Dora Maria Tellez was asked how she compared the revolutionary struggle with running the government. "It's an absolute difference," she replied. "If they gave you the task of demolishing this house, you would knock down the walls and then the windows, etc. But if later they tell you 'now build the house,' you must first become a stonemason, then learn the proportions of cement to stone, and so on. You must take out the old foundation, put down the new foundation, and when you've put up the columns, walls, and a roof, you still have to fix up the interior of the house, put in furniture. It's the same difference."

Until 1983, when the economy began reeling under the strain of war, decapitalization, and regional economic crisis, Nicaraguans made rapid progress in rebuilding their national home. Nicaragua registered the highest rate of economic growth in the region. The literacy crusade slashed adult illiteracy. The World Health

Organization gave Nicaragua its 1982 award for the greatest achievement in health by a Third World nation. Washington has failed to overthrow the government, but it has sabotaged progress in health care, education, and other social services and fueled the economic crisis wreaking havoc in Nicaragua today. War-related economic damage is now over $12.2 billion. Economic warfare has been compounded by the devastating Hurricane Joan.

Minister Tellez described the impact of U.S. intervention this way: "First, we knocked down the house. We ripped out the foundation and began to set a new foundation, to install the pilings and erect the walls. While we're erecting one wall, [the U.S.] comes along and knocks down the one we put up on the other side. So, we leave this one to go rebuild the fallen wall. . . . Meanwhile, [the U.S.] knocks down a different one. What would we do if they weren't doing this to us? We would get the walls up and even put the roof on!"

Americans have to learn to view the changing house of Nicaragua as neighbors, not landlords. Washington must recognize the Nicaraguan's right to control their own destiny.

Self-Determination South and North

An alternative U.S. policy respectful of international law, sovereignty, and self-determination would support the Central American Peace Accords; comply with the World Court; cease contra aid; support efforts to establish a UN peacekeeping force to monitor the Honduras-Nicaragua border; lift the embargo (called for in House bill HR418); respect Nicaraguan elections; and end war-related aid to El Salvador, Honduras, and Guatemala. Taking the longer view, peace activists should call for the outlaw of covert action as a tool of U.S. policy which is incompatible with civil liberties and democracy at home and abroad.

We should be clearer about the link between domestic and international McCarthyism (or Trumanism in recognition of Truman's loyalty statute). Most Americans don't know the FBI functions as a national thought police. Most people don't know about the surveillance, break-ins, and intimidation tactics (given only limited scrutiny with exposure of the FBI CISPES [Committee in Solidarity with the People of El Salvador] investigation). The Bush administration must be challenged to respect democracy and human rights in the United States.

Peace activists have to make anti-intervention work more comprehensive going beyond a country-by-country and regional approach to a multi-regional approach. We should be more consistent in our opposition to the contras in Nicaragua and the UNITA [National Union for the Total Independence of Angola] contras in Angola, to U.S.-supported state terrorism in El Salvador, Guatemala, and the Philippines. We should bolster specific causes with a common agenda for alternative policy that supports self-determination, challenges racism and sexism, ends debt peonage, and supports equitable and ecological development. We need a common agenda to cut the military budget, much of which is directed to intervention in the Third World, and redefine mutual security and progress as the national interest.

The Peace Movement

However strong the peace movement becomes, it will not be strong enough to stop military intervention, much less economic and political intervention, if it remains largely isolated from domestic struggles for change. The Latin American debt crisis and the redlining of U.S. inner cities, for example, are two sides to the same coin. It's self-defeating to support the empowerment of workers and farmers in Central America without forging mutually empowering coalitions in the United States. We have to build on efforts – such as the Rainbow Coalition, MADRE, and the Nicaragua Network's Oats for Peace campaign with the Federation of Southern Cooperatives – to practice mutual solidarity in domestic and international terms.

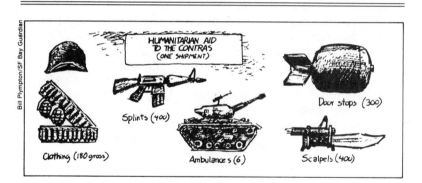

Bill Plympton. Reprinted with permission.

Ultimately, intervention in other countries will not stop unless progressive forces win power in this country – the power to implement alternative policies, not just protest the policies that be. To take Congress as an example, it's self-defeating to demonstrate and lobby Congress without doing voter registration and running accountable candidates to remake Congress. Without real self-determination in the United States, self-determination in the Third World will always be at risk.

a critical thinking activity

Evaluating Sources of Information

A critical thinker must always question sources of information. Historians, for example, distinguish between *primary sources* (eyewitness accounts, documents, or artifacts) and *secondary sources* (writings or statements based on primary sources or other secondary sources). The diary of a nuclear arms negotiator recording arms control discussions is an example of a primary source. A book written by a historian on the arms race between the superpowers is an example of a secondary source.

Interpretation and/or point of view also play a role when dealing with both primary and secondary sources. An American arms negotiator and a Soviet arms negotiator might both keep diaries of the same discussions, but they may differ in their reports of what happened. Likewise, books published in the Soviet Union and the United States might differ in their assessments on the causes and effects of the nuclear arms race. It is up to the researcher to keep in mind the potential biases of his/her sources.

Test your skill in evaluating sources of information by completing the following exercise. Imagine you are writing a report on the weapons the superpowers have deployed in Europe. Listed below are a number of sources which may be useful for your research. *Place a P next to those descriptions you believe are primary sources. Second, rank the primary sources assigning the number (1) to what appears to be the most accurate and fair primary source, the number (2) to the next most accurate, and so on until the ranking is finished.* Next, *place an S next to those descriptions you believe are secondary sources and rank them also, using the same criteria.*

If you are doing this activity as a member of a class or group, discuss and compare your evaluation with other members of the group. Others may come to different conclusions than you. Listening to their reasons may give you valuable insights in evaluating sources of information.

P = *primary*
S = *secondary*

P or S		Rank In Importance

_____ 1. A book entitled *US/Soviet Relations: The Reagan Years.* _____

_____ 2. The text of the intermediate-range nuclear forces (INF) treaty between the US and USSR _____

_____ 3. A magazine article on Mikhail Gorbachev's arms control proposals by a professor of Soviet politics. _____

_____ 4. An interview with the commander of the North Atlantic Treaty Organization on the arms balance between NATO and the Warsaw Pact. _____

_____ 5. A television documentary about the peace movement in the US, Europe, and the USSR. _____

_____ 6. A written agreement between Soviet and US generals outlining procedures to prevent the accidental start of nuclear war. _____

_____ 7. A speech by Mikhail Gorbachev to the United Nations concerning the arms race. _____

_____ 8. A speech by Mikhail Gorbachev to the Soviet Parliament concerning the arms race. _____

_____ 9. A speech by George Bush in Germany calling for a united and peaceful Europe. _____

_____ 10. An article in *Conservative Digest* accusing the Soviets of cheating on arms control treaties. _____

_____ 11. A proposed budget for 1990 US military spending drawn up by the US secretary of defense. _____

Periodical Bibliography

The following articles have been selected to supplement the diverse views presented in this chapter.

Michael H. Armacost	"Regional Issues and US-Soviet Relations," *Department of State Bulletin*, September 1988.
Alvin H. Bernstein	"Insurgents Against Moscow," *Policy Review*, Summer 1987.
Pavel Bogomolov	"When Will the Fighting Stop?" *New Times*, no. 5, January 1988.
James Chace	"Inescapable Entanglements," *Foreign Affairs*, Winter 1988/1989.
Commonweal	"Crimping the Accords," April 21, 1989.
Morton Kondracke	"The World the Candidates Forgot," *The New Republic*, November 21, 1988.
Charles Krauthammer	"America Drowns Soviet Retreat in Sympathy," *Los Angeles Times*, April 9, 1989.
Yuri Kudimov	"A Farewell to Arms?" *New Times*, no. 9, February 28/March 6, 1989.
Yuri Kudimov	"Contras, Bankers and Inflation," *New Times*, no. 10, March 7/13, 1989.
Yuri Kudimov	"Time To Move Towards a Settlement," *New Times*, no. 46, November 1988.
John Lukacs	"Soviets Aren't the Point of Conflict," *Los Angeles Times*, October 2, 1987.
The New Republic	"A Done Deal," April 24, 1989.
Pravda	"Statement by the Soviet Foreign Ministry," February 22, 1989.
Rigoberto Padilla Rush	"Central America: Thorny Path to Peace and Liberation," *World Marxist Review*, April 1988.
Alan Tonelson	"The End of Internationalism," *The New Republic*, February 13, 1989.
Casper W. Weinberger	"Low-Intensity Warfare," *Vital Speeches of the Day*, February 15, 1986.

How Has the New Detente Affected Arms Control?

Chapter Preface

Arms control proposals in the 1980s have centered around arms in Eastern and Western Europe. The Intermediate-Range Nuclear Forces Treaty was an important breakthrough in arms control. In signing the treaty on December 8, 1987, the superpowers agreed to reduce intermediate- and short-range nuclear missiles in Europe. The efforts continued one year later when Soviet General Secretary Mikhail Gorbachev offered to reduce forces in the USSR and Eastern Europe by 500,000 soldiers and 10,000 tanks, in addition to other reductions in conventional arms. In the spring of 1989, US President George Bush proposed cutting US troops stationed in Europe by 20 percent, reducing assault helicopters and aircraft by 15 percent, and reducing the number of tanks and armored troop carriers.

Whether these superpower arms control initiatives will end the threat of nuclear war and bring peace remains to be seen. The authors in this chapter debate how arms control will affect the superpower relationship.

"We are witnessing a new historic reality: the principle of excessive arms stockpiling is giving way to the principle of reasonable sufficiency for defence.

Soviet Arms Reductions Are Genuine

Mikhail Gorbachev

Mikhail Gorbachev is the general secretary of the Communist Party and president of the Soviet Union. Gorbachev argues in the following viewpoint that the Soviet Union has undergone a fundamental change in its worldview. He proposes a significant reduction in both conventional and nuclear forces. Gorbachev asserts that the reductions are lasting, genuine, and will enhance global security.

As you read, consider the following questions:

1. What reductions does Gorbachev propose for the Soviet military?
2. What reasons does Gorbachev give for reducing Soviet forces?
3. How does the author believe the US should respond to the new Soviet military strategy?

Mikhail Gorbachev, "USSR Arms Reductions," a speech delivered to the United Nations on February 1, 1989. Copyright © Novosti Press Agency Publishing House, 1988.

What will humanity be like as it enters the 21st century? Thoughts about this already very near future are engaging people's minds. While we look forward to the future with the anticipation of change for the better, we also view it with alarm.

Today, the world is a very different place from what it was at the beginning of this century, and even in the middle of it. And the world and all of its components keep changing.

The emergence of nuclear weapons was a tragic way of stressing the fundamental nature of these changes. Being the material symbol and the bearer of the ultimate military force, nuclear weapons at the same time laid bare the absolute limits to this force.

Humankind is faced with the problem of survival, of self-protection, in all its magnitude. . . .

The International Situation

In thinking all this over, it becomes clear that we have to look for ways together to improve the international situation, to build a new world—that is, if we are going to take into consideration the lessons of the past, the realities of the present, and the objective logic of world development.

If this is really true, it would be worthwhile to reach an understanding on the basic and genuinely universal principles of this search, and the prerequisites for it.

It is evident, in particular, that force or the threat of force neither can nor should be instruments of foreign policy. This mainly refers to nuclear arsenals, but not to them alone. All of us, and first of all the strongest of us, have to practice self-restraint and renounce the use of force in the international arena.

This is the cornerstone of the ideal of a non-violent world proclaimed by the Soviet Union and India in their Delhi Declaration. We invite all to adopt this ideal.

It is clear even today that no country can achieve omnipotence, no matter how much it builds up its military might. Furthermore, emphasis on that might alone will in the final analysis undermine other aspects of that country's national security. . . .

The Arms Race

International developments and affairs have been distorted by the arms race and the militarization of thought.

As you will no doubt be aware, on January 15, 1986 the Soviet Union advanced a programme to construct a world free from nuclear weapons. Efforts to translate this programme into negotiations already have produced some tangible results.

December 8th is the anniversary of the signing of the Treaty on the Elimination of Intermediate-Range and Shorter-Range Missiles. And I am pleased to say today that the implementation of the Treaty—the destruction of missiles—is proceeding normally, in an atmosphere of trust and constructive work.

A large breach has been made in the wall of suspicion and hostility, which once seemed to be impenetrable. And we are witnessing a new historic reality: the principle of excessive arms stockpiling is giving way to the principle of reasonable sufficiency for defence.

We are witnessing the first efforts to build a new model of security through the reduction of armaments on the basis of compromise, not through their build-up, as was almost always the case in the past.

Soviet Leadership

And the Soviet leadership has decided once again to demonstrate its willingness to encourage this healthy process not only in words but in actions.

I am able to inform you of the fact that the Soviet Union has decided to reduce its armed forces.

Their strength will be reduced by 500,000 men, and substantial cuts will be made in conventional armaments. These cuts will be made unilaterally.

By agreement with our Warsaw Treaty allies, we have decided to withdraw six tank divisions from the German Democratic Republic, Czechoslovakia and Hungary by 1991, and to disband them.

Defensive Sufficiency

Western governments have been skeptical of Soviet statements about the principles of defensive sufficiency and defensive defense because, until Gorbachev's U.N. speech, they had seen no sign of a major redeployment or restructuring of conventional forces, or of a major reduction in defense expenditures or weapons procurement. Gorbachev's decision (in apparent disregard of military advice) to cut the Soviet armed forces by 500,000 men indicates, however, that there is more to the new thinking than words alone.

David Holloway, *Foreign Affairs*, Winter 1988/1989.

In addition, assault-landing formations and units and some others, including assault-crossing support units with their armaments and combat equipment, will be withdrawn from the Soviet forces stationed in these countries.

The Soviet forces stationed in these countries will be reduced by 50,000 men and 5,000 tanks.

The Soviet divisions which still remain on the territory of our allies will be reorganized. Their structure will be changed: a large number of tanks will be withdrawn, and they will become strictly defensive.

At the same time we shall cut troops and armaments in the European part of the U.S.S.R.

The total reductions of Soviet armed forces in the European regions of the U.S.S.R. and on the territory of our European allies will amount to 10,000 tanks, 8,500 artillery systems and 800 combat aircraft.

We shall also make considerable reductions in the armed forces grouping in the Asian part of our country. By agreement with the Mongolian government, a large number of the Soviet troops temporarily stationed there will return home.

In taking these important decisions the Soviet leadership is expressing the will of the Soviet people, who are engaged in the radical overhaul of their entire socialist society.

We shall maintain the country's defence capability at a level of reasonable and dependable sufficiency, so that no one is tempted to encroach upon the security of the U.S.S.R. or its allies.

By this action and by all our efforts to demilitarize international relations, we want to draw the attention of the international community to yet another urgent matter, the problem of converting the armaments economy into a disarmament economy.

The Conversion of Arms

Is the conversion of arms production possible? I have already spoken on this score. We believe it is.

The Soviet Union, for its part, is prepared

• to draft and present its own internal conversion plan as part of its economic reform effort;

• to prepare plans for the conversion of two or three defence plants as an experiment;

• to make public its experience in re-employing defence personnel and using defence facilities and equipment in civilian production.

We consider it desirable for all countries, especially the great military powers, to submit their national conversion plans to the United Nations.

It will also be beneficial if a team of scientists is formed and entrusted with the task of analyzing the problem of conversion in depth, both in general and with regard to individual countries and regions, and reporting its findings to the U.N. Secretary-General.

Later, this question should be discussed at a session of the General Assembly.

Lastly, since I am on American soil, and for other understandable reasons, I cannot help speaking about our relations with this great nation. I was able to fully appreciate its hospitality during my memorable visit to Washington.

The relations between the Soviet Union and the United States stretch back over five and a half decades. As the world has changed, so have the character, role and place of these relations in world politics.

For too long these relations were characterized by confrontation and sometimes hostility, be it open or concealed.

But in recent years people all over the world have sighed with relief as the essence and atmosphere of relations between Moscow and Washington have taken a turn for the better.

Soviet Sincerity

The Soviet Union has demonstrated its sincerity for peace and peaceful relations by significant unilateral measures for disarmament. . . .

The Soviet Union keeps coming up with deeds. Washington keeps coming up with rhetoric. It's time to stop stalling. . . . It's time to get on with the disarmament process.

Jim West, *People's Daily World*, April 26, 1989.

I am not underestimating the seriousness of our differences or the complexity of the problems yet to be resolved. However, we have learned our first lessons in mutual understanding and in searching for solutions that meet both our own and general interests.

Nuclear-Missile Arsenals

The U.S.S.R. and the United States have built up immense nuclear-missile arsenals. But they have also managed to clearly acknowledge their responsibility and become the first to conclude an agreement on the reduction and physical elimination of some of those weapons, which have threatened their own countries and all the other nations of the world.

Our two countries have the greatest and most sophisticated military secrets. But it is precisely they who have laid the basis for and are developing a system of mutual verification of the destruction of armaments, their limitation and a ban on their production.

It is precisely they who are accumulating experience for future bilateral and multilateral agreements.

We cherish this experience, and we appreciate and value the contribution made by President Ronald Reagan and the members of his administration, especially Mr. George Shultz.

All this is capital which we have invested in a joint venture of historic significance. It most not be wasted or left idle.

The U.S. administration . . . will find in us a partner prepared, without procrastination or backsliding, to continue the dialogue in the spirit of realism, openness and goodwill, and determined to achieve practical results on the agenda which now embraces key issues of Soviet-American relations and international politics.

Fifty Percent Arms Reduction

I am referring, above all, to the consistent movement towards a treaty on a 50 percent reduction in strategic offensive arms, while retaining the ABM [Anti-Ballistic Missile] Treaty;

• the work on drafting a convention for the elimination of chemical weapons;

• the negotiations on the reduction of conventional arms and armed forces in Europe.

I am also referring to economic, ecological and humanitarian problems in the broadest context.

It would be wrong to ascribe all the positive changes in the international situation to the U.S.S.R. and the United States alone.

The Soviet Union highly values the great and original contribution made to the improvement of the international situation by the socialist countries.

In the course of negotiations, we constantly feel the presence of other great states, both nuclear and nonnuclear.

Many countries, including medium-sized and small ones, and, of course, the Non-Aligned Movement and the intercontinental Group of Six play an invaluable, constructive role.

We in Moscow are pleased that more and more government, political, party and public leaders, and—I would like to particularly emphasize this—scientists, cultural figures, representatives of mass movements and various Churches, activists of what is called people's diplomacy, are prepared to shoulder the burden of general responsibility.

In this context, I think the idea of convening an Assembly of Public Organizations on a regular basis under the aegis of the United Nations also deserves consideration.

We have no intention of over-simplifying the situation in the world.

The Drive for Disarmament

True, the drive for disarmament has received a strong impetus and is gaining momentum, but it has not become irreversible.

True, there is a strong desire to end confrontation in favour of dialogue and cooperation, but this trend has not become a permanent feature in the practice of international relations.

True, the movement towards a non-violent world free from nuclear weapons can radically change the political and moral aspect of our planet, but we have only made the very first steps, and even these steps have been met with distrust and resistance in some influential circles.

The heritage and inertia of the past are still at work, and deep

contradictions and the root causes of many conflicts have not yet disappeared.

The fundamental fact remains that the shaping of a period of peace will be accompanied by the existence and rivalry of the different social, economic and political systems.

However, the aim of our efforts in the international arena, and one of the key provisions of our concept of new thinking, is that we must transform this rivalry into sensible competition on the basis of respect for freedom of choice and balance of interests.

"Soviet leaders speak increasingly of 'reasonable sufficiency' and a new 'defensive doctrine,' but we have seen no signs the Soviets are putting this new doctrine into practice."

Soviet Arms Reductions Are Not Genuine

Ronald F. Lehman II

The proposed Soviet military cuts and weapons reductions are merely rhetorical and designed primarily to gain equal cuts and reductions from the US, according to the author of the following viewpoint, Ronald F. Lehman II. Lehman argues that alleged Soviet arms reductions are not a genuine attempt to reduce the military threat against the West. Lehman is the Bush Administration's assistant secretary of defense for international security policy. Prior to that, he was the chief US strategic arms negotiator for the Strategic Arms Reduction Talks (START), and was deputy assistant to the president for national security affairs.

As you read, consider the following questions:

1. How do the latest Soviet arms cuts differ from previous Soviet initiatives, according to Lehman?
2. According to the author, how should the US respond to the Soviet arms initiatives?
3. What does Lehman believe the USSR should do to prove that the latest Soviet proposals are genuine?

Ronald F. Lehman II, "Continuity and Change in Soviet Defense Policy," *Defense 89*, January/February 1989.

As in Soviet politics and society, the Soviet Union talks of change in its approach to its military power and doctrine. Nevertheless, we see continuity as the main trend in Soviet security policies. *Perestroika* and *glasnost*, from our vantage point, have made few inroads to date in the Soviet defense sector. Soviet defense policy could perhaps change somewhat on some issues as the result of the so-called "new thinking." Again, however, we have heard less bellicose words in the past, often in the context of "peace campaigns" designed to encourage the West to neglect its defenses. In most cases, change has been faltering, uncertain and largely rhetorical. Soviet force structure, for example, remains offensively oriented, conventional and strategic forces continue to be expanded and modernized, and military spending continues to increase. At the same time, Soviet leaders speak increasingly of "reasonable sufficiency" and a new "defensive doctrine," but we have seen no signs the Soviets are putting this new doctrine into practice in terms of force structure, resources or deployment of forces. . . .

Soviet Continuity

Continuity has also characterized many aspects of Soviet arms control policy, such as its continuing non-compliance with the Anti-Ballistic Missile [ABM] Treaty and other arms control agreements. But change has been evident in its more sophisticated public diplomacy efforts and its more flexible strategy in negotiating the Intermediate-Range Nuclear Forces Treaty [INF], including its acceptance of reduction of asymmetries favoring the USSR, equality in residual forces and an on-site verification regime.

The Soviets have continued to engage in military activities that endanger the lives of U.S. and allied military personnel, such as the shooting at one of our military liaison mission teams in September of 1988 and the "bumping" in early 1989 of U.S. ships exercising the right of innocent passage through Soviet territorial waters in the Black Sea. But they have also agreed to discuss ways to prevent dangerous incidents.

We have seen no let-up in Soviet efforts to gain access to sensitive U.S. technology through all available means, legal and illegal. This continues to be a major area of concern. . . .

Much has been said about a major change in Soviet military doctrine from its traditional reliance on offense to a new emphasis on defense. President Mikhail Gorbachev and other Soviet officials have emphasized the principle of "reasonable sufficiency" and the military claims that Soviet armed forces are now guided by a new "defensive doctrine."

We have sought in discussions with the Soviets to learn if, under a "defensive doctrine," they plan to redirect their forces to a defen-

117

sive orientation and to reduce resources going to the military. We have not learned all that much, either about the status of any "defensive doctrine" or any implications for changes in military forces and resources, and what we have heard has been contradictory. Some civilian officials, for example, have hinted that shifting some resources from military programs to civilian sectors might be warranted. Soviet military leaders, on the other hand, say that "sufficiency" is determined by the extent of the "threat" from the West and seem to imply that any reduction of the Soviet military effort and force levels will occur only in the context of an East-West negotiated agreement. Others have suggested changes in force structure are coming, but will take time.

In spite of all the talk of a "defensive doctrine," we have seen no change in the level of effort and resources devoted to the Soviet military. Soviet spending on the military amounts to 15 percent to 17 percent of gross national product, and we estimate that for each of the last several years, Soviet military spending has increased by about 3 percent per annum.

Soviet military force improvements are taking place across the board—nuclear and conventional. For example, despite recent Soviet statements that appear to reject traditional Soviet thinking that nuclear war could well be fought and won, improvements to the USSR's strategic rocket forces, which are already capable of conducting global nuclear strikes, continue unabated. By the mid-1990s, the Soviets will be fielding a completely new generation of increasingly accurate missiles (particularly the SS-18 follow-on), many of them mobile (e.g., SS-25s and SS-24s), posing a heightened threat to U.S. strategic and other military forces.

A Cutback in Resources

Some analysts believe that we can expect a cutback in the level of resources the Soviets will direct to their defense establishment. This may be small cause for comfort, however, because the motive for any cutback in military investment—if there is a cutback—seems likely to be to assure future military competitiveness, not a retrenchment in expansionist goals or a diminution of the power of the military in the state.

Robert C. McFarlane, *Foreign Affairs*, Summer 1988.

The single-warhead SS-25 and 10-warhead SS-24 are currently being deployed, and the SS-18 follow-on is undergoing extensive testing. At the same time, the Soviets continue to modernize their nuclear-powered, ballistic-missile submarine force, the world's largest, with Typhoon and Delta IV ballistic-missile submarines and are enhancing their bomber forces with the expected introduction of the Blackjack, the world's largest and heaviest bomber, and the recent introduction of the longer-range AS-15 cruise missile, which has substantially improved the flexibility and survivability of the Bear H. We expect the Soviets to continue to improve their strategic nuclear weapons, especially for accuracy, mobility and survivability. . . .

Policy Debate

The contradiction between continuing Soviet efforts to increase their military might and claims to have adopted a "defensive doctrine" may suggest the leadership is embroiled in a policy debate between advocates and opponents of cutting back the Soviet military effort. It is also possible a new "defensive doctrine" has been accepted by the leadership, but that more time is needed to implement it; historically, implementation of changes in Soviet military doctrine has been a process that takes years. Or the leadership may merely be engaged in a rhetorical campaign designed to undermine Western security efforts. Whatever the reason, we have seen no sign of a diminution of the Soviet military threat, which is a function of force structure, resource allocation and deployment of forces, rather than political-military pronouncements or intentions. . . .

Arms Control

Soviet policy on arms control has demonstrated greater flexibility and sophistication under Gorbachev, at least on some issues such as INF, but we still see much continuity here as well. And even on intermediate-range nuclear forces, changes in the Soviet approach were slow and inconsistent.

After Gorbachev's rise to power, the Soviet government at first simply continued to repackage previously tabled, one-sided positions in the INF negotiations that rejected the U.S. offer of global elimination of long-range, ground-launched ballistic and cruise missiles. These early positions sought to maintain a monopoly in such missiles for the Soviet side. . . .

Changes in Soviet negotiating strategy initiated by Gorbachev clearly helped pave the way for concluding the INF treaty, but I believe the U.S. policy of patient diplomacy and negotiating from strength was even more important. While adroit at maneuvering to capture public attention, Gorbachev also recognized the need to reach agreement in intermediate-range nuclear forces with the United States and its NATO [North Atlantic Treaty Organization] allies and that earlier Soviet positions were not sustainable in the face of solidarity. . . .

Similarly, with regard to defense and space issues, the Soviets have altered some positions—admitting in public for the first time in December 1988 that the Soviet Union, like the United States, has a research and development program addressing the same technologies as SDI [Strategic Defense Initiative] and agreeing to a joint statement that constituted an acceptance of the right of both parties to deploy strategic defenses following an unspecified ABM treaty non-withdrawal period. Subsequently, however, the Soviets have retreated from this and other positions agreed to in the joint statement and have continued their efforts to kill SDI.

The Soviets continue to press a number of other issues we cannot accept as well, including an immediate ban on nuclear testing and nuclear and chemical weapons free zones. With regard to nuclear testing, we believe that as long as the United States must rely on nuclear weapons for its security, we must continue to test to ensure their safety, security, reliability, effectiveness and survivability. . . .

The Beginning of Arms Control

The reality is, since the beginning of the contemporary age of arms control, the Soviets have developed and deployed the very force capabilities that were to have been prevented by arms control. They have seen how to utilize the arms control process to depress Western military programs, while the USSR continues with its own. They now look to the prolongation of the process as a means to maintain and expand their nuclear superiority and to prevent the United States and its allies from developing and deploying the defenses that would offset Soviet advantages.

William R. Van Cleave, *Global Affairs*, Spring 1989.

Continuity has also marked Soviet negotiating goals and tactics on conventional arms control, although we have heard some interesting ideas from the Soviets. Gorbachev's proposal to eliminate disparities from the Atlantic to the Urals is one example. It is new in that the Warsaw Pact is admitting that it is ahead in some categories of equipment—tanks, for instance. We would certainly be interested in having the Warsaw Pact nations reduce the number of their tanks in Europe down to NATO's level, but, frankly, I find it difficult to believe that the East is ready to cut its tank forces by 30,000. Gorbachev has also proposed cutting troops in Europe to equal levels. We have, of course, been pursuing that goal in the mutual and balanced force reductions negotiations for years. Expanding the zone of reductions and limitations form the Central Region of Europe to an area stretching from the Atlantic to the Urals will be a step forward, but this in itself will not solve the basic definition and verification problems that continue to stymie the mutual and balanced force reductions negotiations. . . .

Continued Soviet failure to comply with the ABM treaty

seriously complicates U.S.-Soviet negotiations on arms control issues. We must not permit the USSR to think it can violate existing arms control agreements without appropriate U.S. response. . . .

US Response

In sum, we see some change in the USSR that has contributed to an improvement in U.S.-Soviet relations, but it is too early to tell exactly where the Soviet Union is going—domestically, internationally and militarily. What is clear, however, is that the Soviet Union under Gorbachev still poses a tremendous challenge to U.S. and Western interests—a challenge that requires that we remain watchful and vigilant but at the same time receptive to dialogue and energetic in our efforts to work out our differences.

The Soviet Union's continuing buildup and modernization of its military even while it professes to be adopting a "defensive" military doctrine makes it imperative that we and our allies maintain a credible deterrent by improving, modernizing and deploying our own strategic and conventional forces. We must not diminish U.S. or allied military capabilities on the basis of Soviet public statements. We must be prepared to stand up to inevitable Soviet outcries that our nuclear modernization programs run counter to improved East-West relations and the "spirit" of arms control.

For NATO, we must continue implementation of the Conventional Defense Improvement initiative and the programs stemming from the 1983 Montebello Decision. We must also be prepared to turn down Soviet proposals that seek to "denuclearize" Western Europe. We should also continue to press the Soviets to remove asymmetries, especially in ground forces in Europe that threaten the territory of other nations.

Soviet Agreement

The Soviet agreement to withdraw from Afghanistan is a positive move, which we rightfully should applaud, but we should also carefully monitor Soviet adherence to the terms of the Geneva Accords. We will also be carefully watching Soviet policy on other regional conflicts to see if Moscow will live up to professed willingness to cooperate in the peaceful settlement of such conflicts. In many cases, such as with Angola, Ethiopia and the Sandinistas, the Soviets have considerable influence they could bring to bear to resolve the situation. In most cases, our differences—although wide—are not intractable and can, we believe, be resolved through determined, thoughtful and astute diplomacy, reinforced by appropriate vigilance, preparedness and support for our friends and allies.

In the arms control area, as we negotiate with the Soviets in the priority areas of the Strategic Arms Reduction Talks and conventional arms reductions, we need to keep in mind the factors that accounted for our success in negotiating the INF treaty—patient diplomacy, consistency and negotiating from strength. Despite Soviet propaganda efforts to create artificial deadlines for arms control negotiations, the United States should build on its successes with a steady, comprehensive approach to arms control. An acceptable Strategic Arms Reduction Talks Treaty must satisfy four main U.S. objectives: deep reductions, enhanced strategic stability, verifiability and equal force levels of the two sides.

"START treaties can clear the way for a very large reduction in nuclear weapons."

The US Should Reduce Its Nuclear Forces

Hans A. Bethe

Hans A. Bethe argues in the following viewpoint that the USSR has become less of a military threat to the US. Bethe believes Mikhail Gorbachev's program of reform has resulted in a fundamental change in Soviet nuclear strategy to which the US should respond by reducing its nuclear arsenal and promoting arms control. Bethe is a theoretical physicist at Cornell University in Ithaca, New York, and was chief of the theoretical division at Los Alamos during the Manhattan Project, the World War II effort to design and build the first nuclear bomb.

As you read, consider the following questions:

1. According to Bethe, what changes in Soviet security policy permit the US to reduce its nuclear forces?
2. According to the author, what kinds of cuts should the US make in its nuclear arsenal?
3. How would the US and the USSR benefit from arms reductions treaties, according to Bethe?

Hans A. Bethe, "Chop Down the Nuclear Arsenals," *Bulletin of the Atomic Scientists,* March 1989. Reprinted with the author's permission.

Polls indicate that the mainstream wants arms control: More than 80 percent of the respondents in an October 1988 survey by Daniel Yankelovich supported a bilateral freeze on nuclear weapons. Some 80 percent of the respondents in a *Wall Street Journal* poll—including those who called themselves conservative—believed military spending should either decrease or stay constant. So I take the optimistic view that President Bush will build on Ronald Reagan's arms control initiatives and will pursue a 50 percent reduction in strategic nuclear weapons.

There are problems with the strategic arms reduction talks [START], some real and some imaginary. The real problems arise from the question of how U.S. strategic weapons should be structured following an agreement; the imaginary ones arise from feeling rather than analysis, as I will discuss later. Ultimately, I believe, START treaties can clear the way for a very large reduction in nuclear weapons.

Soviet Changes

My optimism derives in large part from the tremendous changes that have been occurring in the Soviet Union. The leader in these changes is Mikhail Gorbachev. But Soviet intellectuals have apparently realized for a long time that change was necessary, chiefly because the Soviet economy simply did not work. By fall 1988, evidence of change was rapidly accumulating:

• On October 4 Vadim A. Medvedev, the new chief ideologist, announced a major reversal in Soviet thought. In a speech to political scientists from communist countries, he said: "Present-day realities mean that universal values such as avoiding war and ecological catastrophe must outweigh the idea of struggle between classes." And he added another signal that the Soviet Union would become easier to live with: "Peaceful coexistence is a lengthy, long-term process whose historic limits are difficult to determine."

Medvedev, an economist, called for major decentralization of the economy. A socialist country, he said, must learn from other socialist countries and even from the capitalist West.

• On October 14, Gorbachev proposed that farms be leased back to farmers who would pay a fixed rent to the government and keep the remainder of the proceeds for themselves.

Arms Concessions

• Andrei Sakharov, who had earlier been permitted to return to Moscow from his Gorky exile, was made a member of the Presidium of the Soviet Academy of Sciences in October. In November he was allowed to travel to the United States.

• The Soviet's tremendous concessions on intrusive arms control inspections made possible the treaty on intermediate-range nuclear forces and by fall, missiles were being destroyed in the presence of witnesses from both sides. Inspectors have been stationed permanently on the periphery of factories that formerly manufactured INF missiles. Soviet inspectors in Utah were reportedly impressed by the friendliness of local citizens.

In the same spirit of friendly cooperation, nuclear weapons tests in Nevada and Semipalatinsk were observed and measured jointly by the host country and guest scientists. These observations made it possible to compare the equipment used to measure the yield of weapons tests.

• Finally, in a dramatic speech to the United Nations on December 7, Gorbachev promised major unilateral reductions in Soviet conventional forces. He offered to reduce Soviet armed forces by half a million men and 10,000 tanks and to cut several other important weapons. While this does not make Soviet forces equal to NATO's [North Atlantic Treaty Organization], at least in quantity, it is a very good and generous start.

Peaceful Revolution

Gorbachev's peaceful revolution and pragmatism were chiefly responsible for the INF Treaty and the good beginning in START, although the U.S. policy of "negotiating from strength" may have helped reveal to the Soviets the futility of continuing the arms competition, just as their economic policy had entered a blind alley.

Nuclear Forces

We and the Russians have been profligate in the amount of money we have spent on nuclear forces. . . . Fifty percent reductions under START would be a large step in the right direction. Reducing the sum of our strategic arsenal from about 25,000 warheads to 12,500 would leave neither side lacking for destructive power.

Stansfield Turner, *The New York Times Magazine*, March 27, 1988.

But Gorbachev and the reform party may lose power. It remains to be seen whether the domestic changes will work, and until the ordinary Soviet citizen feels that life has improved, the reforms will remain fragile. One can only hope that the transfer of farms to private initiative will improve food production, and that the loans from Western Europe will improve the production of consumer goods.

Some analysts recommend that the United States proceed with caution in arms control negotiations until Gorbachev's future is more certain. I believe, on the contrary, that this is a time of extraordinary opportunity, and that we must use it. If Gorbachev and company were, unhappily, to be replaced by a hardline regime, we would all be better off with an agreement in place that reduced the absurd numbers of strategic weapons. An agreement that permitted additional intrusive inspection would be even better. It would be a big step toward an open world and a complete break with the policy of secrecy for which Tsarist Russia was already noted.

The Soviet government has recognized, as the Western arms control community did long ago, that neither side can be safe unless both are safe. And the Soviets now want arms control more urgently than the U.S. government does. . . .

A Survivable Force

But while their numbers are being reduced, the weapons should be made more survivable, so that there is less incentive to use them in a preemptive strike. Submarines are the best choice for a survivable U.S. nuclear force, because they are difficult to detect. Fortunately for strategic stability, it is highly unlikely that effective means can be developed to detect and attack deeply submerged missile-carrying submarines. Even if antisubmarine warfare were to become possible someday, it will not happen overnight. There would be ample time to shift emphasis to the land and air legs of the triad. . . .

Another stumbling block is ship-based cruise missiles. It would be best to eliminate nonstrategic nuclear weapons on ships altogether, as Reagan's arms control adviser Paul Nitze proposed. But this leads to difficult verification problems. Perhaps the best we can do is limit the number and take it on faith that both sides will obey the agreement. Sidney Drell of Stanford University has suggested that this might be acceptable for sea-launched cruise missiles because they are rather slow and thus not first-strike weapons.

With submarines secure for the present, one may question the need for land-based intercontinental ballistic missiles (ICBMs). For a long time ICBMs were the most accurate missiles, but with the introduction of the accurate D-5 (Trident II) submarine-launched missile, there is no longer a good reason to emphasize ICBMs. Land-based missiles are needed only as insurance against unforeseen advances in antisubmarine warfare, or against failure of communication with submarines. But what kind of ICBMs should the United States deploy?

• *MIRVs.* Even Henry Kissinger, who approved of the decision to introduce MIRVs (multiple independently targetable reentry vehicles) around 1970, now admits that they must be eliminated on land-based missiles. MIRVed missiles are first-strike weapons, threatening to the enemy and inviting preemptive attack. In the 50 percent reduction, both sides should move decisively toward single-warhead ICBMs.

• *Mobility.* The Soviet Union has an enormous land mass, lots

126

of open space, and few coasts on the open oceans. The United States has long coasts and is more densely populated. To have a survivable force, the Soviets need mobility on land, while the United States does not. I like Drell's idea for improving the survivability of the U.S. land force: to put small, single-warhead missiles ("Midgetman") in silos, for the time being. They would be unattractive targets, because the Soviets would have to use two warheads to destroy each missile, and they would still be exposed to the much more numerous U.S. submarine missile force. Putting Midgetman in silos would save a great deal of money. The missiles could be designed in such a way that they could be put on an all-terrain vehicle if this were ever to become necessary. A force of, say, 400 small silo-based missiles would bring us closer to an ultimately desirable force than would the 10-warhead MX in a rail-garrison mobile basing system.

US Deeds

There is an urgent need to
• speed the conclusion of a treaty to reduce strategic nuclear weapons by 50 percent, preserve the ABM [Anti-Ballistic Missile] treaty and scrap SDI [Strategic Defense Initiative]; for a nuclear-weapon-free world by the year 2000;
• end all nuclear weapons' tests; establish nuclear-weapon-free zones;
• remove all nuclear weapons from foreign soil and bring our troops home.

Jim West, *Political Affairs*, February 1989.

• *Yield.* Now that both sides have achieved great accuracy, heavy missiles such as the Soviet SS-18 are no longer necessary, and all ballistic missiles should be limited in yield. The Soviets have promised to reduce numbers of SS-18s by half and also to reduce the total throw weight of their missile force by half. U.S. Minuteman II and III missiles are much smaller, but their yield should be further reduced, in line with their increased accuracy. One reason for such reduction is to make sure that there will not be a "nuclear winter" if the missiles are ever launched: whether the temperature falls by four degrees or twenty, it would be a global catastrophe.

Congress has supported the move toward smaller missiles. But the Midgetman has been conceived as a mobile missile, which is unnecessary. And the air force has proposed putting three warheads on each missile instead of one, in order to save money. This would defeat its purpose. Survivability, not cost, should be the decisive factor. Arms reduction will not necessarily save much money at first, but savings will come later with reduced maintenance costs.

Once START is concluded, other important arms control initiatives can follow:

• Restricting the number of permissible missile tests would be a powerful measure, although it is seldom mentioned. Missile tests are above ground and are therefore easy to verify by satellites and other "national technical means." Limiting missile tests would more effectively halt the development of new weapons than would a comprehensive nuclear test ban.

• Tactical nuclear weapons, with a range less than 500 kilometers, should be reduced: each side now has thousands. If war broke out in Europe, the U.S. doctrine of flexible response envisages possible escalation to tactical nuclear war. This would be extremely dangerous for Western Europe, especially since nuclear artillery, a large part of the tactical force, is not very mobile and may present the commander with the well-known dilemma, "use them or lose them." And tactical nuclear war may quickly lead to a full, strategic nuclear war.

• During the long period that will be required to implement START, negotiations should begin to reduce strategic weapons further. A reasonable goal is another 50 percent reduction, to 3,000 warheads on each side. MIRVs must continue to be eliminated and survivability must be emphasized.

• At this stage, China, France, and Great Britain must be brought into the negotiations. This will not be easy: France may be the most resistant, and there will presumably be long haggling about the number of warheads permitted to each country. Other suspected weapons countries, such as India and Israel, will need to join the third round.

The Ultimate Goal

The ultimate goal should not be zero nuclear weapons but some low number like 200-1,000 on each side. Fortuitously, the Committee of Soviet Scientists for Peace has come up with a similar number, 600. One reason for retaining some weapons is residual mistrust between the superpowers which requires a hedge against possible treaty violations. Dozens of missiles may be concealed, but it would be very difficult to conceal hundreds, ready to launch. A second reason is that rogue countries might start small nuclear arsenals. Finally, nuclear weapon design is well known, and there is little difference between having the design and having a small residual force. . . .

Security for both sides ultimately depends on freedom from fear of attack. At present the main Western concern is the apparent superiority of the Warsaw Pact over NATO in conventional weapons. The perpetual Soviet concern is invasion from the West, repeating that of the Nazis in 1941-43, the Germans in 1914-17, and Napoleon in 1812. . . .

An important first step has already been achieved in the agreement signed by 35 nations in Stockholm in 1986, providing for notification and observation of maneuvers. This builds confidence that neither side will be able to launch a massive surprise attack with conventional weapons. And the concepts of nonoffensive defense spelled out by West European analysts and taken up by the Soviets raise encouraging possibilities but some questions as well—about the role of planes, for instance. The initial data exchanges agreed to in the May 1988 Moscow summit will be important, since there has been persistent disagreement on the numbers of weapons each side possesses. And the West will have to decide what it wants to give in exchange for reductions in Soviet tanks, motorized artillery, and perhaps interceptor planes. Perhaps NATO might agree to reduce fighter bombers like the F-16.

Conventional Forces

Reconciling the divergent European views will require strong leadership on the part of the U.S. president. Even so, the talks will be difficult, and it would be fatal to hold START hostage to success in conventional force negotiations.

A fundamental change in the attitude and character of a country—or *Bewussteinswandel*, to use the title of a recent book by Carl Friedrich von Weizsäcker—is possible: we have seen it in Germany's transformation from Nazi empire to federal republic. This is happening today in the Soviet Union, fortunately without a war.

But the West must undergo its own *Bewussteinswandel* and realize that the Soviet government has changed and is no longer an "evil empire." We may pursue and stabilize this mutual, basic attitude change in joint enterprises—environmental problems, especially the control of carbon dioxide and ozone, should be top priorities—and in agreements not to excessively arm opposing parties in local conflicts. If "avoiding war and ecological catastrophe" really does outweigh the idea of a class struggle in the Soviet Union, then peaceful coexistence is possible.

4

"Arms control is not a solution. It is part of the problem."

The US Should Not Reduce Its Nuclear Forces

Angelo M. Codevilla

In the following viewpoint, Angelo M. Codevilla argues that the US should not be deceived by Soviet calls for military reductions. Even if the Soviets reduce the number of nuclear and conventional weapons, the USSR will still be more powerful than the US, according to Codevilla. The author believes the US should not reduce either its conventional or its nuclear forces. Codevilla is a fellow of the Hoover Institution at Stanford University in Stanford, California, and author of *While Others Build: The Common-Sense Approach to the Strategic Defense Initiative.*

As you read, consider the following questions:

1. Why does Codevilla mistrust Soviet arms initiatives?
2. What strategy should the US have for maintaining its national security, according to Codevilla?
3. How does the author suggest the US respond to Soviet arms proposals?

Angelo M. Codevilla, "Is There Still a Soviet Threat?" Excerpts reprinted from *Commentary*, November 1988, by permission; all rights reserved.

The case for the proposition that "peace is breaking out all over" rests, at best, on American hopes attached to Soviet actions. And there are indeed a few Soviet actions that may (or may not) be part of trends that may (or may not) lead to real peace in the long run: for example, Soviet troops have left Afghanistan. The case also rests on American interpretations of the general Soviet situation, especially the economic situation, which, it is believed, should force profound changes in the direction of disarmament and peace. Finally, the case rests on American hopes attached to Soviet words—in particular on what Soviet officials say about a new defensive emphasis in Soviet military doctrine and about a total pullback in Angola and Nicaragua.

The now highly unfashionable case to the contrary—that the Soviet Union is as much of a threat as ever, maybe more—is based on a different set of assessments: Soviet military power *relative to that of the United States* continues to grow, while Soviet efforts to cushion the consequences of military spending by acquiring Western capital and technology are more successful now than they have been in many years.

Military Budget

The contest between these views is of the greatest significance for U.S. policy in the years ahead, regardless of which party controls the White House or the Congress. Shall we continue to cut our military budget in real terms, as (contrary to what many people imagine) we have done every year since 1985; or shall we spend whatever is needed to deter a war by preparing to fight, survive, and win one if it should nevertheless break out? Shall we help to finance and build up the Soviet economy; or shall we work to cut off its access to Western credits and expertise? Shall we help those who are fighting Soviet and Soviet-supported regimes, from Angola to Nicaragua to Poland; or shall we advise them to work as best they can within a Soviet empire that may be evolving in a good direction?

Another consideration is even more important. Ever since the Founding, we Americans have defined ourselves in opposition to tyranny. Since World War II, the ongoing need to counter the Soviet Union has served to remind us that the United States of America is not just another nation among nations but a beacon and a help to free men everywhere. Are we going to live by, or put aside, the concerns with political, personal, and religious liberty that the struggle against Soviet Communism has energized among us? A host of commitments, including our geopolitical relationship with Europe and Japan, make sense only in the context of opposition to Soviet Communism. Have they become obsolete?

In truth, much of the controversy in this country over what is and is not happening in the Soviet Union is really about what

131

directions American policy should take. The focus is less on ascertaining Soviet reality than on vindicating one or another side in an intramural American quarrel. This sort of solipsism is unfortunate, because the extent to which the Soviet Union actually threatens us makes a big difference. It would be worse than wasteful to base our policy on opposition to the Soviet Union if that country were on its way to a true political transformation. But if that is not the case, we would by the same token be criminally foolish to repeat our mistakes of the 1970's (a succinct summary of which was offered at the time by Harold Brown: "When we stop, they build"). A serious, prudent evaluation of the Soviet threat must begin by eschewing the temptation to treat our own hopes or fears about the future as if they were an incontestable reality. . . .

SURPRISINGLY, JUST WHEN THERE SEEMED TO BE A HUGE OPENING, THE PRESIDENT WALKED OUT. BUT, THE SOVIETS SAY THE DOOR IS STILL WIDE OPEN! BACK TO YOU, DAN...

SOVIET ARMS DEAL

Dick Wright. Reprinted by permission of UFS, Inc.

Consider the military balance. If the Soviets were becoming our partners in security, military capacity would not matter. But Soviet thaws can turn to frosts as quickly as smiles can change to frowns, and far more quickly than missiles and anti-missile devices can be built. Moreover, military opportunities have been known to tempt men less inured to violence than the current crop of Soviet leaders. Hence it is important to note that the military balance is continuing its long-term shift in the Soviet Union's favor, and that recent American cutbacks are accelerating that trend.

Contrary to widespread belief, the U.S. has not become militarily stronger over the past decade *relative to the Soviet Union*. True, during the early Reagan years the American military waxed. As a result, our Navy is now substantially bigger and much improved. The Army, while shrinking a bit, has largely switched to a new generation of tanks and attack helicopters. U.S. fighter-bombers, though fewer, are better than they were. As for American strategic forces, they have benefited from the addition of 99 new B-1 bombers, the loading of air-launched cruise missiles on old B-52s, and the much-delayed arrival of a small fleet of 50 new MX missiles. Finally, electronic command links have also been much improved.

Overall, then, our forces are stronger than they were ten years ago. Yet this is quite irrelevant, since the only comparison that matters is between U.S. and Soviet forces. Here, *all* the tangible evidence says that we are much worse off than before.

Tank Inequalities

The latest edition of the Secretary of Defense's annual report to Congress tells the tale. Over the past decade, the U.S. has produced 7,600 tanks to the Soviet Union's 25,300. . . . With regard to artillery pieces, the figures are 3,200 for us and 27,300 for them. We do better with fighter planes and fighter-bombers, where we are down only 2 to 1 (3,600 to 7,700). But where nuclear-capable artillery and rocket launchers are concerned, we do worse: there the ratio is 17 to 1 against us.

The days are long gone when we could discount such figures by referring to Soviet technical backwardness. The equipment coming off Soviet production lines today is roughly as good as our best. Often, especially in infantry fighting vehicles, it is superior. And in the field of defense against aircraft, cruise missiles, and ballistic missiles, the Soviets have equipment the likes of which we simply do not possess. . . .

Concerning intercontinental missiles and bombers, where subjective factors do not apply, it is much more difficult to slight the numbers. This is perhaps why the Secretary's report does not mention that whereas a decade ago the Soviets had only about 4,000 warheads with the necessary combination of nuclear yield and accuracy to destroy America's own strategic forces, today they have about 6,500. Thus, we have gone from roughly two Soviet ICBM [intercontinental ballistic missiles] warheads per American missile silo, bomber base, command-and-control center, and submarine port, to roughly three nuclear warheads pointed at each of these American targets.

How does Frank Carlucci, the Secretary of Defense, deal with such facts? Our strategy, he says, is "to hold at risk those assets that the Soviets value most." But those assets—their strategic forces and command apparatus—are precisely the ones we are *unable* to hold at risk. In fact, the only targets we can still confidently hold at risk are the civilians and the industries that the Soviet

133

government has chosen not to protect. Yet as the Secretary's report also acknowledges, the Soviets "are continuing their enormous investment in expensive and technically demanding active and passive defense systems designed to limit damage to the USSR in the event of war." These include "industrial preparations for nuclear war," a massive shelter program, a pervasive air defense, and full production of every part of a comprehensive anti-missile system—all on the back of a "strapped" economy. Thus, little by little, not only the military but even the civilian sectors of the Soviet Union need fear us less and less. . . .

The Secretary says that in the 1990's the new Trident II submarine-launched missiles "will permit us to hold at risk a greater proportion of the *hardened, fixed* Soviet target base" (emphasis added). That is literally true—except that such coverage will not be anything like the coverage which the Soviets have of our targets. Moreover, the hardened, fixed target base vulnerable to U.S. retaliation is vanishing, and by the 1990's substantially all Soviet strategic-force reserves will be mobile; the key parts of the mechanism for control of Soviet society will be out of reach; and Soviet anti-missile defenses will be in place.

Armed Power

To fulfill its obligations to collectivism, the U.S. must maintain its share of armed power to deter those who would violate the valid interests of tranquil nations. The world may yearn for a more stable peace, but is still imperiled by hostility, aggression, subversion and terrorism.

Military stability, including conventional and nuclear defenses, is a prerequisite for collective management of a troubled political situation.

Both the U.S. and its allies in Europe and Asia believe that a nuclear deterrent is an essential political measure and military instrument to prevent war while diplomacy works to lessen the deep political divisions between East and West.

Elmo R. Zumwalt and Worth H. Bagley, *Conservative Chronicle*, May 3, 1989.

So far, the only actual (rather than rhetorical) initiative by the U.S. government to change this situation has been to pursue the series of arms-control agreements which Mikhail Gorbachev proposed at the Reykjavik summit of 1986: a 50-percent reduction in each side's long-range nuclear warheads, and adherence to the ABM [Anti-Ballistic Missile] treaty for at least ten years.

The first problem here is that such a reduction would further increase the ratio of Soviet warheads to American strategic targets. Moreover, while the U.S. has interpreted the ABM treaty as a prohibition against producing anti-missile devices, the Soviet Union has not.

Second, while the U.S. has charged that the Soviet Union has violated and circumvented every arms-control agreement it has ever signed, we have neither compelled the Soviets to undo the gains they have made thereby, nor have we matched or offset those gains by new armament programs of our own. Instead, in the words of Kenneth Adelman, the former director of the Arms Control and Disarmament Agency, having received rotten oranges from the store, we have gone back to the same store for more oranges.

Suppose that the U.S. were to obtain an arms-control agreement from the Soviet Union that would "fix" every one of the looming strategic problems I have mentioned. Any Soviet official who suggested that the USSR abide by it would be derelict in his duty to his country. That is because the U.S. has granted the USSR a license to have its arms-control cake while eating it too, and no American has suggested any way of revoking that license. No, arms control is not a solution. It is part of the problem. . . .

Military Operations

One of the uses of superiority at the highest level of military operations is to cover military operations or threats at lower levels.

Consider Europe, where some 300,000 U.S. troops are stationed. These represent the bulk of our ground and air-force operational units. Estimates vary, but we spend somewhat over half our military budget on the defense of Europe. The expense notwithstanding, however, the official U.S. judgment is that whereas a decade ago NATO [North Atlantic Treaty Organization] ground forces were inferior to the Warsaw Pact by an overall ration of 1.5 to 1, today the ratio of ready forces is roughly 2 to 1 against NATO, and almost 3 to 1 against us one month after mobilization. NATO's disadvantage in the air is perhaps only 1.3 to 1. But Soviet overall superiority on the central front is at least 3 to 1. (Actually, the raw figures are worse than these summary final assessments because the usual "intangibles" are thrown into the balance on the U.S. side.)

The Secretary of Defense concedes that the U.S. has "not been able to calculate adequately" what effects a Soviet combined-arms attack on Europe would have, and that the Soviet Union has reason to believe that it could conquer NATO quickly. Nevertheless, he concludes that "the Soviets may not be confident that their forces are sufficient to guarantee them a high probability of success." Why? Because of "capabilities NATO is pursuing" (but does not have). . . .

Meanwhile, as Europe looks East it sees a Red Army with more divisions in East Germany than are in the entire active U.S. Army, and more divisions in Czechoslovakia than there are U.S. divisions in all of Europe. All of these Soviet divisions have forward-deployed mobile bridging equipment that is useful only for offense. *Under Gorbachev, not one of these divisions has been eliminated or even neglected. All continue to be improved. . . .*

Strategic Weapons

The proposed cut of strategic weapons by 50 percent could upset the strategic balance and leave the United States less secure than it is now. Soviet military deployments and new weapons developments clearly indicate that Moscow will be in a better strategic posture than the U.S. after the proposed START [Strategic Arms Reaction Talks] agreement takes effect.

National Security Record, May 1988.

The Soviet Union's claim that it has a brand-new, defensive doctrine rings hollow. As anyone knows who has followed the Soviet military over the years, the Soviet Union has *always* proclaimed that its operational doctrine is strictly defensive. The words of the current leadership on this subject are no different from those of its predecessors; the difference lies in the willingness of Westerners to accept them, a willingness that comes, significantly, at a moment when Soviet offensive capacity has never been higher, and when the numbers of tanks, planes, missiles, and so forth emerging from Soviet factories are steady at levels several times our own. The effort may be breaking the Soviet Union economically, but it is not broken yet. And, as Gorbachev's words help cut down the U.S. military, they raise the marginal efficiency of every Soviet military ruble.

Disarming the US

Indeed, Gorbachev's foremost political act has been to disarm (in every sense) the U.S. As he himself explained on the 70th anniversary of the October revolution, "Our *perestroika . . .* is eliminating the fear of the 'Soviet threat,' with [American] militarism losing its political justification." Georgi Arbatov has been even more specific: "Without this bugaboo [of the Soviet threat], the $300-billion-per-year American military presence in the Atlantic, Pacific, Indian Ocean, Mediterranean, and Near East would be meaningless. Take away the 'Soviet threat' and this entire costly edifice will crumble like a house of cards." The Soviet magazine *New Times* has described *glasnost* and *perestroika* as "marvelous keys to American hearts."

If Soviet leaders were removing the *substance* of their threat to the rest of the world, and then simply reporting, say, that Warsaw Pact military production had dropped to NATO levels, that would be one thing. But this is not what they are doing. Rather than cutting their own military production in reality, they are attempting to do away with the reality of *American* military forces by convincing American leaders to accept a certain image of the "Soviet threat." *Glasnost* and *perestroika* have certainly resulted in disarmament—but of the U.S., not of the Soviet Union. There is no reason to confuse what is, after all, a traditional "peace offensive" with peace itself. . . .

This is not the place for a discussion of internal Soviet politics, but we must keep in mind that the Soviet system is peculiarly stacked against a peaceful evolution to either traditional Russian conservatism or Western-type liberalism. *Perestroika* and *glasnost* seem to be stimulating anyone who has both a following and a grievance to assert himself, yet none of the people doing so is a moderate in the Western mold. And in the meantime, the food lines are lengthening.

In such a volatile situation, various kinds of violent struggles are likely to break out, followed by the victory of one faction and then a crackdown on the others. We can dream, if we care to, that when the smoke clears the "leader" will suppress his own faction's interests as well as the others, blame all the country's sufferings on his own people, exonerate the "imperialists" who have been every faction's whipping boy for three generations, ignore the massive military power at his command, and be nice to the wealthy and underarmed West. But we dare not stake our future on it. If Gorbachev himself were the winner, how would he and his band act once they had caused the "house of cards" of Western defense to come tumbling down or at least to suffer from neglect? Is there anything in their background to suggest they would hesitate to raise the price of their forbearance in order to pay off their supporters and avoid another round of unsettling domestic reforms?

No Reduced Threat

For us, faced with such uncertainties, the prudent course is to pay the hardest attention to the hardest facts. Secretary of Defense Carlucci reiterated that Soviet words about a reduced military threat are entirely belied by Soviet deeds. Carlucci's point is clear enough: keep your powder dry. But although he makes a convincing case that the Soviets are lying, and in ways calculated to increase the danger we are in, the administration he has served does not act as if we were being bilked. Instead, pouring cold water on the "powder" of public opinion, it praises the Soviets for relative candor, and looks forward to putting them to the test.

"Europeans are able to eventually take responsibility for their own defenses."

The Superpowers Should Withdraw from Europe

Doug Bandow

In the following viewpoint, Doug Bandow argues that recent Soviet peace initiatives could lead to a mutual US-Soviet withdrawal from Europe. A US withdrawal would save the US money and would not endanger Europe, he believes. Bandow served as a special assistant to President Reagan and is now a senior fellow at the Cato Institute, a public policy research foundation in Washington, DC.

As you read, consider the following questions:

1. What Soviet changes allow the US to propose withdrawing its military from Western Europe, according to Bandow?
2. What changes does the author argue NATO must make so the US can withdraw?
3. After the US withdraws its troops from Western Europe, how should Western Europe defend itself, according to Bandow?

Doug Bandow, "What Next for NATO?" Reprinted, with permission, from the April 1989 issue of *Reason* magazine. Copyright © 1989 by the Reason Foundation, 2716 Ocean Park Blvd., Suite 1062, Santa Monica, CA 90405.

The Western alliance . . .is in disarray. The fissures among its members were growing even before Mikhail Gorbachev's accession to power in the Soviet Union. But now the Soviet "great communicator," who used a speech to the United Nations in December 1988 to announce unilateral troop reductions in Eastern Europe, is threatening to emasculate NATO [North Atlantic Treaty Organization].

Observes foreign policy analyst Christopher Layne, "Gorbachev has been able to manipulate Western European perceptions of the Soviet threat and in so doing undermine NATO's cohesion and support for nuclear force modernization and conventional military buildup." In fact, a poll in West Germany, the front-line state most at risk, found that 75 percent of respondents didn't believe the Soviets pose a threat to their nation; people ranked defense spending last among the 17 listed budget priorities.

A Weakening NATO

Not that the formal collapse of NATO is imminent. But the alliance is increasingly incapable of responding to the Soviet challenge. "We are continually allowing ourselves to be caught off guard and put on the defensive," says Layne. Unless the United States develops its own initiatives for reducing continental military tensions, NATO threatens to become an expensive but militarily ineffective alliance torn by constant squabbling.

There is an alternative. Washington should immediately press for unrestricted arms reduction talks to build on Gorbachev's proposal. By advocating mutual superpower disengagement, the United States should indicate its willingness to fundamentally transform the European military landscape. That goal is ambitious, but nevertheless worth pursuing. "Gorbachev has given us virtually everything we've wanted," says Hudson Institute analyst Jeffrey Record, including elimination of the SS-20 missiles, withdrawal from Afghanistan, and pullbacks in Central Europe. So "maybe he's prepared to give us more."

Four decades ago, Europe was still digging out of the rubble left by six years of total war. Stalin's Red Army quickly subjugated the states it had "liberated." The only thing that blocked Moscow from imposing its rule on Western Europe was America's threat to intervene. But no one believed that Europe would not one day recover and thereafter be able to look after its own affairs. In fact, Secretary of State Dean Acheson told Congress that American troops were to be stationed in Europe only temporarily, to act as a shield until Europe was able to stand on its own.

But a crutch once relied on is not easily abandoned. Even as Britain and France rebuilt their economies and West Germany regained its sovereignty, U.S. forces remained. And NATO chose to respond to Soviet conventional superiority with the threat of massive nuclear retaliation. As long as the United States maintained an overwhelming nuclear advantage, extended deterrence was viable. But during the 1960s and 1970s, as the United States lost that decisive superiority, the threat of a nuclear response to a conventional attack lost credibility.

No Global Nuclear War

In fact, in 1983 former Defense Secretary Robert McNamara revealed that he had advised both Presidents John Kennedy and Lyndon Johnson not to initiate the use of nuclear weapons to save Europe. And today, while the possibility that Washington would ignite a global nuclear war in response to a Warsaw Pact invasion may have some deterrent effect on the Soviet Union, the Europeans would be foolish to assume that an American president would commit national suicide, sacrificing dozens of U.S. cities to prevent the Soviet flag from flying over Bonn and Paris.

Dismantle NATO and the Warsaw Pact

NATO was organized to thwart a perceived Soviet threat, not to keep Europe permanently divided and armed. Germany and France were traditional enemies. Today their border is like Sweden and Norway's. Wouldn't it be wonderful to have similar borders all over Europe. I have yet to meet a Hungarian who does not want the Warsaw Pact dismantled.

There's only one way to do that. And that is to dismantle NATO. I think it can be done. We can dismantle the Warsaw Pact and NATO gradually, responsibly, so that at each step both sides feel militarily far more secure.

William Sloane Coffin, *Time*, June 5, 1989.

As a result of its reliance on the nuclear threat, NATO has been left with an apparent conventional inferiority that the Pentagon has used incessantly to justify increased U.S. military spending. In reality, the gap—expressed in such hideous ratios as 1.4 to 1 in troops, 1.5 to 1 in helicopters, 2 to 1 in combat aircraft, 3.1 to 1 in tanks, and 3.1 to 1 in artillery—has always looked worse on paper than it really is on the field. The West possesses better-trained soldiers and more-advanced equipment; its units are more combat ready, and it has roughly as many reservists as the Warsaw Pact. NATO's decentralized command structure would operate better in fluid combat situations. And the Eastern European states are dubious allies at best: since World War II the Soviets have had to crush outright rebellions in East Germany and Hungary, forcibly suppress reform in Czechoslovakia, and threaten an invasion of Poland. . . .

To assuage any doubts that NATO does indeed possess a deterrent capability, the member states could easily augment their forces. The Western nations spend less than half as much per capita as does the Eastern Bloc, and the problem is not the United States. On almost every measure the Europeans' performance is simply dreadful. West Germany, for instance, spends barely 3.0 percent of its GNP [gross national product] on defense, half the U.S. level. While the United States devoted $1,164 per capita to defense in 1986, Germany spent $454. . . . Britain, France, and Norway contributed slightly more; everyone else spent less. Since roughly half the U.S. defense budget goes for NATO, American citizens are spending more per person than the Europeans to simply defend Europe.

Were the Europeans to take the Warsaw Pact seriously, they could easily overwhelm the East: NATO's collective GNP is two-and-a-half times that of the Warsaw Pact and its population is 50 percent greater. Even without the United States the Europeans exceed the entire Soviet alliance economically and nearly equal it in population. Moreover, Europe faces no other continental threat, while the Soviet Union has to maintain significant forces on its border with China. . . .

Saving NATO Money

Gorbachev, however, may have saved NATO a lot of money. Though his U.N. speech was clearly aimed at making diplomatic points and putting the Bush administration on the defensive, Gorbachev's initiative was, first and foremost, a major military retreat. If the Soviet leader did not propose to unilaterally disarm, his plan was nevertheless "good news," says the Hudson Institute's Jeffrey Record. "On the basis of what he said, and I think we can rely on him to carry out his program, it is a fairly substantial reduction. It is more than military tokenism."

Gorbachev pledged to reduce total Soviet manpower by 500,000 and tank inventories by 10,000; disband 6 Soviet tank divisions (along with their short-range nuclear weapons, said foreign minister Eduard Shevardnadze in January 1989); withdraw from East Germany, Czechoslovakia, and Hungary 50,000 soldiers, 8,500 "artillery systems," 5,000 tanks, and 800 combat aircraft; and pull out an unspecified number of assault-landing and river-crossing units from the same three front-line states. The overall manpower reduction may be the least significant, since total Soviet forces are estimated to number 5.2 million, of which some 1.5 million are in noncombatant labor units. But, observes Record, "if you look at what he's cutting where, it substantially reduces the Soviet capacity to do the one thing that NATO has most feared for years—launch a surprise attack."

For instance, withdrawing 10,000 tanks will unequivocally

degrade the Soviet Union's offensive capability. Of course, Moscow may demobilize the oldest tanks, of Korean War vintage, but their age has never stopped the Pentagon from including them in the military balance figures in order to show NATO's need for more money. Moreover, in January 1989 Gorbachev said that half the tanks to be withdrawn would be "the most modern ones." Says Anthony Cordesman, a Washington, D.C.-based military analyst, "no matter how you slice it, Gorbachev can't make these tank cuts in these areas without seriously affecting their offensive capability."

While leaving the Soviets with clear numerical superiority, the artillery and aircraft reductions, too, will reduce the edge that would be useful, and probably necessary, in any attempt to overwhelm the West. Disbanding 6 of the 16 Soviet tank divisions in Eastern Europe may be even more important, since NATO has always feared a blitzkrieg through Germany's central plains.

The Red Army

The cement that holds Moscow's European empire together is the Red Army. Remove that; the empire collapses. We should offer to negotiate the removal of the Red Army, first from Berlin, then, Germany, Czechoslovakia, Hungary and Poland, offering in return total U.S. troop withdrawal back across the Atlantic. Here is a proposal Europe could not reject: Europe for Europeans!

Patrick J. Buchanan, *Manchester Union Leader*, May 18, 1989.

But perhaps most significant of all is Gorbachev's pledge to reduce the Soviet's assault forces. Though less glamorous than tank divisions, these units would be at the forefront of any invasion. Admits one NATO official, "this certainly helps stability by reducing the chances of a bolt-from-the-blue attack." Even Christopher Donnelly, head of Soviet Studies Research at Great Britain's Sandhurst Military Academy, and a Gorbachev skeptic, acknowledges that a major cutback in this area "could make a lot of difference in their ability to attack."

CIA [Central Intelligence Agency] Director William Webster made a similar point in December 1988. Though the withdrawal would eliminate only part of the Warsaw Pact's military edge, he said, "they will substantially reduce the ability . . . to launch a surprise, short-warning attack." In sum, as a dramatic change in past Soviet policy, Gorbachev's plan should be used to initiate efforts to substantially reduce military spending in both West and East and to eventually eliminate America's role in defending Europe. . . .

Instead of fighting over "cuts in this or that," argues David

Calleo, director of European Studies at the Johns Hopkins School of Advanced International Studies, our approach should be to decide "what we want for the final security arrangement that will make us all feel and be more secure." Given Europe's ability to stand on its own, that goal should be complete withdrawal of superpower military forces from the continent. Layne, for instance, suggests that the Bush administration propose removing all U.S. and Soviet nuclear and conventional forces from Central Europe (East and West Germany, Czechoslovakia, Hungary, and Poland), demobilizing significant portions of the conventional troops, and pledging not to be the first to reintroduce units in the region. Such a plan, argues Layne, would "wrest the diplomatic initiative from Moscow, casting America as the champion of pan-European aspirations for an end to the continent's artificial division." It would also guarantee the security of both the West and the Soviet Union, since the Eastern European states would pose no threat to West Germany or its neighbors, while operating as a buffer for Moscow.

Mutual Disengagement

Of course, the USSR might reject mutual disengagement, since withdrawal would reduce the Politburo's influence in Eastern Europe. Yet Gorbachev has already measurably loosened Moscow's reins over the satellite states, and his planned troop reductions are clearly "driven by domestic economic concerns," says Record, a factor that is likely to grow ever more important. Anyway, we will never know whether such a program is viable unless we propose it. And it is a no-lose proposition: should the Soviets reject mutual disengagement, they would be blamed for the continued superpower militarization of Europe.

If the continent-wide proposal initially fails, Moscow might agree to more-limited cuts. In 1988, for instance, Soviet and Czechoslovakian officials suggested creating a "depletion zone" in the central front, with fewer offensive weapons. In 1987 Poland's Wojciech Jaruzelski proposed reducing battlefield nuclear weapons with "the greatest strength and strike precision, which could be used for a sudden attack." Since Gorbachev's initiative includes cuts in assault forces and forward tank divisions, further progress in this area seems possible. And partial withdrawals today could lead to a full pullout tomorrow.

Even with a complete superpower disengagement, Europe would, of course, have to possess some defense capability. "Unless the Soviet state collapses, the chances of which seem remote," says Calleo, "Europe will need a military balance to live in reasonable comfort next to the USSR." But Europeans themselves should increasingly provide those forces. Irrespective of Moscow's reaction to a proposal for mutual disengagement, part two of a new U.S. defense strategy should be the steady Europeanization of NATO.

The process has already begun. Germany and France plan to create a joint brigade, and Bonn has suggested establishing an air cavalry division made up of Belgian, British, Dutch, and German troops; more such steps should be encouraged. So, too, should ongoing efforts to make the Western European Union, established in 1948 to encourage cooperative defense efforts among the Europeans, into a more potent organization.

Burden-Sharing

Simple burden-sharing—getting the Europeans to spend more—is not the goal, however. In late December 1988 Deputy Defense Secretary William Taft argued that even if the other NATO states do more, the United States must maintain present expenditure levels. "Our view—and we have been emphatic about this throughout the discussion—is that the United States needs to do at least as much as it is doing, that it can afford to do what it is doing."

This argument only "proves the public choice economic theory," says Ted Galen Carpenter, director of foreign policy studies at the Cato Institute. "These people are out to protect their bureaucratic interest. They don't recognize that changes in the world necessitate changes in military posture; they're just adjusting their justification for the status quo."

After all, Europe has the capability to defend itself. Were the wealthier NATO states simply to spend as much per capita as does the United States, the alliance would move steadily toward parity with the Warsaw Pact. They don't because they can rely on American aid. "Permanent troop establishments abroad," warned Dwight Eisenhower in 1963, will "discourage the development of the necessary military strength Western European countries should provide for themselves."

What conceivable justification is there for the United States to impose nearly triple the defense burden on its citizens as does Germany, which faces the greatest invasion threat? Bonn argues that mere statistical measurements undervalue its contribution, which includes the fact that it hosts the bulk of NATO's forces and suffers from constant maneuvers and training missions. However, 245,000 American troops are not stationed in that nation because Bonn selflessly agreed to accept units otherwise destined for, say, Luxembourg. The forces are there to protect Germany. Since that nation derives the most direct benefits from the alliance, it should, in turn, spend the most proportionately on defense.

Indeed, a process of Europeanization would fulfill the original intent of the Western alliance. America's involvement in NATO was supposed to be merely temporary, until the Europeans had recovered. For example, Eisenhower, NATO's first supreme commander, wrote in 1951 that the United States should "establish clear limits" regarding how long America would station troops in Europe. Even Harry Truman, who pushed the treaty through a skeptical Senate, would undoubtedly be shocked to learn that Washington was still subsidizing its wealthy friends. The policy simply doesn't make sense. . . .

Some analysts fear that though Europe could defend itself, it won't. The result of an American withdrawal would then be the "Finlandization" of Washington's closest international friends. Yet the Europeans have battled each other for centuries to defend their independence; their experience reflects what Layne calls "the historical tendency of states to balance power centers rather than join a bandwagon." The Europeans are especially unlikely to accede to domination by a power that is visibly decaying. If anything, it is Eastern Europe that seems to be moving toward the Finland model, with greater national autonomy and a growing Soviet reluctance to meddle in internal disputes. (After Gorbachev's U.N. speech, Hungary and East Germany announced that they were reducing their military budgets: Poland, too, is considering military cutbacks.)

Gorbachev's unilateral troop withdrawal program comes at a particularly propitious time. But the opportunity will be wasted if the West simply presses for some additional cuts in a few weapon and troop totals. Instead, Washington should push for total, mutual superpower disengagement, a program that would provide enormous economic benefits for both the United States and the Soviet Union while sharply reducing the risk of war in Europe. Such an agreement may seem unlikely, but in 1987 no one would have predicted Gorbachev's latest initiative, Moscow's interest in troop reductions in East Asia, the INF [Intermediate-Range Nuclear Forces] agreement, the Soviet withdrawal from Afghanistan, or Moscow's sharp reduction in naval spending. Today it appears the more far-reaching the proposal, the greater its likelihood of success.

6

"The continued presence of the United States in Europe is . . . essential to the survival of West European independence."

Europe Needs US Protection

Arnulf Baring

In the following viewpoint, Berlin professor Arnulf Baring explains how the historical split of Germany into two parts—one communist and one democratic—proves the US should not withdraw its troops from Western Europe. Baring argues that the USSR remains a threat to West Germany and the rest of Western Europe. He teaches modern history and international relations at the Free University in West Berlin.

As you read, consider the following questions:

1. Why did US President Truman station American troops in Europe, according to Baring?
2. According to the author, how has US military support for NATO affected the Soviet Union?
3. Why does Baring argue that US troops must remain in the NATO countries?

Arnulf Baring, "Transatlantic Relations: The View from Europe," *NATO Review*, No. 1, February 1989. Reprinted with permission.

As the Cold War began, the United States was a country virtually without troops and without weapons, not only in Europe but also in America itself; the atom bomb was out of the question as a serious means of exerting political pressure, and even more so as a military weapon against former wartime allies.

Abandoning a Venerable Tradition

The outbreak of the Korean conflict in 1950 was seen in the Federal Republic of Germany, and also in the United States, as conceivably the start of a generalized 'hot' war that could spread into Europe. This threatened outbreak of World War III prompted the Americans to request from their Alliance partners the raising of West German troops and it likewise prompted the West European Allies, especially France, to ask the US to station American troops in Europe immediately. The fear on the European side of the Atlantic was that, in the event of a Russian blitzkrieg action, i.e. a Soviet surprise attack, it would take the Americans far too long to arrive on the scene if their troops had to be brought all the way from the United States after hostilities had already begun. . . .

In 1950 the Europeans were not only urging that American troops should be stationed immediately on our continent, but were also requesting that there should be a permanent American Supreme Allied Commander in Europe. Together, it was felt, the two factors would guarantee the recently created and now indissoluble bond between the Old and New Worlds.

In agreeing to these requests, the United States was making a sharp about-turn. All at once, it was abandoning a venerable tradition of isolationism that dated back to its origins in the 18th century, discarding its deep-seated reluctance to allow itself to become embroiled politically and militarily in European differences on a long-term basis. Instead, it was now prepared to forge a permanent link, to join its own destiny with that of Europe—at the urgent request of the West Europeans, but also in its own interest and of its own accord. . . .

A Military Threat

It is my conviction that Western Europe now, just as much as ever, is still under threat militarily and politically and unable to ensure its common defence adequately by means of its own strength. True, the Western part of the continent has long since recovered economically; and today, the Soviet Union presents no ideological or social danger or temptation. But what has changed since 1950 is that it has turned itself into a real superpower, a major nuclear power with, at the same time, overwhelming conventional superiority in Europe.

Since the 1960s, when a nuclear war became increasingly risky

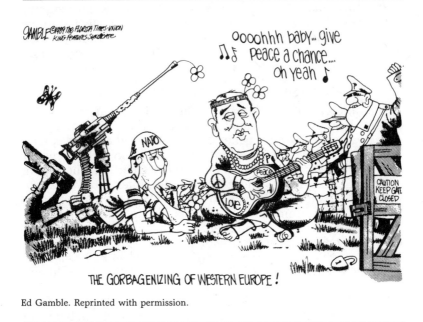

Oooohhh baby... give peace a chance.... oh yeah ♪

CAUTION KEEP GATE CLOSED

THE GORBAGENIZING OF WESTERN EUROPE !

Ed Gamble. Reprinted with permission.

and therefore increasingly unlikely because of the balance of fear and the mutual nuclear vulnerability of the world powers, the Soviet Union has concentrated its European strategy on conventional, non-nuclear warfare after the manner of the German 'blitzkrieg', waged so successfully by Hitler against Poland, France, Norway and other European countries. Accordingly, the offensive capability of the powerful Soviet forces in the GDR [German Democratic Republic] has been constantly increased and improved. This is evident in their deployment, *matériel* and logistics. Lothar Rühl, former State Secretary in the Bonn Ministry of Defence, calls the Soviet concept 'an offensive strategy of overthrow'. The Red Army, he says, has improved its potential for breakthrough and widespread offensive deployment against Western Europe and so achieved a 'strategic invasion capability against Western Europe as a means of offensive warfare'. According to Rühl, political statements in Moscow and at Warsaw Pact meetings are aimed at masking this capability and denying the latent preparedness for attack.

New Soviet Tone

Unquestionably, the Russians have, for some years now, been adopting a new tone: more peaceable, more disposed towards mutual understanding and more receptive to ideas. To date, unfortunately, this has still done nothing to alter the aggressive deployment, *matériel* and logistics of their forces in Central Europe, or their enormous conventional superiority or, again, their blitzkrieg concept in spite of steps that could lead to the adoption of their newly formulated 'defensive sufficiency' doctrine, and the stated intention to reduce the size of their forces. Today, as yesterday, it would still take them only a brief period of preparation to enable them to be at the Rhine within a few hours and at the Atlantic within a few days. Certainly, they are willing to hold talks with the West, even about strategy. But up till now these have been merely declarations of intent which are not binding and which do nothing to alter the hard facts.

Of course, we must test and explore every promising and sound starting point for future agreements, catch at every thread of mutual understanding and follow it up. No end to the threat is yet in sight, however, and true peace is no more than a dream of the future. For the time being, we therefore have to be wary of exaggerated and premature hopes. Even Theo Sommer, Editor of *Die Zeit*, who vigorously advocates a positive Western response to the present moves toward an easing of tension, is realistic in stressing that, in favourable circumstances, i.e. with a smooth continuation of the processes of détente that have been initiated, it will take two or three decades before the alliances become superfluous. Reaching a true *rapprochement*, where the differences would no longer have any real significance, will, he says, take even more decades. By then we shall be 'with a bit of luck, far into the next century'. Thus far, the Soviet Union is still striving for absolute security—something altogether different from peace in Europe. For, as the former American Secretary of State Henry Kissinger has said more than once, the Soviet Union's absolute security is to be had only at the price of the absolute insecurity of all other countries.

Soviet Danger

And most important of all, the danger posed by the Soviet Union is frequently mistakenly viewed in terms that are too strictly military. The prospect of suddenly being over-run by Soviet troops is in fact only a small part of it. Far more pressing are the political repercussions of overwhelming military superiority. Today, the formidable, threatening potential of the Soviet Union is a political power factor of the first order, from which strong political shock waves spread out over the whole of Europe, not just in the Eastern bloc but in the Western part of our continent as well.

What does this imply? What can we West Germans, we West Europeans do, what should we do?

In the first place, we should make up our minds, soberly, what the alliance with the United States means for us—now and in the future. On both sides of the Atlantic it is time for a debate on the

149

rôle and purpose of the Alliance in the years to come.

On our side, there is a growing conviction that the Soviet Union no longer poses a threat to Western Europe. In the United States, on the other hand, the view is that, despite all the hoped-for détente and disarmament, the power struggle between Moscow and Washington will inevitably persist. If these fundamentally contrasting perceptions continue, they will set aside what has hitherto been the basis of the Alliance. Forty years ago, this was the certainty of a common task. No alliance is viable without commonly perceived dangers, without commonly assumed obligations. Only if the interests of both sides remain broadly identical can the Alliance endure.

Invading Western Europe

Arthur Schlesinger wrote: 'Anyone who thinks that an invasion of Western Europe is high on the list of Mr Gorbachev's priorities should have his head examined.' No quarrel with that. The more relevant question is what kind of suzerainty the Soviet Union could establish *without* having to invade, if it ever acquired unchallenged military power. And Gorbachev is no foundation for our future. Clearly, the Bolshevik Party cannot revert to messianic communist imperialism. The faith is dead. But nor can it find legitimacy in the hodge-podge of incoherent half measures known as *perestroika*. . . . All we know is that turbulent, declining empires with large armies are exceedingly dangerous.

Ambrose Evans-Pritchard, *The Spectator*, June 3, 1989.

In addition to the original objective of checking the influence of the Soviet Union in Europe, new challenges have since arisen which confront Americans and West Europeans alike. With good reasons, therefore, the US is demanding that the Europeans, and particularly the Federal Republic of Germany, should take on a greater share of responsibility for global policy. This includes coordinated aid programmes for the Third World and military contributions toward the stabilization of crisis areas outside Europe. The Federal Republic, especially, must examine carefully the extent to which, for example, its worldwide trade interests might be endangered in the future and thus need military protection. For it has become increasingly evident over the past few years that the United States is no longer in a position to continue to bear the burden of its rôle as a world power on the present scale. . . .

At the moment, it does not look as if we West Europeans will, within the next few years, possess a sufficient joint concentration of power and political determination to guarantee the security of Western Europe by our own means, much less play an independent rôle in the world. We must be pleased and thankful if, by 1992, we actually bring about the single internal Market. Not until we then, in addition, become united politically and stand on our own feet militarily, will we be able to confront the Soviet Union's hegemonic ambitions, which even under Gorbachev still exist and continue to pose a danger. That may take us decades to achieve.

Continued US Presence

The continued presence of the United States in Europe is therefore essential to the survival of West European independence, freedom and self-determination. The alliance with the US must remain alive and strong into the future. The corollary of this is the stationing of a sufficently large number of American troops in Europe. These American divisions are not only indispensable for our security but are also important for what we may hope will be Eastern Europe's growing scope for manoeuvre. The US presence in Europe has positive repercussions for the Eastern part of our continent—a fact that we mostly fail to appreciate—since it compels the Kremlin to afford its satellites some measure of consideration. To that extent, prominent East Europeans are likewise vitally interested in the continued stationing of strong American forces in the Western part of the continent.

A withdrawal of American troops would, on the other hand, allow Moscow greater freedom of action in Eastern Europe and also, in the longer term, greater influence in Western Europe. No clear-sighted person among us can want that. There are many in the United States, too, who are opposed to such a development. We must give them our support. If we do not, we shall only be acting against our own interests.

Distinguishing Between Fact and Opinion

This activity is designed to help develop the basic reading and thinking skill of distinguishing between fact and opinion. Consider the following statement: "In 1985 Mikhail Gorbachev became leader of the Soviet Union." This is a fact which can be verified by many published sources. But consider this statement: "Mikhail Gorbachev is a great leader." This statement expresses an opinion about Gorbachev. Many people may have a different assessment of the Soviet leader.

When investigating controversial issues it is important that one be able to distinguish between statements of fact and statements of opinion. It is also important to recognize that not all statements of fact are true. They may appear to be true, but some are based on inaccurate or false information. For this activity, however, we are concerned with understanding the difference between those statements which appear to be factual and those which appear to be based primarily on opinion.

The following statements are related to topics covered in this chapter. Consider each statement carefully. *Mark O for any statement you believe is an opinion or interpretation of facts. Mark F for any statement you consider a fact. Mark U if you are uncertain.*

If you are doing this activity as a member of a class or group, compare your answers to those of other class or group members. Be able to defend your answers. You may discover that others come to different conclusions than you. Listening to the reasons others present for their answers may give you valuable insights in distinguishing between fact and opinion.

O = opinion
F = fact
U = uncertain

1. Socialism possesses vast possibilities for self-development and self-perfection that have yet to be revealed.

2. Japan's 120 million people produce more than one and a half times as many goods and services as 280 million Soviet citizens.

3. There are some Americans who believe that socialism is in crisis and has led the Soviet Union to a dead end.

4. Soviet influence in the world has peaked, and is headed towards decline.

5. Evidence from countries around the world has shown that rigid, centralized institutions are incapable of producing modern, efficient economies.

6. Any objective observer must admit that Soviet history is in general a history of indisputable progress, despite losses, setbacks, and failures.

7. Everywhere it has been tried, communism has failed.

8. Societies with severe domestic problems also tend to be the most dangerous internationally.

9. In Lenin's day Western techniques in business management were used in Soviet factories.

10. The Soviet Union's world trade totaled $170 billion in 1987.

11. The Soviet Union is a major industrial power.

12. A stronger Soviet economy means a stronger Soviet military.

13. The Soviet Union spends twice as high a percentage of its gross national product on arms as the US.

14. Western banks have loaned the Soviet Union billions of dollars.

15. Among major industrial nations, the Soviet Union is unique in that its monetary currency cannot be easily exchanged into dollars.

16. Western money and technology has allowed the USSR to avoid cutting back its military spending.

17. Over 90 percent of Soviet hard currency exports consist of oil, gas, gold, and arms.

18. More conciliatory US trade policies toward the Soviet Union might encourage more Soviet reforms.

Periodical Bibliography

The following articles have been selected to supplement the diverse views presented in this chapter.

William M. Arkin	"Gorbachev Talks but Who Listens?" *Bulletin of the Atomic Scientists,* March 1989.
Lev Bezymensky and Nikita Zholkver	"A Visit Is Hard Work," *New Times,* no. 25, June, 1989.
Gregory Flynn	"Problems in Paradigm," *Foreign Policy,* Spring 1989.
Makhmut Gareyev	"Soviet Armed Forces and Glasnost," *Soviet Military Review,* March 1989.
Colin S. Gray	"The Gorbachev Offensive," *Society,* July/August 1987.
John Greenwald	"The Big Shake-Up," *Time,* August 8, 1988.
Simon Head	"The Battle Inside NATO," *The New York Review of Books,* May 18, 1989.
Jerry F. Hough	"A Flawed View of Future Europe," *Los Angeles Times,* May 3, 1989.
Max M. Kampelman	"Arms Control and Soviet Relations," *Vital Speeches of the Day,* April 15, 1989.
Alexei Kireyev	"The Price of Disarmament," *New Times,* no. 37, September 1988.
Igor Malashenko	"Ideals and Interests," *New Times,* no. 45, November 1988.
Thomas Moore	"Who's Afraid of Tearing Down the Iron Curtain?" *U.S. News & World Report,* May 15, 1989.
William E. Odom	"Soviet Military Doctrine," *Foreign Affairs,* Winter 1988/1989.
David J. Trachtenberg	"INF: The Soviets Cheat," *National Review,* May 19, 1989.
Henry Trewhitt with Jeff Trimble, Robyn Knight, and Robert Kaylor	"A Different Call to Arms," *U.S. News & World Report,* March 13, 1989.
Stansfield Turner	"Winnowing Our Warheads," *The New York Times Magazine,* May 27, 1988.

CHAPTER
4

Is More Economic Cooperation Between the Superpowers Possible?

THE SUPERPOWERS
A NEW DETENTE

Chapter Preface

Perestroika, Gorbachev's reform program, provides an opportunity for more economic ties between the US and the USSR.

An increasingly common example of cooperation is a joint venture, in which an American company and a Soviet company manufacture a product together. The product sells on the Soviet market and the two companies share the profits. Archer Daniels Midland Company, Coca-Cola, PepsiCo, Nike, and Honeywell are only a few of the more than fifty US companies involved in US-Soviet joint ventures. Joint ventures and other forms of economic cooperation are controversial, however.

Those who favor joint ventures agree with US Representative Don Bonker, who contends that this increased economic cooperation will promote a more peaceful relationship between the superpowers. Bonker asserts that joint ventures and trade strengthen bonds between the superpowers, making it less likely that they would revert to hostile relations. Some experts would disagree, however. Economist Judy Shelton, for example, argues that joint ventures and other US economic ties with the USSR will strengthen the Soviet economy. She believes this would permit the Soviets to devote more money to strengthening their military, thus endangering US security.

The authors in this chapter debate whether economic cooperation with the Soviet Union is beneficial.

"A Soviet Union more engaged in the global economy would be less prone to backsliding in its economic and political evolution."

The US Should Trade with the Soviet Union

Adlai E. Stevenson and Alton Frye

Adlai E. Stevenson is a former US senator from Illinois. He is now with the law firm of Mayer, Brown, and Platt in Chicago, Illinois. Alton Frye is the vice-president of the Council on Foreign Relations, an organization that studies the international aspects of American political, economic, and strategic problems. In the following viewpoint, the authors describe how the United States should respond to reforms in the Soviet Union. The authors believe that lifting restrictions against loans and trade to the USSR would improve economic cooperation and relations between the two superpowers.

As you read, consider the following questions:

1. What economic policies should the US change, in the authors' opinion?
2. According to the authors, how have past economic policies affected US relations with the Soviet Union?
3. How would the changes benefit the US and the USSR, according to Stevenson and Frye?

Adlai E. Stevenson and Alton Frye, "Trading With the Communists." Reprinted by permission of *Foreign Affairs*, Spring 1989. Copyright 1989 by the Council on Foreign Relations, Inc.

In Moscow bold minds are asking where Marxism-Leninism went wrong. Were its premises flawed? Was the execution inept? Communist governments are experimenting with the answers. Americans would do well to pose similar questions about U.S. economic policy toward these nations. Are the premises correct? Do changes in their policies require new assumptions and changes in our policy?

The candor of Soviet self-criticism demands a comparable dose of introspection on our part. We have never expected mea culpas from the Soviets, and we have always prided ourselves on a capacity for self-correction. Yet the United States has been slow to acknowledge evident shortcomings in its economic policy toward the Soviet Union and other communist countries.

An Expansionist Imperial State

Policies framed to deal with an expansionist imperial state driven by authoritarian ideology and marked by the sacrifice of its citizens' well-being to the appetites of its military establishment are not appropriate for a state being reshaped in the image projected by the architects of perestroika and glasnost. As evidence mounts that the reforms of Mikhail Gorbachev are real, the West is challenged to rethink its approach to the Soviet Union....

The Reagan Administration began a gradual movement toward more normal economic relations with the Soviet Union. Led by the late secretary of commerce, Malcolm Baldrige, the U.S.-Soviet Joint Commercial Commission in 1985 resumed sessions that had been suspended indefinitely in 1978. Various trade promotion activities have ensued, with hundreds of American businessmen visiting Moscow. Reagan lifted a ban on sales of some oil and gas equipment to the Soviets, a sanction tightened at the time of the Afghanistan invasion. He also allowed imports of Soviet nickel and furs to resume. Before leaving office Secretary Shultz recommended that COCOM [Coordinating Committee for Multilateral Export Controls] end the "no exception" ban on high-technology exports after the Soviets withdrew from Afghanistan. The European allies support this return to a case-by-case review of such sales. U.S. reticence on this point could revive European fears of more "light switch" diplomacy — and Soviet suspicions that concessions only invite demands for more concessions. The ban should be lifted.

Increased commerce with the Soviet Union has been slow, but some developments are potentially significant. Several major firms have formed an American Trade Consortium and negotiated arrangements to permit repatriation of profits from operations in the Soviet Union, perhaps a model arrangement that will permit more income and capital flows to and from joint ventures there. In December 1988 the Soviets further adjusted their rules for joint ventures to permit foreign participants to hold equity majorities and to delay taxation until several years after initial profits are realized. They also increased the number of Soviet organizations authorized to deal directly with foreign partners and suppliers. These attempts to accelerate the pace of the Soviet economy's engagement with foreign investors and markets reveal an alertness to the weaknesses of Moscow's first steps in this direction. American firms were involved in only about 15 of some 200 joint ventures....

This policy flaw bears on export controls. The United States pays a high price for the quaint notion that trade is a privilege. By some estimates export controls have cost U.S. firms between $7 billion and $9 billion in exports and 180,000 jobs annually. A National Academy of Sciences survey of almost 200 firms found that over half claimed to have lost sales because of these controls. Such controls also hurt U.S. sales with non-communist countries; 26 percent of the companies surveyed said they had lost deals with free world customers because of export controls, and over a third of the companies reported such customers preferred to shift to other suppliers outside the United States. In 1985 the control process handled proposals approaching $80 billion in value. This gives an idea of how far it ranges beyond direct trade with the Soviets.

Conciliatory Policies

More conciliatory U.S. trade policies toward the Soviet Union might give added impetus to *perestroika*.

Thomas M. Magstadt, *USA Today*, July 1988.

In a wide-ranging review of COCOM's record, the National Academy of Sciences studies have urged a new balance between national security export controls and commercial considerations. They called into question the feasibility of enforcing the extensive COCOM list of controlled items and pressed for stronger enforcement of more limited restraints— "higher fences around fewer items." These studies and consultations within COCOM have helped build a consensus to shrink the export control list. In addition, the verdict emerged that, however compressed the list, the executive branch had to pick up its own tempo to reach timely decisions on export applications. With that goal in mind, the 100th Congress trimmed the Department of Defense's authority to delay the process, limiting DOD export license evaluations to "national security" as distinct from "foreign policy" considerations. It remains questionable whether such exhortations will be more effective than those in the past.

In the end, there must be some recognition that technology is inherently difficult to control. It travels on paper and in the human mind, as well as in tangible products. It is usually available from many sources. Security requires control of exports with clear military applications to adversaries. But the West's technological supremacy depends upon its economic and intellectual environment, resources for the development of inventions and their rapid application to commercial and military uses. The United States must stay ahead through a nurtured process of basic research and technological innovation.

Should We Help Gorbachev?

It is essential to state the issues confronting U.S. policy with some precision. Posing the question "Should we help Gorbachev?" tends to divert discussion into narrow byways. If all the change that is transpiring in the Soviet Union rests on a single individual, if it has no roots beyond Gorbachev's alluring rhetoric, then there is little ground for optimism about its durability, or his. If the innovations are tentative and perishable, one would not be wise to argue for shifting American policy onto sandy terrain.

The dawning consensus, however, is that the changes within the Soviet Union are erupting from sources too deep to permit their suppression even if Gorbachev's tenure turns out to be relatively brief. He is a creature of economic and strategic necessities already recognized in China and other communist countries. What is remarkable is that this historical inevitability has been so slow in coming and that it has not yet appeared in many communist countries. Fidel Castro and Nicholae Ceausescu are defiant. . . .

For policy purposes, it is not necessary to predict an outcome with certainty in order to prefer it. Surely, from the Western standpoint, a Soviet system that must become more benign in order to become more powerful is preferable to one that joins excessive military capability with the malign impulses of totalitarianism in decline.

But to welcome perestroika is not to advocate paying for it. In truth, there is little likelihood of excessive American investment in the still risky Soviet economy. The U.S. business community has long since discounted forecasts of easy or early profits in the Soviet market. There is impatience with the sluggish bargaining required to close deals with Soviet bureaucrats and enterprises. Permitting U.S. investment in the Soviet economy is not payment for perestroika. It merely means repealing provisions that hamper commerce and penalize American companies.

Soviet Exports

As far as Soviet exports to the United States are concerned, the range of candidates remains limited. Over 90 percent of Soviet hard currency exports consist of oil, gas, gold and arms, not manufactures that would displace major domestic sales by U.S. firms. It is conceivable that buried deep in Soviet archives and laboratories are ingenious developments waiting to be commercialized, but so far the examples are few, e.g., sales of electromagnetic casting technology and an ion-gun hardening system for industrial cutting tools.

Understandably Moscow hopes that the joint ventures it now encourages will concentrate on exports to generate hard currency revenues, but the projected scale of such enterprises remains relatively modest. The volume of trade with communist countries may be small, but these are nations with which the United States can run a needed trade surplus.

The apprehension that the United States might be lured into paying for perestroika seems to focus on official credit arrangements, perhaps reflecting concern about methods once employed to pursue détente. If Moscow were to become eligible for Export-Import Bank financing, as agreed in 1972, today it would face stiff competition for the bank's limited resources. There is no disposition in either Congress or the executive branch to allow Export-Import Bank guarantees to become a surrogate for foreign aid, for example, underwriting development in Soviet Siberia. In the midst of U.S. budget stringencies and chronic trade imbalances the bank is obliged more than ever to husband its authority and to devote its efforts to improving American export performance....

US-Soviet Trade

The Soviet Far East and Siberia are rich in raw materials such as oil, natural gas, timber and many nonfuel minerals. The U.S. has the machinery, technology and management skills to extract, process and export these resources. A natural complementary of economic interests is waiting to be exploited.... An enlightened, carefully conceived [U.S.] economic policy would not only prove profitable for Amercian business but would encourage further reform in the Soviet Union.

Foreign Policy Institute, in *The Washington Spectator,* March 1,1989.

To preclude Export-Import Bank participation in business with communist countries discourages exporters, investors and private lenders from exploring opportunities. In any case, the bank's primary function is not to do the whole job but to lubricate the larger process. To the extent that there develops a need for selective use of Export-Import Bank assistance in trade, the option should be open. Otherwise American traders and financiers carry a handicap that their counterparts in other Western countries do not.

There appears to be a good understanding at the highest levels in Moscow that one way to energize Soviet domestic enterprises is to subject them, albeit gradually, to the stresses of international competition.

The emphasis on opening the Soviet Union to foreign investment and on working toward convertibility of the ruble reflects this insight. More than nostalgia lies in the recollection that Lenin had a convertible currency. This opening is a farsighted appeal for a return to pragmatism, coupled with a straightforward acknowledgment that the transition from the current 6,000 variations ("currency coefficients") to a unitary ruble exchange rate will take a decade or more.

For the West the prospect of convertible currencies and an end to the Council for Mutual Economic Assistance poses interesting policy questions. Few measures would contribute more to the predictability of transactions with communist countries than the shift to currencies readily traded on world markets. Such a development could testify to the growing strength and independence of communist economies. It could help to stabilize East-West economic relations. . . .

Communist Economies

But do we want communist economies to be integrated into the world capital and trading system? Certainly not the Soviet economy we have learned to distrust. The economy Gorbachev envisages, however, would be a different matter. A Soviet economy that had undergone the transformations now contemplated could become a constructive participant in the international economic system arduously constructed by the free market countries. . . .

Looking ahead, there has been speculation regarding future Soviet involvement in the International Monetary Fund [IMF]. Leaders in Moscow have pointed out that an IMF relationship could expedite the country's graduation to currency convertibility. They note that a place in IMF would not give a veto to the Soviet Union and that, given the IMF structure, Moscow would hardly have enough leverage to disrupt its functions. Hungary and Poland are already members and the prospect of an eventual Soviet connection to IMF warrants examination.

As we evaluate these issues, it is reasonable to argue that a Soviet Union more engaged in the global economy would be less prone to backsliding in its economic and political evolution. In the phrase of one close observer, Brezhnev wanted foreign investment to avoid reform, Gorbachev wants it to foster reform. . . .

Does the communist countries' pursuit of foreign investment threaten U.S. interests? One can imagine scenarios in which it might do so. Gullible Western investors, shown the green light by changes in public policy, might divert so many resources to Soviet projects and joint ventures that they deprive other needy nations of capital. That redirection of capital flows could drive up the cost of funds to everyone, including the United States. Reverse leverage could come into play, with the American government and its allies under pressure to do nothing that might prompt the Soviets to default. These concerns are valid, but not conclusive. Western banks' painful over-exposure in Latin America and Eastern Europe, especially Poland, has bred a healthy caution about concentrating too many eggs in the Soviet basket. Most lenders have relearned the old banker's adage that "if a man owes you a hundred dollars, he's got a problem; if he owes you a million dollars, you've got a problem."

Worst-Case Anticipations

Present evidence makes worst-case anticipations implausible. The Soviets and Chinese historically have been prudent, cautious, even reluctant borrowers. Sovereign borrowers, no less than others, cannot afford to antagonize the big players in Western capital markets. Besides, the West always has its assets to sequester, as Iran discovered. The risks are not exorbitant. . . .

Moscow has begun to dabble with bond issues underwritten in the West, and during 1988 Western lenders extended lines of credit amounting to several billion dollars, most of which are thought to be tied to purchases of consumer goods and equipment. The U.S. government believes that the majority of these credits are officially guaranteed, export-related borrowings permissible under OECD [Organization for Economic Cooperation and Development] guidelines. This contrasts with the pattern of Soviet loans earlier in the 1980s, which appeared to be generally untied. Two-way trade with nonsocialist countries slackened somewhat, but Wharton Associates projects volume reaching $95 billion in the early 1990s. In the estimate of Soviet economist Abel Aganbegyan, removal of trade barriers could bring bilateral U.S.-Soviet trade levels up to a range of $10 billion to $20 billion within five to seven years. . . .

Inadequate Trade

American trade with the Soviet Union is clearly inadequate and there are possibilities for expanding it on mutually advantageous terms. The U.S.S.R. is an industrial power which trades on the world market to the tune of about 170 billion dollars a year.

Michael Nite, *New Times,* no. 47, November 30, 1987.

All things considered, alarm over Soviet penetration of Western capital markets is premature. From a policy standpoint the important objective in the near term is to improve the means of monitoring Moscow's activities in those markets. That task is part of the more general need to develop adequate information about capital flows—now so rapid and dominant an element in the global economy—as a building block for intelligent policy and for government interventions, when necessary to maintain stability. The United States will have more clout in extracting that information from the Soviets if it is a player, rather than a bystander, in Gorbachev's enterprise.

Policy Shifts

The shift in policy emphasis recommended here does not prejudge whether American firms will discover enticing and large-scale opportunities in the Soviet Union. Our contention is simply that the government should not strangle their search for such opportunities by policies that preempt consideration of mutually acceptable economic possibilities. The message is: let businessmen strike bargains they deem profitable—and keep enough steerage over U.S. policy to hold a safe and steady course in our overall relationship with communist states.

It is often the essence of political decision-making that governments must choose before there is a confident basis for judgment. So it is in shaping the next phase of U.S. economic relations with communist countries. The mistakes of the past 15 years are clearer than the path into the next century. But, while remaining alert to the dangers, American policy should lift the impediments barring its citizens from exploring that path actively. In today's world economy, inertia is a recipe for neither prosperity nor security. There is no standing still.

"We should applaud perestroika. But not finance it."

The US Should Not Trade with the Soviet Union

Judy Shelton

Reforms in the USSR have prompted some US commentators to argue that the US should loan money to and increase its trade with the Soviets to encourage further reforms. The author of the following viewpoint, Judy Shelton, disagrees with this suggestion. She believes the USSR would use the extra money for a military build-up which would threaten the US. Shelton is a research fellow at the Hoover Institution on War, Revolution, and Peace at Stanford University in Stanford, California.

As you read, consider the following questions:

1. Why has the Soviet Union liberalized and begun to reduce its nuclear arsenal, according to the author?
2. According to Shelton, what economic assistance could the US provide for the USSR?
3. Why does Shelton believe the US should not provide loans and trade opportunities for the Soviet Union?

Judy Shelton, "The Western Economic Response: Should We Help Gorbachev?" a speech given to the National Strategy Information Center at the National Press Club on March 14, 1989.

Should we help Gorbachev? All the hopes and dreams of the members of the Western Alliance in terms of our vision for peace in the world with our long-term military rival seem riveted on a single man. It is natural that we would focus on Gorbachev as an individual because, after all, he is the leader of the Soviet Union and he clearly is making a difference. But if Gorbachev were to be replaced tomorrow by the head of the KGB, or by the Soviet Minister of Defense, would we in the West feel compelled to restructure our entire foreign policy stance toward the Soviet Union? Surely we should be dealing with the system, not the man. And we should not buy into the bogey-man notion that, should Gorbachev be replaced, there will automatically be a return to ominous, threatening behavior from the Soviet Union. Any pragmatist who emerges to assume the leadership of the Soviet Union will find himself facing the same set of economic, social and political circumstances that are now confronting Gorbachev – and will likely feel compelled to carry through with the reforms that have been initiated.

Western Response

I would like to proceed with an examination of economic and financial conditions in the Soviet Union.

Not that the two perspectives, political and economic, can be easily separated; when the subject of East-West trade is discussed in political circles – most particularly, the issue of Soviet borrowing – the talk typically does turn to such matters as human rights, regional conflicts, or arms control. Indeed, purely financial questions about the Soviet Union's internal budget crisis and its credit-worthiness as a borrower tend to be downplayed in the broader debate over East-West political relations.

This is unfortunate; it may well prove dangerously shortsighted for members of the Western Alliance. Understanding the budgetary pressures facing the Kremlin at this time is key if we are to understand Soviet motives in world affairs. Only by comprehending the magnitude of the financial and economic problems now confronting Moscow do we gain proper perspective for interpreting Soviet global behavior, and specifically, Gorbachev's political initiatives toward the West. . . .

One can draw a rough linkage to identify the connection between chronic budgetary shortfalls and resulting economic and political fallout. The Soviet domestic budget, i.e., the internal state budget, regulates the monetary and financial system in the Soviet Union. The distribution of internal resources is directly affected by the amount of credit within the Soviet system, and thus is vulnerable to the consequences of monetary distortions caused by having to cover internal budgetary deficiencies. . . .

166

H. Payne. Reprinted by permission of UFS, Inc.

When economic difficulties reach the point of severity where citizens feel stressed due to, say, widespread consumer shortages, the situation can lead to social turmoil. Anti-social behavior in the Soviet Union is already observable in the form of widespread corruption and black market activities; it may well be manifested in the future as mass strikes by workers. Social turmoil is generally the precursor to political upheaval, which unfortunately is often accompanied by violence. Should conditions in the Soviet Union reach the point where widespread violence was imminent, it would be socially and politically destabilizing....

At the heart of the problem is the internal budget deficit. To put it in the most straightforward terms: The Soviet government is currently running a massive budget deficit and, despite assertions to the contrary, has been for years....

A Startling Disclosure

It was no less than a startling disclosure when Soviet Finance Minister Boris Gostev told an assembly of the Supreme Soviet that the 1989 budget would show a 36 billion ruble deficit (about $58 billion), over 7 percent of the total state budget. Even more shocking, Gostev revealed that the problem of deficits had not just now emerged, but had been going on for years.

For the Soviet Union to admit to a budget deficit, given that it has always held up the U.S. budget deficit with its attendant scourge of inflation as the ultimate symbol of capitalist mismanagement, is a radical shift indeed. It was prompted, it would seem, by the sheer desperation of the Soviet financial situation. Strongly reinforcing that conclusion, Leonid Abalkin, one of Gorbachev's closest economic advisors, made the statement in January 1989 that the actual Soviet budget deficit is three times higher than the figure admitted by the Finance Minister in October 1988; according to Abalkin, the deficit amount for 1989 is over 100 billion rubles.

To put that in perspective: The U.S. budget deficit is roughly 3 to 4 percent of gross national product. The original deficit figure cited by Gostev would have put the Soviet deficit at a comparable level of 3.9 percent of gross national product. However, the revised figure for the Soviet budget deficit revealed by Abalkin and subsequently corroborated by Abel Aganbegyan, another leading economic advisor to Gorbachev, represents some 11 percent of Soviet gross national product. (My own calculations indicate that the actual amount of the Soviet budget deficit arising from domestic economic activities is closer to 18 percent of gross national product, and that revenues from foreign imports play a substantial, though as yet unacknowledged, role in offsetting the nominal deficit amount.)

A Considerable Problem

Obviously, many countries are carrying a budget deficit including, of course, the United States. But when it comes to financing the deficit—and all governments must finance their revenue shortfalls, either internally or by borrowing from abroad—the Soviet Union has a considerable problem. Among major industrial nations, the Soviet Union's problem is rather unique: Its currency is not convertible. One can only use rubles to buy Soviet-produced goods. So whereas the United States can get investors in other countries to finance its deficit directly because they are willing to hold dollar-denominated bonds, the Soviet Union does not have this option. It must bear the entire impact of financing its deficit internally. And deficit spending, whether in a capitalist system or a socialist one, spawns inflationary pressures.

In the United States and other Western countries, the term inflation is considered practically synonymous with the idea of rising prices. Under free markets, when there is too much money in the system, the prices of goods rise to accommodate the excess money in the hands of consumers. But in the Soviet Union, prices are fixed by the government. Inflation is therefore manifested differently.

Soviet consumers today are holding too many rubles because, since the 1960s, wages overall have been increased through the inflationary practices of the Soviet government. With all these extra rubles, however, they can hardly buy anything; at the fixed prices, all available consumer goods tend to sell out immediately. In other words, wages have been increased in the Soviet Union without there having been a concurrent increase in productivity. The additional rubles that have been printed are now chasing the same basic level of goods as before. Inflation under socialism, therefore, does not result in higher prices, but rather shows up in the form of longer lines. . . .

Revenue Shortfalls

To reiterate the problem: There are significant and chronic revenue shortfalls in the state budget; the Soviet government has been running an enormous budget deficit; the government finances this deficit internally by printing excess money. How is this excess money actually infused into the Soviet system? It is generally accomplished through the state-owned enterprises, which, whether they are productive or not, are required to contribute certain amounts to the state budget out of their so-called "profits."

When a Soviet firm has not earned sufficient money to make its requisite payment back to the state budget, i.e., to the Soviet government, it looks to the state-owned banking system to provide the necessary funds. The deposit accounts of Soviet enterprises are administered by the State Bank (Gosydarstvennyi Bank or Gosbank), the same state bank that also takes in the deposits of the people. Gosbank traditionally has been empowered not only to handle all financial transactions, but also to have supervisory authority over the operations of enterprises. Such a mandate carries with it an inherent responsibility for the performance of the enterprises – and therein lies a serious conflict of interest. . . .

Trade Policy

Why spend $300 billion on defense if we're going to underwrite the Soviet military too? With a tough trade policy, the West could cripple the Kremlin's ability to project its power beyond its own hemisphere. Cut off Soviet access to hard currency and Western technology, and we can undo the Evil Empire without firing a single shot.

R. Cort Kirkwood, *The National Review,* April 29, 1988.

Since Gosbank is owned and administered by the state, the mechanical granting of credits means that the Soviet government is making loans to itself to make up for inadequate revenues from production at state-owned enterprises. In the financial statements prepared by the Central Statistical Administration (Tsentral'noye Statisticheskoye Upravleniye or TsSU), unwarranted credits mas-

169

querade as phantom contributions to the budget; they are buried under accounting entries such as "deductions from profits and other payments" and carried as budget revenues in the official published statistics. . . .

The Soviet budget crisis is essentially an internal financial problem. Due to chronic revenue shortfalls, the Soviet government is tightly constrained in its spending at this point; if Kremlin officials want to spend additional money on consumers, or on fixed capital investment, or on the military sector (not necessarily in that order), they need first to increase the productivity of the Soviet economy to extract additional real revenues.

But there are only two methods, according to classic economic theory, for improving productivity. The first is to increase the productivity of labor, the second is to increase the productivity of capital. Increasing the productivity of labor is accomplished by getting people to work harder or longer; it is conventionally achieved by offering to pay them more money for their extra effort.

Gorbachev's Dilemma

Herein lies the primary component of the internal economic dilemma Gorbachev is facing. Because of the inflationary consequences of financing an internal deficit, Soviet workers already have too much worthless money that is virtually inconvertible, even within Soviet borders, into desired consumer goods. An offer to reward them with more money as the reward for additional work carries little incentive appeal. It is necessary to have the consumer goods in place first if people are to be persuaded to work harder to earn the money to buy them. Yet, until Soviet workers start working harder, it is unlikely that significantly higher levels of consumer goods can be produced in the Soviet Union. Thus, when it comes to improving Soviet labor productivity, there exists a catch-22 situation.

The other path, which calls for increasing the productivity of capital, requires the application of technology to improve existing production methods. Technological breakthroughs are normally achieved through research and development efforts; these tend to be costly and time-consuming. Investment in research and development is not something the Soviet government can well afford at this time. (While Moscow has spent considerable sums for R & D related to military application, it has neglected to devote sufficient amounts to improving manufacturing techniques in the consumption sector.) . . .

In short, the two inputs the Soviet system needs to break out of its financial and economic conundrum—consumer goods to motivate workers, technology to increase productivity—must come from outside the Soviet Union. If the West does not furnish them, Gorbachev (or his replacement) will be forced to make a fundamental and wrenching change within the Soviet system to transfer resources out of the military sector, which is basically unproductive, and into manufacturing for the consumption sector, which is the source of real economic production. The alternative is to permit the Soviet economy as a whole to continue to deteriorate, and, in so doing, incur the grave risk of social and political unrest.

Assistance from the Outside

In light of this analysis, it becomes apparent that deliveries from the West of consumer goods and technology, financed with Western credits, have the effect of relieving the pressure on the Kremlin to implement a decision to divert resources from producing guns to producing butter. If we in the West take it upon ourselves to supply the consumer goods for the Soviets, and make available to them the benefits of our own research and development by furnishing the technology outright, we effectively grant the Kremlin a reprieve.

Assistance from the outside serves to alleviate the internal economic pressure that is the compelling force behind perestroika; it enables Soviet authorities to continue to devote scarce internal resources to the military as before. Thus, aid from the West has the effect of forestalling the very transition process we presumably like to see taking place in the Soviet Union: a switch in priorities from military spending to improving the quality of life for the Soviet people. . . .

A Desperate Situation

Clearly, Gorbachev is dealing his best cards: unilateral arms reductions, increased emigration, withdrawal from Afghanistan. All of these should be seen as reflections of the desperate financial situation in the Soviet Union. By understanding that, we maintain an informed perspective for evaluating proposed political arrangements whereby economic rewards and trade benefits from the West are exchanged for specific concessions by the Kremlin.

What is important to keep in mind is that any such deals are no tribute to Western diplomacy; they are being driven from the Soviet side. It is Gorbachev who, by holding out the possibility of reduced military tensions and Soviet improvement on human rights as bait, is coercing the West into providing the desperately needed financial help. . . .

Since I started out by focusing on that rather loaded phrase — "Should We Help Gorbachev"– as a shorthand means of expressing the policy aspects of a very complex issue, I would like now to finish up with another useful short phrase, that for me, captures the thrust of the conclusion I have come to after analyzing these issues. The phrase comes from General William Odom, who was quoted in a Bill Safire op-ed piece published in *The International Herald Tribune* on May 17, 1988. That was, you will recall, just before the Reagan-Gorbachev summit in Moscow. The question posed in the Safire article was whether or not it is in America's national interest to bail out the failing Soviet system. General Odom's answer, the one to which I likewise sign onto, was this: "We should applaud perestroika. But not finance it."

"The West should support Gorbachev's reforms because a more open and democratic Soviet Union will be a less expansionist and more responsible actor on the world stage."

Aiding Soviet Reforms Increases US National Security

George G. Weickhardt

In the following viewpoint, George G. Weickhardt proposes a plan to increase US-Soviet economic cooperation. He suggests that American businesspeople volunteer to teach Soviet managers to increase productivity. This plan will encourage understanding and mutual support between the two countries and decrease the likelihood of war, according to Weickhardt. Weickhardt is an attorney at the firm of Feldman, Waldman, and Kline in San Francisco, California.

As you read, consider the following questions:

1. How would Weickhardt's plan disarm the USSR?
2. In what ways would Weickhardt's plan benefit both the US and the USSR?
3. What does the author believe the US can teach the Soviet Union?

George C. Weickhardt, "Capitalists for Peace." Reprinted by permission of the *Bulletin of the Atomic Scientists*, a magazine of science and world affairs. Copyright © 1988 by the Educational Foundation for Nuclear Science, 6042 South Kimbark Avenue, Chicago, Illinois 60637.

Now that the Soviet Union has a pragmatic leader, it is time for Washington to devise new policies to help end the Cold War. Because Mikhail Gorbachev is gradually redirecting Soviet foreign policy along a less expansionist and aggressive course, the United States has a vital interest in the Soviet leader's domestic political fortunes. By finding ways to assist Gorbachev in his domestic reforms, particularly in his efforts to rescue the Soviet economy from its Stalinist legacy, the United States could advance its own interests.

Gorbachev is a bold reformer who has shown interest in recruiting Western management and technical expertise, so he would probably be receptive to a form of U.S. assistance similar to the International Executive Service Corps. This nonprofit organization, based in Stamford, Connecticut, was founded by David Rockefeller to send retired executives to aid businesses in developing countries. The service corps has completed over 9,000 projects and currently has executives working in 33 countries. Also, some 8,500 volunteers have signed up for further projects.

Entrepreneur Corps

A government-sponsored version of this type of service corps could send retired or unemployed U.S. managers and executives to the Soviet Union to serve as advisers or consultants to Soviet factory managers, who are weak in entrepreneurial skills. Such an "entrepreneur corps" would facilitate Gorbachev's program to transform Soviet managers from bureaucrats into independent entrepreneurs....

Although much of this program is vague in outline, it will apparently allow a market economy to operate side by side with the existing command economy. The consumer goods and services sectors and the farm economy will probably play larger roles in the market economy than will heavy and defense industries. Because there is only one customer for armaments – the Ministry of Defense – and because one would expect the state to retain tight control over defense plants, freely negotiated contracts in this sector are unlikely. How much a true market economy develops elsewhere will largely depend on legislation yet to be drafted and on its effective implementation.

In agriculture, Gorbachev's most promising reform is the so-called family contract, under which a plot of land or herd of animals is to be assigned on a long-term basis to a single family. The family would then work as an autonomous unit within the existing collective farms, to be compensated according to how much it produced but with some minimum income guaranteed. In current practice, however, the family is not free to determine what crops to grow. The limits of this reform remain ambiguous, but it could develop into something like China's responsibility system, in which collective farms were eventually parceled out on long-term lease to the peasants. In China this has meant the de facto decollectivization of agriculture. . . .

Entrenched Bureaucracy

While there is nothing the West can do to help Gorbachev overcome the power of this entrenched bureaucracy, it can assist him directly in overcoming the other principal obstacle to reform: the mindset of individual Soviet managers and collective farmers. Trained in a system where most key business decisions are made for them, they themselves have long taken the role of functionaries rather than entrepreneurs. Traditionally, much of their time and energy has been consumed by their efforts to have production quotas set low and their materials allocations set high. Further, a significant amount of managerial energy is required to insure that the plant actually receives the materials allotted to it. Because investment and new product decisions have long been made at the center rather than at the plant level, Soviet managers have acquired little expertise in analyzing how product changes and new investment in equipment affect profitability. . . .

Economic Relations

Improved economic relations between the superpowers can provide important new markets for U.S. exporters and possibly give the United States more leverage to influence Soviet actions in the future. Even more importantly, increased trade could help to build cultural bridges, reduced suspicion and hostility and lay the foundation for superpower harmony in the future.

Don Bonker, *Multinational Monitor*, November/December 1987.

This would be the function of an entrepreneur corps, whose consultants could teach U.S.-style management to Soviet factory managers. Such advisers might go to the Soviet Union for one- or two-year tours, much like Peace Corps volunteers; or they could be sent only to work on particular projects. On longer tours they would live in Soviet cities and towns and be employed in Soviet factories.

The relatively small cost to the U.S. government of this program – recruiting qualified participants, teaching them Russian in a four-month "total immersion" program, and flying them to the Soviet Union – could be recouped by charging the Soviets a fee for each consultant. The factories to which they were assigned would pay them salaries or retainers, and provide them with housing, medical care, and the other benefits that Soviet employees generally receive. U.S. consultants could teach Soviet managers how to increase their productivity through improved techniques and through introducing new or better consumer goods, which would meet international standards.

Economic Reform

While many have argued that the United States has much to gain from Soviet economic reform, others have questioned how it can possibly enhance U.S. security for the Soviets to solve their economic problems. Well-designed reforms may accelerate the growth of the Soviet economy and improve its innovative ability. Ultimately, it is argued, such improvements will be harnessed for the production of more and better weapons. While a Soviet Union absorbed in domestic reforms may temporarily pose less of a threat, it may eventually become a much more serious threat. This is perhaps why the Soviet military has, by and large, shown a keen interest in most of the reforms to date.

There is no doubt that an economically healthier and more innovative Soviet Union may have the capacity to compete better in the arms race, but on balance it appears that the West has a serious stake in the success of Gorbachev's reforms for six basic reasons:

While Gorbachev's decentralizing reforms may improve economic performance, they are also likely to greatly disperse economic decision making and, ultimately, economic power. An autonomous manager of a facility that provides consumer goods or services will want to produce something for which there is a market. Decentralization is therefore likely to increase the importance of consumer preference and of local, as opposed to central, economic power. It is also likely to enhance the economic power of such traditionally underrepresented groups as the peasants and the non-Russian nationalities.

Growth Acceleration

Any serious effort to accelerate Soviet economic growth will necessarily involve a shift of priorities and resources – away from the military sector and toward consumer goods and services, better food, and more housing. Gorbachev understands that his reforms are unlikely to succeed unless he can give the population such a payoff in the near term. He knows that it will be difficult to motivate Soviet workers to work harder for monetary rewards if there is little to buy with the additional income. Thus more resources will have to be allocated to goods and services that consumers demand. Since only a finite amount of resources is available overall, the logical place to find the additional amount for workers' incentives is in the bloated military budget, which according to CIA [Central Intelligence Agency] estimates now consumes at least

176

15 percent of the Soviet gross national product (GNP). Reform, therefore, is in the U.S. interest because it will probably bring about reductions in Soviet defense expenditures.

Businessmen Diplomats

Businessmen are in a sense diplomats; they help to improve relations between countries. Theirs is a diplomacy of peace. For the closer economic ties are, the greater the interest of countries in maintaining normal political relations. . . .

One big Washington department store sells T-shirts with portraits of Lenin and Gorbachev. The shirt-makers are quick to profit by the growing interest in our country. But businessmen understand that interest in the Soviet Union should be encouraged in every way, for the strengthening of commercial contacts with the U.S.S.R. is good for business. And not only for business.

Michael Nite and Vladimir Zhitomirsky, *New Times*, no. 47, November 30, 1987.

A third point is closely related to the first two: If Gorbachev can create a reasonably autonomous and healthy consumer goods sector, it will itself compete more vigorously with the defense sector for scarce economic resources. Today the consumer goods sector is so underdeveloped that it drags down the entire economy. The military, on the other hand, pays the best salaries and attracts the best people. It also has a priority claim on material inputs. Largely because of these two factors it performs better than the rest of the economy, turning out large volumes of well-designed weapons. Its very success strengthens its claim on resources, because there is a tendency among planners to prefer the economic sector that seems to perform the best.

If Gorbachev can get the consumer sector working at anywhere near the efficiency level of Western economies, a manager providing a consumer-oriented product in high demand will bid up the price for resources now being diverted to the military economy at subsidized prices. He will also bid up salaries for engineers and highly skilled workers who might otherwise find their most lucrative employment opportunites in the military economy. (There is already a relatively free labor market in the Soviet Union.) . . .

Economic and Political Reform

Gorbachev apparently realizes that economic and political reform are inseparable. While he initially emphasized discipline (the anti-alcohol and anti-corruption campaigns) and moderate reforms, he now seems to have concluded that he cannot inspire and motivate the population without very open discussion of the country's problems and some limited choice of electoral candidates, at least within the party. Gorbachev has transformed glasnost, which started as a tool for exposing corruption, into a debate about the Soviet future. The Soviet leader also understands that a modern, technologically oriented economy must enlist the talent, energy, and independent spirit of the technical intelligentsia, such as electronic engineers and microbiologists. To capture the imagination and loyalty of this group, Gorbachev is even willing to take such extraordinary risks as releasing prominent intellectuals like Andrei Sakharov.

There are signs that Gorbachev believes in the need for international tranquility to create the proper environment for his reforms. His principal objective in foreign policy has been to relax tensions between the superpowers in order to give the Soviet Union the breathing space it needs to embark upon the risky and perhaps destabilizing venture of economic reform. In a word, the Gorbachev package – economic reform, political liberalization, and international tranquility – is an attractive one for the West, and Gorbachev is the best Soviet leader the West could have hoped for. But it is a package deal: disruption or discrediting of any of his goals is likely to disrupt others and to undermine his entire position. The other side of the coin is that successful economic reform will probably reinforce Gorbachev's program of limited political liberalization. Few would deny that such democratization is in America's interest.

Societies with severe domestic problems also tend to be more dangerous internationally. To date, the strong suit of the Soviet Union in superpower competition has been its ability to produce large quantities of highly serviceable weapons. The Soviet Union has long preferred to compete in the area of military power because it has had little ability to compete with the West economically, culturally, or ideologically. In the words of Zbigniew Brzezinski, it is a one-dimensional power; that is, it can influence world events only through its military might, and the temptation to do so will be all the greater if its economy continues to stagnate.

Domestic Problems

A regime unable to deal with its domestic problems is especially inclined to strengthen its legitimacy by successes in foreign military ventures, like the Soviet proxy wars of the 1970s in Ethiopia and Angola. War scares have traditionally been used by Soviet leaders to divert attention from domestic problems and to exact and justify greater sacrifices from the population.

Decentralization and a market economy will thus make the Soviet Union a less totalitarian or authoritarian society. As Sakharov suggested to British Prime Minister Margaret Thatcher in April 1987, the West should support Gorbachev's reforms because a more open and democratic Soviet Union will be a less expansionist and more responsible actor on the world stage.

If its economy were heavily involved in world trade of

nonmilitary goods the Soviet Union would have a greater interest in international stability. Here the Chinese example is particularly instructive. The current period of reform in China has coincided with a less aggressive foreign policy, cordial relations with a wide spectrum of nations, reduced military expenditures, and dramatic increases in China's stake in world trade.

Would the Soviet Union really want a "fifth column" of capitalist managers operating within its economy? Certainly in the past the country was too closed a society to accept the type of spontaneous people-to-people contact that an entrepreneur corps would involve. Under Gorbachev, however, things have been changing. Western Sovietologists and other experts have gained increased access to their Soviet counterparts. And the Chinese example demonstrates that a dogmatic and xenophobic society can open up quite rapidly once a dynamic leader has made the decision to encourage new ideas for economic management.

Management Assistance

In fact, Gorbachev has already shown that he is interested in direct management assistance from some unusual sources, including Western companies. In January 1987, the Soviet Union published its ground rules for joint ventures with Western – capitalist – firms; and even though few firms have found these rules attractive enough to conclude deals with the Soviets, the concept of trying to bring in Western expertise and technology by such joint ownership is nothing short of revolutionary.

Increased Trade

Spurred by General Secretary Gorbachev's economic reforms, many U.S. companies have recently sought to establish business contacts with the Soviet Union. These initial contacts may be only the tip of the iceberg. Increased trade within certain guidelines serves the best interests of both nations and improves prospects for reduced tensions.

Don Bonker, *Multinational Monitor*, November/December 1987.

Not only does the joint venture program fly in the face of many Soviet ideological precepts; it also seems to recognize the benefit of free contact between Soviet citizens and Western business executives at the plant level (presumably without heavy-handed stage management by the KGB). With much fanfare, the Soviets have also hired a Western management consulting firm. Within the Soviet Union the demand for management expertise is in fact so great that Soviet economists have been allowed to sell their services to plant managers, presumably under a November 1986

179

statute allowing individual enterprise in certain limited areas. There is also talk now of setting up "business schools." . . .

The Soviets have never had an ideological problem with adopting advanced management techniques developed by capitalist enterprises. Even in Lenin's day Western techniques in time-and-motion studies were used in Soviet factories. More recently Western management science – including operations research, the systems concept, and network methods – has been widely studied and accepted, at least in form, by the Soviets. . . .

Whatever the economic success of the program, it would, like the Peace Corps, be of inestimable symbolic value as a gesture of goodwill. Eventually, a large contingent of articulate people would emerge in both the United States and the Soviet Union who would understand each other's ways quite well. Soviet society would also be opened up to spontaneous contact with foreigners in an unprecedented way so that even if the economic benefits prove meager the personal contacts are likely to serve the cause of peace. In U.S.-Soviet relations it might be the equivalent of Anwar Sadat's trip to Jerusalem to speak to the Knesset.

One of the best arguments for offering the entrepreneur corps to the Soviet Union is that Gorbachev has seized, and for nearly two years has kept, the initiative in U.S.-Soviet relations. . . . Washington is constantly reacting, usually negatively, to his proposals.

It is time for the United States to regain the initiative with its own bold program. And fortunately, the Soviet leader does not dismiss radical or unconventional ideas. In fact, the West has learned not to make sweeping proposals to Gorbachev just for propaganda purposes, because he is likely to accept them. This proposal might be precisely the type of restructuring of relations that would appeal to him.

"Gorbachev understands that a stronger Soviet economy means a stronger military machine."

Aiding Soviet Reforms Endangers US Security

Irwin M. Stelzer

The Soviet economy is in trouble despite Mikhail Gorbachev's reform program, according to the author of the following viewpoint. Irwin M. Stelzer argues that any economic aid the US gives to the Soviet Union strengthens the USSR, making it easier for it to dominate the world. Stelzer is monthly business correspondent for *The American Spectator*, and is director of the Energy and Environmental Policy Center of the John F. Kennedy School at Harvard University in Cambridge, Massachusetts.

As you read, consider the following questions:

1. How do Gorbachev's reforms compare with the reforms undertaken by previous Soviet leaders, according to Stelzer?
2. Why does Stelzer believe the US has contributed to perestroika?
3. According to the author, how do the Soviet reforms endanger the US?

Irwin M. Stelzer, "Gorby's Cash Grab," *The American Spectator*, August 1988. Reprinted with permission.

That the Soviet economy is in serious trouble there can be no doubt. Gorbachev himself has conceded that the Soviet Union is suffering from "economic failures," "slowing economic growth," "a shortage of goods," and that its economy is one in which "the consumer found himself totally at the mercy of the producer." And the mess is getting steadily worse. Abel Aganbegyan, his chief economic adviser (chairman of the Commission for the Study of Productive Forces and Resources, and head of the economics section of the Soviet Academy of Sciences), says that in 1981-85, "there was practically no economic growth." Per capita income actually declined. Since January 1986, when the new five-year plan was launched, growth is reported to have been about 2 percent per year; that's half of the plan's target rate. One expert on the Soviet economy says that perestroika is "beginning to look like a disaster."

New Economic Policy

This comes as no surprise to anyone even vaguely familiar with the history of failed efforts by a succession of Soviet rulers to get the country's economy moving. Lenin was himself the first "reformer": his New Economic Policy (NEP) was inaugurated in 1921 in response to widespread unrest among the starving peasants. It included many of the features we now associate with Gorbachev's perestroika – greater reliance on markets, joint ventures between the Soviet state and foreign capitalists, encouragement of cooperatives. But it most definitely did not include a permanent abandonment of authoritarian, central direction of the economy. As Lenin pointed out, "We are retreating...in order... to take a running start and make a bigger leap forward." The essence of NEP, in Theodore Draper's words, "was to use capitalists...against capitalism, to use capitalism against itself.... This was the rationale for inviting foreign capitalism into Soviet Russia in the form of mixed enterprises and economic concessions."

The NEP didn't long survive Lenin, and the improvements it brought in economic performance were soon swamped by Stalinism and World War II. Four subsequent efforts at reform – by Khrushchev (1957), Kosygin (1965), and Brezhnev (1973 and 1979) – all "proved disappointing," according to Ed Hewitt, author of *Reforming the Soviet Economy.*

And now we have perestroika. I say "we" because without Western help its already-slim chances of success would be reduced to zero. Gorbachev needs foreign businessmen to invest in his country's factories, so that he can have goods to export and to sell to the Soviet workers he hopes will now work harder (they won't, unless they can buy something with the incentive wages they will receive); he needs hard-currency loans to finance the purchase of state-of-the-art Western machinery and capital goods; and he needs Western technology, especially computers.

The factory investment will have to be in the form of joint ventures with the Soviet state (only one of the ways in which perestroika borrows from NEP), and on stiff terms. The share of foreign capital may not exceed 49 percent. The manager of the enterprise must be a Soviet citizen. Profits will be taxed at a rate of 30 percent, with an additional 20 percent taken if they are transferred abroad. Most important – and contrary to the impression created by press reports about the opening of mobile pizza parlors and McDonald's – the areas in which foreigners will be permitted to invest are those chosen by the Soviet government for their strategic importance to its economy and security. Capitalists willing to serve the purposes of the Soviet state are welcome; others need not apply.

Vladimir Kamentsey, deputy chairman of the Soviet Council of Ministers responsible for foreign trade, is quite specific in identifying the areas in which the Soviet Union will allow large-scale joint ventures: oil and gas production, instrument making, automotive construction, medical equipment (seen as a potential export market and hard-currency earner), and farm equipment. To this list Aganbegyan adds chemicals.

Inadequate Security

Many of the challenges the United States faces in the world today are underpinned, directly or indirectly, by economic and financial resources made available to the Soviet Union and its client states by the West. The ability of the USSR to get things done at the national and international levels depends to a great extent on the availability of financial resources, especially hard currencies. Yet there has been inadequate unity and concern within the Western Alliance with regard to the security dimensions of East-West economic and commercial relations.

Roger W. Robinson, *National Security Record,* April 1986.

American business is rushing to oblige. Although only some forty-six joint ventures worth only $30 million have been concluded since the beginning of 1987 (the figure comes from Ivan Ivanov, the number-two Soviet foreign trade official), more are in the works, some 300 if the Soviets are to be believed. Their long-time favorite industrialist, Occidental's Armand Hammer, has announced a number of big new oil and petrochemical projects, including a plastics facility in Western Siberia, this to be financed by a new multi-national chemical consortium. (Hammer also signed an agreement to build the Soviet Union's first golf course.) And the newly formed American Trade Consortium, which numbers among its members RJR Nabisco, Ford, Eastman Kodak, Johnson

& Johnson, Chevron, and Archer Daniels Midland, expects at least a dozen joint ventures.

In addition, the Soviet Union plans to step up its own investment, particularly in machine building and metal working. There are three ways Gorbachev can finance this. He can divert resources from his country's enormous arms program and costly foreign adventures. He can forcibly raise the rate of domestic savings by cutting workers' already miserable consumption levels. Or he can borrow from foreign capitalists.

The first of these solutions is a real option only if the West continues to reduce its own defense establishment, something it is under no economic compulsion to do. Unlike the USSR, we can afford guns and butter. The second—reducing workers' living standards—is risky: there are already rumblings of discontent at the below-Third World living standards experienced by most Soviets.

So borrow Gorbachev must. And can. The Soviet Union has already increased its debt to the West from $15 billion in 1983 to twice that level. What has Western financiers drooling is that this may be only the beginning. A leading Soviet economist, Nikolai Shmelev, estimated in a 1988 article in *Moscow News* that the Soviet Union could, over the next few years, safely borrow $35-$50 billion to support perestroika.

Western bankers are eager to finance this strengthening of the Soviet economy. . . .

Euromarket Financing

Indeed, the Germans are the most active in beating the Russian bushes for business. But others are not far behind. Britain's Lloyds has lead-managed four Euromarket financings for Soviet institutions in recent years; Barclay's has set up a trade-finance subsidiary; and NatWest and Morgan Grenfell have Moscow representatives looking for deals. Even Michael Milken, the Drexel Burnham partner who created the junk-bond market, is interested. He suggested to Gorbachev that resource-rich Russia issue bonds backed by gold or oil.

There are, of course, skeptics—some of whom remember the Bolsheviks' repudiation of the $75 million debt run up by the czars, and others of whom won't play until the Soviets publish sufficient financial information to permit them and the rating agencies to appraise the so-called Red Notes. But most observers expect a steady increase in Soviet borrowing, with a dollar-denominated bond issue in London and, the political climate permitting, a "Gorbibond" issue in the U.S. thereafter.

While two of Gorbachev's desires are being met—more joint ventures, some Western financing—his third wish, access to Western technology, is being thwarted, at least for now, by the United States.

Most members of the seventeen-nation Coordinating Committee for Multilateral Export Controls (COCOM) want to relax restrictions on the export of high-technology products to the Soviet Union, but the U.S. has held out. The betting is, however, that the jovial atmosphere of the Moscow summit . . . will soften the American position. Pressure for such relaxation is coming primarily from the French and West Germans, and order-hungry computer manufacturers of all nations.

MAJOR REFORMS
OF THE
NEW SOVIET OPENNESS:

ESTABLISH NEW TIES

BEFORE   AFTER

From the February 27, 1987 *Washington Times.*

The real question is whether the West should oblige Gorbachev, and, if so, on what terms. At the moment, the Soviet Union is spending about twice as much of its shriveled GNP [gross national product] on arms as the U.S. Indeed, it was the inability of the Soviet economy to match Reagan's defense build-up that brought the USSR to the disarmament bargaining table, forced it to withdraw from Afghanistan, and is compelling it to reduce support of client states such as Cuba. Without foreign financing of his perestroika, Gorbachev will be under even greater pressure to make concessions on arms control in order to lighten his military burdens.

Fortunately, sober observers have begun to question the wisdom of President Reagan's statement to a group of Soviet students that "nothing will please my heart more than...to see a growing, exporting, exuberant Soviet Union." Lord Carrington, the departing NATO [North Atlantic Treaty Oranization] secretary general, speaking at the NATO Council's spring 1988 meeting, warned that "the Soviet. . . military machine is still, so far, operating at exactly the same level as it was in the days before perestroika and glasnost." Colin Powell, Reagan's national security adviser, also cautioned the West not to help the USSR modernize its economy until there is hard evidence that it had cut defense expenditures. And Defense Secretary Frank Carlucci, hardly a hard-liner, had this reaction to the summit's rosy glow: "If the end result is that. . . the Soviet Union modernizes its industrial and technological base, and if sometime in the 1990s it. . . can produce enormous quantities of weapons even more effectively than it does today, then we will have made an enormous miscalculation."

Military Machine

Clearly, Gorbachev understands that a stronger Soviet economy means a stronger military machine. Hewitt is on target when he points out, "Gorbachev knows full well that military and economic capabilities are intertwined. . . . For Gorbachev, a dramatic improvement in Soviet economic performance is not only good politics; it is an important component of his approach to Soviet national security."

But the West's capitalists are blinded by the prospects for huge profits. Charles Hugel, the president of Combustion Engineering – which hopes to participate in perhaps $20 billion worth of chemical plants in Siberia – has begun to speak out for the repeal of the Jackson-Vanick amendment. That legislation, which ties preferential trade status for the Soviet Union to its emigration policies, is an increasing source of irritation to Gorbachev, and an increasing inconvenience to American firms who want to do business with his country. Those firms will undoubtedly also oppose Senator James McClure's effort to make the Soviets pay with political concessions for the cash and technology they so badly need. McClure would link trade concessions not only to the Soviet Union's willingness to let its imprisoned Jewish population emigrate, but to its compliance with the Helsinki agreement on human rights.

"They really need Western help and they're reaching out for it," Hugel told reporters. He and others in the world's business and financial community have apparently forgotten Lenin's frank admission that cooperation with capitalists is to be pursued only so long as it contributes to their eventual destruction. Forgotten, too, is the simple fact that poorer, backward countries are, after all, less dangerous adversaries than richer, advanced ones.

*"Every part of our program of perestroika—and
the program as a whole, for that matter—is
fully based on the principle of more socialism
and more democracy."*

Perestroika Proves
Socialism's Success

Mikhail Gorbachev

Mikhail Gorbachev is the general secretary of the Communist
Party of the Soviet Union. In the following viewpoint, Gorbachev
argues that perestroika, the system of economic, political, and
social reforms currently underway in the Soviet Union, is not a
rejection of socialism. Gorbachev instead believes that it is a
reaffirmation of the system.

As you read, consider the following questions:

1. What changes in the economy does Gorbachev describe?
2. For what reasons did the Soviets implement reforms,
   according to Gorbachev?
3. According to the author, what results do the Soviets hope
   to produce by restructuring?

The adoption of fundamental principles for a radical change in economic management was a big step forward in the program of perestroika. Now perestroika concerns virtually every main aspect of public life. Of course, our notions about the contents, methods and forms of perestroika will be developed, clarified and corrected later on. This is inevitable and natural. This is a living process. No doubt, changes will pose new major problems which will require unorthodox solutions. But the overall concept, and the overall plan of perestroika, not only from the point of view of substance, but also of its component parts, are clear to us.

Perestroika means overcoming the stagnation process, breaking down the braking mechanism, creating a dependable and effective mechanism for the acceleration of social and economic progress and giving it greater dynamism.

Mass Initiative

Perestroika means mass initiative. It is the comprehensive development of democracy, socialist self-government, encouragement of initiative and creative endeavor, improved order and discipline, more glasnost, criticism and self-criticism in all spheres of our society. It is utmost respect for the individual and consideration for personal dignity.

Perestroika is the all-round intensification of the Soviet economy, the revival and development of the principles of democratic centralism in running the national economy, the universal introduction of economic methods, the renunciation of management by injunction and by administrative methods, and the overall encouragement of innovation and socialist enterprise.

Perestroika means a resolute shift to scientific methods, an ability to provide a solid scientific basis for every new initiative. It means the combination of the achievements of the scientific and technological revolution with a planned economy.

Perestroika means priority development of the social sphere aimed at ever better satisfaction of the Soviet people's requirements for good living and working conditions, for good rest and recreation, education and health care. It means unceasing concern for cultural and spiritual wealth, for the culture of every individual and society as a whole.

Socialist Ethics

Perestroika means the elimination from society of the distortions of socialist ethics, the consistent implementation of the principles of social justice. It means the unity of words and deeds, rights and duties. It is the elevation of honest, highly-qualified labor, the overcoming of leveling tendencies in pay and consumerism.

This is how we see perestroika today. This is how we see our tasks, and the substance and content of our work for the forthcoming period. It is difficult now to say how long that period will take. Of course, it will be much more than two or three years. We are ready for serious, strenuous and tedious work to ensure that our country reaches new heights by the end of the twentieth century.

We are often asked what we want of perestroika. What are our final goals? We can hardly give a detailed, exact answer. It's not our way to engage in prophesying and trying to predestinate all the architectural elements of the public building we will erect in the process of perestroika.

But in principle I can say that the end result of perestroika is clear to us. It is a thorough renewal of every aspect of Soviet life; it is giving socialism the most progressive forms of social organization; it is the fullest exposure of the humanist nature of our social system in its crucial aspects – economic, social, political and moral.

Renovation and Acceleration

I stress once again: perestroika is not some kind of illumination or revelation. To restructure our life means to understand the objective necessity for renovation and acceleration. And that necessity emerged in the heart of our society. The essence of perestroika lies in the fact that *it unites socialism with democracy* and revives the Leninist concept of socialist construction both in theory and in practice. Such is the essence of perestroika, which accounts for its genuine revolutionary spirit and its all-embracing scope.

The goal is worth the effort. And we are sure that our effort will be a worthy contribution to humanity's social progress.

Economic Development

In the last 70 years socialism has shown itself to be a growing and forceful society. It has become a system which has developed in a number of countries and continents with one-third of the world population. For many nations, socialism has become the only road to fast economic development, sovereignty, independence. Socialism has proved such advantages as non-cyclical development of the economy, full employment and elimination of compulsory unemployment, vast expansion of social security and public services, including free medical care, free education, low-cost housing, pensions for everybody, wide access to recreation facilities.

Stanislav Menshikov, *World Marxist Review,* January 1988.

Perestroika is closely connected with socialism as a system. That side of the matter is being widely discussed, especially abroad, and our talk about perestroika won't be entirely clear if we don't touch upon that aspect.

Does perestroika mean that we are giving up socialism or at least some of its foundations? Some ask this question with hope, others with misgiving.

A Deep Crisis

There are people in the West who would like to tell us that socialism is in a deep crisis and has brought our society to a dead end. That's how they interpret our critical analysis of the situation at the end of the seventies and beginning of the eighties. We have only one way out, they say: to adopt capitalist methods of economic management and social patterns, to drift toward capitalism.

They tell us that nothing will come of perestroika within the framework of our system. They say we should change this system and borrow from the experience of another socio-political system. To this they add that, if the Soviet Union takes this path and gives up its socialist choice, close links with the West will supposedly become possible. They go so far as to claim that the October 1917 Revolution was a mistake which almost completely cut off our country from world social progress.

To put an end to all the rumors and speculations that abound in the West about this, I would like to point out once again that we are conducting all our reforms in accordance with the socialist choice. We are looking within socialism, rather than outside it, for the answers to all the questions that arise. We assess our successes and errors alike by socialist standards. Those who hope that we shall move away from the socialist path will be greatly disappointed. Every part of our program of perestroika – and the program as a whole, for that matter – is fully based on the principle of more socialism and more democracy.

More socialism means a more dynamic pace and creative endeavor, more organization, law and order, more scientific methods and initiative in economic management, efficiency in administration, and a better and materially richer life for the people.

More Democracy

More socialism means more democracy, openness and collectivism in everyday life, more culture and humanism in production, social and personal relations among people, more dignity and self-respect for the individual.

More socialism means more patriotism and aspiration to noble ideals, more active civic concern about the country's internal affairs and about their positive influence on international affairs.

In other words, more of all those things which are inherent in socialism and in the theoretical precepts which characterize it as a distinct socio-economic formation.

We will proceed toward better socialism rather than away from it. We are saying this honestly, without trying to fool our own people or the world. Any hopes that we will begin to build a different, non-socialist society and go over to the other camp are unrealistic and futile. Those in the West who expect us to give up socialism will be disappointed. It is high time they understood this, and, even more importantly, proceeded from that understanding in practical relations with the Soviet Union. . . .

We want more socialism and, therefore, more democracy.

As we understand it, the difficulties and problems of the seventies and eighties did not signify some kind of crisis for socialism as a social and political system, but rather were the result of insufficient consistency in applying the principles of socialism, of departures from them and even distortions of them, and of continued adherence to the methods and forms of social management that arose under specific historical conditions in the early stages of socialist development.

Developing Socialism

Perestroika is a revolutionary process for it is a jump forward in the development of socialism, in the realization of its essential characteristics. From the outset we realized that we had no time to lose. It is very important not to stay too long on the starting line, to overcome the lag, to get out of the quagmire of conservatism, and to break the inertia of stagnation.

Mikhail Gorbachev, *Perestroika*, 1987.

On the contrary, socialism as a young social system, as a way of living, possesses vast possibilities for self-development and self-perfection that have yet to be revealed, and for the solution of the fundamental problems of contemporary society's scientific, technological, economic, cultural and intellectual progress, and of the development of the human individual. This is indicated by the path our country has taken since October 1917, a path that has been full of innumerable difficulties, drama and strenuous work, and at the same time full of great triumphs and accomplishments.

It is true to say that post-revolutionary development underwent difficult stages, largely due to the rude meddling of imperialist forces in our internal affairs; policy mistakes and miscalculations also occurred. Nevertheless, the Soviet Union progressed, and a society has been created in which people have confidence in their future. And if truth is the guide, any objective observer must admit that Soviet history is in general a history of indisputable progress, despite all the losses, setbacks and failures. We advanced in the absence of roads, literally and figuratively: we would

191

sometimes go astray and make mistakes, and more than enough blood was shed and sweat lost along our path. But we stubbornly marched on and never thought of retreating, of giving up the ground we had gained, or of questioning our socialist choice....

Our fathers and grandfathers overcame everything that befell them and made a crucial contribution to the development and consolidation of our society at a time when its entire future had to be decided.

Industrialization in the twenties and thirties really was a very hard trial. But let's now, with hindsight, try to answer the question: Was it necessary? Could such a vast country as ours have lived in the twentieth century without being an industrially developed state? There was another reason that also very soon made it clear that we had no option but to speed up industrialization. As early as 1933 the threat of fascism began to grow swiftly. And where would the world now be if the Soviet Union had not blocked the road for Hitler's war machine? Our people routed fascism with the might created by them in the twenties and thirties. Had there been no industrialization, we would have been unarmed before fascism....

Origins of Perestroika

But why did everything that made perestroika necessary happen? Why has it been delayed? Why did the obsolete methods of work persist so long? How did the dogmatization of social consciousness and theory occur?

All this needs explanation. And, in analyzing and explaining, we find much proof that the Party and society saw the negative processes growing. Furthermore, awareness of a need for change acutely manifested itself more than once. But the changes did not go all the way and were inconsistent under the weight of the "legacy of the past" with all its dominant attributes.

A major landmark in our history was the 20th CPSU [Communist Party of the Soviet Union] Congress. The 20th Congress of the CPSU was held in Moscow on 14-25 February 1956. The Congress approved the Directives for the Sixth Five-Year Plan for the country's economic development for 1956-60, spelled out the principle of peaceful coexistence between states with different social systems as it applies to the current epoch, and condemned the personality cult of Stalin and its consequences. It made a great contribution to the theory and practice of socialist construction. During and after, a great attempt was made to turn the helm in the country's advance, to impart an impulse to liberation from the negative aspects of socio-political life engendered by the Stalin personality cult.

The decisions taken by the Congress helped through major political, economic, social and ideological measures. But the possibilities that emerged were not used to the full. The explanation is the subjectivist methods adopted by the leadership under Khrushchev. Economic management was dominated by improvisation. That leadership's willful and changing ideas and actions kept society and the Party in a fever. Ambitious and unfounded promises and predictions again produced a gap between words and deeds.

That was why at the next stage, whose hallmark was the October 1964 Plenary Meeting of the CPSU Central Committee, the first step was to overcome these extremes and to combat these extremes. A line towards stabilization was taken. And it was a well-justified line. It received the support of the Party and the people. Some positive results appeared. The decisions that were formulated and adopted were more considered and better substantiated. The start of the economic reform of 1965 and the March 1965 Plenary Meeting of the Central Committee devoted to agriculture were major initiatives aimed at positive changes in the economy. But, having produced a substantial though temporary effect, they petered out. . . .

A Revolutionary Renewal

Perestroika in the Soviet Union is a revolutionary renewal of the whole of Soviet society. It is not confined to economic change. . . . But the economic restructuring that has already begun cannot be separated from all the other aspects of *perestroika*. We plan to step up the pace of growth in the economy, but this cannot be separated from the process of democratization and of what we call *glasnost,* a greater openness in all aspects of government and social organization. The economic changes which are taking place are all based on a re-examination of Soviet history, of the successes *and* the failures, the periods of reform and growth as well as of degeneracy and stagnation, not forgetting a proper appreciation of the appalling destruction of two world wars and the heroic struggle of the Soviet people to survive and rebuild their shattered lives.

Abel Aganbegyan, *New Left Review,* May/June 1988.

What conclusions have we drawn from the lessons of history?

First, socialism as a social system has proved that it has immense potentialities for resolving the most complex problems of social progress. We are convinced of its capacity for self-perfection, for still greater revelation of its possibilities, and for dealing with the present major problems of social progress which arise as we approach the twenty-first century.

At the same time, we realize that improving socialism is not a spontaneous process, but a job requiring tremendous attention, a truthful and unbiased analysis of problems, and a resolute rejection of anything outdated. We have come to see that half-hearted measures will not work here. We must act on a wide front, consistently and energetically, without failing to take the boldest steps.

One more conclusion – the most important one I would say – is that we should rely on the initiative and creativity of the masses; on the active participation of the widest sections of the population in the implementation of the reforms planned; that is, on democratization and again democratization.

"The rhetoric of Soviet reform emphasizes renewal and progress, but the facts that made reform necessary describe failure—the failure of the Soviet system."

Perestroika Proves Socialism's Failure

Robert G. Kaiser

Economic reforms in the Soviet Union may be exciting on the surface, but underneath, the Soviet system of socialism has failed, argues author Robert G. Kaiser. Kaiser is the assistant managing editor of *The Washington Post* and is the author of *Russia: The People and the Power.* According to Kaiser, pervasive bureaucracy, shoddy goods, laziness resulting from guaranteed wages, and the expense of the military all contributed to the downfall of the socialist system.

As you read, consider the following questions:

1. What sign does Kaiser see of socialism's failure?
2. According to Kaiser, how is the rest of the Eastern bloc affected by the Soviet system of government?
3. According to the author, what effect has the system of reforms had on the Soviet economy?

Robert G. Kaiser, "The USSR in Decline," *Foreign Affairs*, Winter 1988-89. Reprinted with the author's permission.

The news from the Soviet Union is enthralling – nothing so interesting or exciting as Mikhail Gorbachev's reforms has happened in Russia in modern times. The world is rightly transfixed by the spectacle of Russians telling the truth about their past and their present, encouraging private enterprise, urging a diminished role for the Communist Party and generally committing mayhem against Marxism-Leninism.

But there is a paradoxical aspect to perestroika that deserves more attention. The rhetoric of Soviet reform emphasizes renewal and progress, but the facts that made reform necessary describe failure – the failure of the Soviet system. For the foreseeable future, the fact of that failure is likely to be more important for the world than Gorbachev's efforts to overcome it.

Economic Hope

That is because the failure is a fact, while the reforms – at least the practical ones affecting the economic life of the country – remain just a hope. It is likely to remain a forlorn hope for years to come.

The failure of the Soviet system – Joseph Stalin's system, which organized Soviet life for more than half a century – is a larger event than many have yet acknowledged. It signals more than the collapse of Stalin's dream of a centrally planned economic powerhouse that might someday dominate the world. We are also witnessing the beginning of the end of the Soviet empire. The fear of Soviet conquest and hegemony that dominated world politics for more than a generation should now dissipate. We have passed the high-water mark of Soviet power and influence in the world.

The crisis in the communist world has provoked radical changes from Beijing to Warsaw, and all of them contain a common ingredient: liberalization. Milovan Djilas describes what is going on as the inevitable consequence of the realization that the Stalinist model does not work in the present age. Its rigid, centralized institutions have proven incapable of producing modern, efficient economies; to fight their rigidity, communist regimes must turn to decentralization and liberalization.

Djilas is convinced that liberalization in the communist world will continue – probably in fits and starts – because the crisis of the old order will continue. "Liberalization, crisis, they are the same thing," Djilas has said. In other words, the only available antidote to the backwardness and stagnation that afflict communist countries is decentralization, loosening of controls – liberalization. It is a shrewd argument, not easy to dispute in light of the evidence from so many different communist countries.

Gorbachev clearly sees the world in similar terms. He speaks repeatedly of the need to democratize his country to make it work better. Economic reform, he has concluded, is impossible without political reform, so he has proposed astounding changes to remove the Communist Party apparatus from day-to-day administration of the economy and society, to replace it with new, elected bodies. He proposes to make the Soviet Union into a society ruled by law, not party, and to assure personal freedoms and the right to privacy. All of this is deliberate – to improve the economy, raise the standard of living and restore the Soviet Union to the front rank of nations.

Similar tactics to achieve similar objectives have been adopted in China, Poland, Yugoslavia and Hungary, and they are surely to come throughout the communist world. Even Vietnam is toying with such changes to modernize its failing economy.

Complete Failure

Everywhere it has been tried, communism has failed. Nowhere has it failed more completely than in the Soviet Union. Marxism-Leninism was supposed to create heaven on earth – a new society free of mankind's destructive and exploitive sins where the state would wither, a new idealistic soviet man would emerge, all would be equal, and the economy and agriculture, centrally controlled for the benefit of all, would ensure plenty. Instead, the state and party are all-pervasive and all-powerful, the masses are demoralized and mistrustful of authority, inequality is institutionalized on a scale that would have impressed the ancient Egyptians, and the economy and agriculture malfunction and barely provide.

Maurice Tugwell, *Vital Speeches of the Day*, August 8, 1987.

Declaring or even initiating a plan to reform is a far cry from achieving its objectives, however. The Chinese have made great but uneven progress; the Poles have made negative progress; the Soviets have made none. In the years ahead, Gorbachev and his allies – or their successors – will discover just how difficult a task they have undertaken.

The Stalinist System

The Stalinist system has done profound damage to Russia – so much damage that a decade or two of reform is most unlikely to put things right. Of all the communist countries, Russia will have the most difficulty finding a new path to real progress, because the foundation on which the Soviet leaders must build is so rotten. No other communist system is even half a century old; the Soviet model has had three or four generations to reach its present, dismal condition. The new openness of the Gorbachev era has illuminated that condition – made it painfully vivid and undeniable.

197

That is the most significant contribution of glasnost. In the West we are fascinated by Soviet truth-telling about historical figures like Bukharin and Trotsky, or revelations about Stalin's crimes in the 1930s and 1940s, but the truly devastating revelations are about contemporary reality. If Gorbachev were ousted by more conservative comrades tomorrow, and they moved at once to shut off glasnost and restore Brezhnevite orthodoxy (something like that could happen – the road to liberalization will not be a straight one), the new leaders could not remove the damning facts that have now been spread across the official record.

Admissions of the failure of the system are now published so often that they are routine. And they are found in much more august forums than the pages of newspapers. The 1988 summer Communist Party conference, convened as a solemn event of great national significance, was filled with vivid confessions of past sins. Until Gorbachev came to power, such events were usually devoted to rosy propaganda. . . .

Economic Restructuring

Perestroika – economic restructuring and reform – is the only way out, the delegates were told. "Either the country is doomed to further stagnation, or we gain strength and forge ahead to progress. That is how the question stands. We have no third course." Those were not Gorbachev's words; they were spoken by Yegor Ligachev, the leading Politburo conservative and Gorbachev rival, whom Gorbachev bumped from the ideology portfolio into new responsibilities for agriculture in his dramatic personnel reshuffle in early October 1988. . . .

Gorbachev is struggling against the consequences of five decades of misrule – and in some of his ambitions, against all of Russian history as well. "Our model failed," one official in Moscow told me. "It took us nowhere." Another prominent intellectual – a well-known member of the avant-garde of glasnost who was a delegate to the party conference – offered an ironic elaboration of that judgment. "We have made one important contribution," he said. "We have taught the world what *not* to do."

The model failed, but it also distorted the life of a huge nation, creating an inefficient, backward society riddled with bad habits, many of them now ingrained over two generations or more. Glasnost has finally allowed thoughtful Soviet analysts to address the distortions of Soviet life directly. Nikolai Shmelyev, an economist, took advantage of the new opportunity to speak bluntly in an article published in *Novy Mir.*

"It is important that we all recognize the degree to which we have gotten out of the habit of doing everything that is economically normal and healthy, and into the habit of doing everything that is economically abnormal and unhealthy," Shmelyev wrote. "We are now like a seriously ill man who, after a long time in bed, takes his first step with the greatest difficulty and finds, to his horror, that he has almost forgotten how to walk." . . .

The Gorbachev Period

The Gorbachev period has changed the thoughts in Soviet citizens' heads. Gorbachev has not yet reformed the economy effectively, but he has enshrined an entirely new set of principles for his countrymen. His most important contribution in this regard may be the destruction of old definitions of "impossible." So much that was once considered impossible is now routine that many thoughtful Soviet citizens have ceased being intimidated by the old taboos. By speaking out with some candor during this period, Gorbachev has accomplished something comparable to the feat of the little boy who shouted out what everyone else knew—that the emperor was naked. It will not be possible for any future, more reactionary Soviet leader simply to announce—as Soviet leaders did for so long—that everything is rosy and wonderful. Gorbachev has eliminated that argument from the usable political vocabulary.

Steve Kelley. Reprinted with permission.

Nor does there appear to be an option of abandoning economic reform and returning to Brezhnevite central controls. Ligachev and his allies have long since acknowledged that the old ways were corrupt and ineffective. Vitaliy Korotich, the editor of *Ogonyek,* one of the loudest trumpets of glasnost, told me: "Without liberalization, the country would just grind to a halt."

His sentiment is widely shared – so widely that no voice can be heard making the traditional, contrary argument. This is Gorbachev's biggest advantage: no element in the party has come forward with a plausible solution for the country's problems that differs from his. Even the traditional bureaucrats most discomfited by what is going on cannot offer a hopeful alternative. So it seems most likely now that Gorbachev's colleagues will give him more time to try to find successful antidotes to economic stagnation.

A Genuine Rival

Russians are coming to terms with the failure of their system, and so should we. Of course they are eager to put it right; many of them would like to return to the days when both they and the outside world saw the Soviet Union as the only genuine rival to the United States for international preeminence. But the return of that day is at best a long way off. In truth, it is unlikely ever to come again.

Stalin's goal was to create an empire tied together by communist ideology, fueled by communist efficiency and dominated by Great Russian ambitions. But the ideology has failed, the efficiency has proven illusory, and the ambitions are anachronistic in the modern world. What is left is a brontosaurus empire, one unfit for survival in a new environment – today's world.

This metaphor was suggested by Lev Kopelev, an extraordinary Russian who was born in Kiev five years before the Bolshevik Revolution, personally participated in many of the most exciting phases of the Soviet experiment, and was driven from his homeland in 1981 because of his own brand of glasnost, then not in favor. He now lives in Cologne, West Germany. In his own lifetime Kopelev has seen the demise of the German, French, British, Austro-Hungarian, Portuguese, Dutch, Italian and Japanese empires – the twentieth century has not been hospitable to such enterprises. This century has been marked by the rise of science, technology and self-knowledge, all of which work against the kind of centralized power needed to maintain an empire or an authoritarian society.

The End of the Empire

The Russians fought against the times despite setbacks that began long ago, with the defections of Yugoslavia and China, and the rebellions in East Germany, Hungary, Czechoslovakia and Poland.

But the fight cannot be waged much longer, because there is no more adhesive to hold the empire together. Even within the borders of the Soviet Union there are signs of grave strain.

Most of the twentieth-century empires collapsed peacefully, but some only fell under the pressure of violence. The French held on too long, at too great a cost; the Russians may do the same. It is hard now to imagine how Gorbachev or any future Soviet leader could gracefully yield to the Poles or the Hungarians – not to mention the Armenians or the Estonians – their independence.

Doomed to Failure

Gorbachev's desperate attempt to make the ossified Soviet system more efficient is so urgently required because, in contrast to the prophecies and plans of the 1961 party program, the Soviet Union failed to overtake the United States by 1980 and is falling ever farther behind the industrial nations of the free world. In 1960, the Soviet Union still produced more than five times as much as Japan; today, 120 million Japanese produce more than one and a half times as much as 280 million Soviet citizens. If Gorbachev today promises that the Soviet standard of living will double by the year 2000, this is – given a continuing socialist dictatorship – doomed to failure in just the same way as the predictions of 1961.

Hans Huyn, *The World & I,* June 1987.

But the entire Gorbachev phenomenon was hard to imagine before it happened. These are amazing times. The most dramatic political experiment of the century is collapsing before our eyes – slowly, but certainly.

Recognizing Statements That Are Provable

From various sources of information we are constantly confronted with statements and generalizations about social and moral problems. In order to think clearly about these problems, it is useful if one can make a basic distinction between statements for which evidence can be found and other statements which cannot be verified or proved because evidence is not available, or the issue is so controversial that it cannot be definitely proved.

Readers should constantly be aware that magazines, newspapers, and other sources often contain statements of a controversial nature. The following activity is designed to allow experimentation with statements that are provable and those that are not.

The following statements are taken from the viewpoints in this chapter. Consider each statement carefully. *Mark P for any statement you believe is provable. Mark U for any statement you feel is unprovable because of the lack of evidence. Mark C for any statements you think are too controversial to be proved to everyone's satisfaction.*

If you are doing this activity as a member of a class or group, compare your answers with those of other class or group members. Be able to defend your answers. You many discover that others will come to different conclusions than you. Listening to the reasons others present for their answers may give you valuable insights in recognizing statements that are provable.

P = *provable*
U = *unprovable*
C = *too controversial*

1. The United States invaded Grenada in 1983.

2. The next challenge Americans face is stopping the moral corrosion of their society.

3. The improvement in relations between Washington and Moscow has significantly reduced the likelihood of nuclear war.

4. The US military establishment is changing its focus from a confrontation with the Soviet Union to war against the Third World.

5. Paul Kennedy's book *The Rise and Fall of the Great Powers* was a best-seller in 1988.

6. Mikhail Gorbachev has called nuclear weapons "the greatest evil."

7. Nicaragua received over one billion dollars in aid from the Soviet Union in 1986.

8. The primary Soviet foreign policy goal is to confine the United States within the Western Hemisphere.

9. Soviet leaders frequently speak as if they were already at war with the US, their principal imperialist enemy.

10. The current international environment does not pose a major threat to Soviet security.

11. The Soviet leadership has decided to substantially cut its commitment of resources abroad.

12. The Soviet Union has no legitimate security interest in Central America.

13. The Esquipulas accord between Central American countries calls for resistance forces to settle their grievances peacefully.

14. US marines fought in Nicaragua in 1927.

15. The World Health Organization gave Nicaragua an award for greatest achievement in health by a Third World nation.

16. The United States has sabotaged the Nicaraguan economy through its support of the contra war.

17. The Soviet Union has intervened in such countries as Vietnam, Afghanistan, and Ethiopia.

Periodical Bibliography

The following articles have been selected to supplement the diverse views presented in this chapter.

Abel Aganbegyan "The Economics of Perestroika," *International Affairs*, Spring 1988. Available from The Royal Institute of International Affairs, Chatham House 10 St. James Square, London, UK SW1Y 4LE.

Mikhail Chernyshov, et al. "We've Got the Cosmos in Our Hands," *Air & Space*, April/May 1989. Available from the Smithsonian Institution, 900 Jefferson Drive, Washington, DC 20560.

Charles Colson "How Open Shall We Be to Glasnost?" *Christianity Today*, May 12, 1989.

Boris Fyodorov "Foreign Loans: Pros and Cons," *New Times*, no. 10, March 7/13, 1989.

Robert M. Gates "A CIA Briefing on the USSR," *Conservative Digest*, December 1988.

Mikhail Gorbachev "Mikhail Gorbachev Meets with US Businessmen," *Soviet Life*, December 7/19, 1987.

Peter Gumbel "Funny Money," *The Wall Street Journal*, September 23, 1988.

P. Edward Haley "East-West Hybrid Is Economics' Mutant," *Los Angeles Times*, June 14, 1989.

Mark Hosenball "Allies Defy US on High-Tech Sales to Soviets," *The Wall Street Journal*, May 3, 1989.

Valentin Kashin "Towards a Healthier Economy," *New Times*, no. 52, December 1988.

Andrei Kuteinikov "Economic and Social Factors," *New Times*, no. 20, May 1988.

Michael Ledeen "The Suave Gorbachev Wears No Clothes," *The American Spectator*, February 1989.

Henry R. Nau "Go Slow in Trade with Moscow," *The World & I*, June 1988.

Ernest van den Haag "Comrade, Can You Spare a Dime?" *National Review*, March 24, 1989.

Is Peace Between the Superpowers Possible?

Chapter Preface

In the last decade of the twentieth century, lasting peace between the superpowers seems possible. Both East and West have discussed the demolition of the Berlin Wall, long a contentious issue in superpower relations. They have also discussed withdrawing troops from Europe, suggesting a possible end to Cold War blocs. And improved relations have led to an increase in citizen and cultural exchanges, further enhancing superpower relations.

Are these hopeful signs harbingers of an era of world peace? Or do they merely signal a breathing space before the superpowers begin yet another phase of the Cold War? The following chapter presents several views on the future of US-Soviet relations.

"The second 'cold war' is ending. *What will come to replace it? I hope it will be extensive dialogue and cooperation.*"

Peaceful Coexistence Is Possible

Georgi Arbatov

In the following viewpoint, Georgi Arbatov argues that Mikhail Gorbachev's reforms have contributed to the end of the Cold War. Arbatov is a member of the USSR Academy of Sciences and director of the Institute for US and Canada Studies in Moscow. He asserts that the US and the USSR have ended the Cold War through summits and treaties. Now the two superpowers should work to ensure that continuation of this present, peaceful relationship.

As you read, consider the following questions:

1. What factors led to the end of the Cold War, according to Arbatov?
2. According to the author, what should replace the Cold War?
3. How has the Soviet reform program contributed to peaceful relations, according to Arbatov?

Georgi Arbatov, "The Cold War Is Ending," *World Marxist Review*, May 1988. Reprinted by permission of *World Marxist Review*, published by Progress Books, Toronto.

Not too long ago, one hardly believed that within three years, four Soviet-American summits would be arranged and that the fourth one, held in Moscow, would perhaps start the clock of an era of genuine disarmament ticking. What made this possible?

I think that serious changes have occurred in the attitudes and policies of both sides – although the Americans had to make bigger changes to normalise relations with us and to curb the arms race.

The erosion of the views about the exclusive nature of American capitalism has long been in progress – a phased process going on by fits and starts – in the United States. At the same time, the reluctance to part with the illusions about America's special role has taken firmer hold there. These views used to have a certain rationale in the past, and they gained particular currency in the wake of World War II, when the United States acquired a monopoly on nuclear weapons and overwhelming economic superiority over other nations. It was widely believed that a Pax Americana had dawned.

Later it became obvious that it had been a transient situation and that it was now a thing of the past. America was vulnerable. There were other powerful nations and the US economic role was not what it used to be. To the United States, the détente of the 1970s was a period of adjustment to new realities. But the Americans – at least many Americans – kept thinking that perhaps old realities could be restored and new ones changed. Ronald Reagan became President riding on the crest of this wistful wave. In foreign policy, this meant attempts to revive the Cold War, restore America's worldwide *diktat* and secure military superiority over the USSR. But did all this work?

The Mass Peace Movement

Ronald Reagan ran into difficulties during the first years of his presidency. The resentment shown by the allies and the upsurge of the mass peace movement sent out warning signals too. The million-strong demonstrations in New York City in 1981-1982 forced the administration to return to the negotiating table for talks with the USSR. True, those were tactical not strategic concessions to the actual realities. But later, things really changed.

There has been virtually no increase in the US military budget for some time now, especially since the October 1987 stock market crash, and several militaristic programmes have ground to a halt – first and foremost, out of economic necessity. Under President Reagan, the Pentagon has spent $2.5 trillion to attain military superiority over the USSR, but to no avail. Instead, the United States has turned from the world's biggest creditor into the biggest debtor. Social problems have been seriously neglected. . . . Jesse Jackson is expressing the discontent not only of black

MELT-DOWN?

Americans but also of all those who object to the growing social polarisation between the rich and the poor. . . .

Turning to the subject of America's swing to the right in the early 1980s and, to a certain extent, even before, let me say that I think this was connected with the noticeable difficulties the Soviet Union was experiencing. They nurtured Washington's hope to put an end to socialism by simply applying crude power pressure. Our foreign policy flaws also played their part: in our thinking, we were lagging behind new realities and overestimated the military ways of ensuring security while underrating political ones. It is not that we were building up offensive forces: our objectives remained defensive during that period too. But for some time, the Soviet Union had accepted the American rules of the game and tried to copy each new US weapon system. It was only later that the concepts of reasonable sufficiency and asymmetrical response matured.

Drawn-Out Negotiations

Besides, we were reconciled too long to fruitless and drawn-out negotiations. In some ways they may have been even harmful because they were used by the other side to try and camouflage the arms race. Take the Vienna talks on reductions of conventional forces and armaments in Central Europe. Launched back in 1973, they have yielded nothing to this day. They opened against a peculiar background with the US Senate taking an increasingly favourable view of the Mansfield Amendment under which a large part of the US troops was to be withdrawn from Europe. To bind the Senate hand and foot, the US administration agreed to start these talks. Naturally, we could not reject them. But we shouldn't have allowed them to degenerate into years of empty talk either. And when Mikhail Gorbachev spoke in Reykjavik about the mothballs and junk covering the negotiating table, we must admit that we, too, permitted it to pile up.

The world is witness to the way political thinking has been changing in the Soviet Union in recent years and to the much greater flexibility of its foreign policy. The impact of these changes is shaking the Cold War foundations of *the entire edifice of international relations*. This edifice was built on the conviction that there existed a 'Soviet threat,' on the image of the USSR as an implacable and terrible enemy. . . .

The talks in Moscow have clearly advanced the cause of *demilitarising and improving Soviet-American relations*. The exchange of the instruments of ratification of the INF [Intermediate-Range Nuclear Forces] Treaty and the signing of several other new and useful accords on cooperation are not the only confirmation of this point. Still more important has been the deepening of the political dialogue on the more acute international issues, above all on issues of disarmament. They were central to the Soviet-American talks. It proved possible to bring the positions of the sides closer together in these matters, although the main obstacles to new agreements were not removed.

What prevented the conclusion of an accord on halving strategic offensive armaments? Of course, SDI [Strategic Defense Initiative] and the sea-based Cruise missiles are important obstacles. But I think both have a deeper motive—the fear of the ruling quarters that disarmament has gone too far.

Indeed, the disarmament process has got off the ground for the first time, and changes are under way on the international scene which are really eroding the foundations underlying the post-war world order, the system of Soviet-American relations. That is something not only the far right or the military-industrial complex but also the traditional establishment fears. Two generations of politicians have been weaned on stereotypes of the past, and now they are asking, "Can we really do without an enemy? Without armed force that cements everything?"

A Serious Policy

I do not doubt that Gorbachev, and allies like Foreign Minister Eduard Shevardnadze, mean what they say. The fact, for example, that the Soviet Union in 1988 paid the UN $200 million in arrears and is showing great support for the UN indicates that the new Soviet globalism is a serious policy. The same can be said on the USSR's new emphasis on international cooperation to protect the environment. The changed Soviet perspective emphasizing peaceful resolution of conflicts, disarmament, nonintervention and participation in the world economy is certainly an important ideological departure.

Bob Guldin, *The Guardian*, February 22, 1989.

As for SDI, at the Moscow summit we moderated our stance somewhat and expressed our readiness to discuss certain issues of testing. I do not think that SDI—as originally presented by Ronald Reagan—is viable. Apparently, it will produce several dangerous and costly weapon programmes. But no one except Ronald Reagan believes in the fantastic notion that it will provide the United States with a shield reliably protecting the nation against nuclear missiles.

One often hears it asked whether we are witnessing a transition from a second 'cold war' to a new détente. I don't know what the coming period will be called. But what is happening before our very eyes means that *the second 'cold war' is ending*. What will come to replace it? I hope it will be an extensive dialogue and cooperation: it has already begun. An impressive step has been taken in the field of disarmament. . . .

The paradox of the current situation is that, for the first time ever, new nuclear weapons are being scrapped while the arms race is continuing. There is now virtually no numerical build-up of strategic nuclear weapons, but improvements of performance characteristics are in evidence.

Regrettably, no radical step has yet been taken towards *ending nuclear tests* either. Besides, the issue of testing has been set somewhat aside, as it were – but not for long, I am sure. In order to neutralise all the trump cards of those who object to a ban on nuclear tests, we have agreed to specify the joint verification procedure, to begin cooperating in this sphere and to ratify the two treaties drawn up in 1974 and 1976 but still remaining unsigned – on the yield threshold and on limiting the number of the tests. After that, we plan to begin lowering the threshold and eventually to cease testing altogether. This will also mean that nuclear weapons will no longer be improved.

What, then, are the current prospects of disarmament, of Soviet-American relations, and of world affairs in general?

Advancing Disarmament

The disarmament process is and will be advancing amid a struggle. This struggle remains complicated. I do not doubt that those who oppose the arms race will become stronger. Economic factors, political education and improvements in the international situation are favourable for them. At the same time, we must not forget that a great deal is at stake and that those who seek to perpetuate this militaristic race are resisting change with increasing stubbornness.

I think that Soviet-American relations will develop positively. But the Soviet Union does not view the world from the angle of these relations only. Relations with other countries, with whole continents are also very important. We are well aware that the combined population of the USSR and the United States makes up only ten per cent of the human race, and that there can be no security for us if the situation throughout the world is not normal or favourable. We also understand that military might does not make right but imposes an enormous responsibilty on us. We have advanced the concept of a comprehensive, all-embracing system of international security and, in the final analysis, we will not accept anything less.

"The Reds 'shall never turn off that road' to world domination."

Peaceful Coexistence Is Impossible

Peter B. Gemma Jr.

The Soviet reform program is designed to deceive the US, according to the author of the following viewpoint, Peter B. Gemma Jr. Gemma is a political consultant in Washington, DC and a contributing editor to *Conservative Digest*, a journal of opinion. Gemma argues that proposed Soviet military reductions do nothing to ensure world peace. He believes that a truly peaceful Soviet-American relationship is impossible.

As you read, consider the following questions:

1. What evidence does Gemma provide to prove that the USSR is still a hostile power and a threat to world peace?
2. According to Gemma, how should the US respond to the Soviet economic crisis?
3. How does the economic crisis affect the Soviet military, according to Gemma?

Peter B. Gemma Jr., "Soviet Seductions," *Conservative Digest*, March/April 1989. Reprinted with permission.

Since Mikhail Gorbachev assumed power over the Soviet Union and its satellites in March of 1985, heads of Western politicians and policy analysts have been swimming. Where there once was predictability in Kremlin substance and style, now the only certainty is the uncertainty of Moscow's next move.

No single Soviet strongman has captured the American imagination and public confidence more than Gorbachev and his *perestroika/glasnost* campaign – not "Uncle Joe" Stalin of the wartime 40s, nor Nikita Khrushchev during his 1959 Disneyland visit, nor Leonid Brezhnev and his long vodka toasts with Richard Nixon in Moscow in 1974.

In just four years Gorbachev has put East-West relations in the fast lane, although there is heated debate over what direction things are going.

The Rules Have Not Changed

However, no matter how quickly the cards are shuffled, the rules of the game stay the same. One step back for each two steps forward has been the Communist march through history. And like most other despots and totalitarian regimes throughout the ages, the Red dictators have given the world clear perspectives during times of heady propaganda. Consider:

Vladimir Lenin once instructed his Red revolutionaries that it "is necessary to combine the strictest loyalty to the ideas of communism with the necessary compromises, agreements, zigzags, retreats, and so on. . . ." Soviet strongman Leonid Brezhnev learned well the lessons of Communist history when he boasted: "We are achieving with détente what our predecessors have been unable to achieve with the mailed fist."

Now enter, from stage left, Mikhail Gorbachev who, in a thundering Kremlin speech to the party faithful in 1987, asserted that Marxists have since "October 1917 [been] moving toward a new world, the world of communism. We shall never turn off that road." And, more specifically, in the opening sentences of his book *Perestroika* (curiously *not* to be found in the American edition) he categorically states: "Perestroika is a continuation of the October Revolution."

No Soviet Change

Apparently *perestroika* is not so much about changes in policy as it is about changes in perception. As foreign policy analyst and author Richard Pipes observes in the Winter 1989 *Policy Review,* "Mikhail Gorbachev has so far failed to bring about any fundamental or structural change in the Soviet political, economic, or social order." Professor Pipes continues: "Despite its widely advertised new thinking, Soviet foreign policy's overriding goal so far appears unchanged: relentless pursuit of tactical and strategic advantages, short of direct military confrontation, in a struggle against Western political and economic interests."

Still, the U.S. faces a different Soviet Union today. Domestically, some dissent is being tolerated, token capitalist experiments are taking place in the Russian marketplace, and some concessions to autonomy are being granted to captive ethnic nations. Meanwhile, Communist combat troops have been withdrawn from Afghanistan and symbolic military reductions may soon be taking place in Eastern Europe.

The Same Ideology

The ideology is the same: that socialism is the future of the world. I don't believe that Gorbachev can be trusted without reservations. Basically it is impossible to imagine really friendly relations with the Soviet Union such as we have with France, let's say, or England.

Boris Shragin, *National Review*, April 7, 1989.

There seem to be two clear economic reasons for the *perestroika/glasnost* PR [public relations] policies.

First, socialist-inspired perennial economic stagnation has turned into a grow-or-die crisis. The 70-year-old workers "paradise" that has yet to feed itself is in danger of total collapse. For years 15 to 17 percent of the U.S.S.R.'s gross national product has been spent on its military machine, and this continues today under Gorbachev. This compares with about six percent in the United States and much less in Western Europe and Japan. The constant siphoning off the cream of Russian production has caught up to the Soviet economy. Again.

Economic Crisis

The second reason for the Kremlin's current economic crisis is that the Soviet Union is collapsing under the weight of its own bureaucracy and rotting from within by corruption. In 1988 alone, more than 18 billion dollars' worth of state-run businesses failed because Marxist ideologues and bureaucrats control the system. As Dr. Yuri Orlov, the distinguished emigré scientist, observed in *Commentary* for October 1988, while "corruption infects all bureaucracies and all governments, [it] is an especially serious threat to the Soviet government because bureaucracy is *built into* the Soviet system with its centralized planning, centralized, tightly controlled classified information, and centralized leadership."

Throughout history successful dictatorships have kept their captive peoples just hungry enough to forestall revolt. With the growing discontent in Poland, Estonia, and Armenia, that careful balance is endangered.

Thus, faced with an economic crisis, now sparking ethnic and ideological unrest, the *perestroika* campaign puts a kinder, gentler face on a Kremlin seized with panic.

West to the Rescue

Enter, from stage right, President Ronald Reagan. Armed with this hard-liner's convincing "I trust but verify" endorsement of *perestroika*, Moscow opened up shop on Wall Street.

In an article for the January 19, 1988, *New York Times*, Clyde H. Farnsworth reported: "President Reagan has opened the door to Soviet membership in the World Bank, the International Monetary Fund, and the General Agreement on Tariffs and Trade." Farnsworth went on to note that "the new position contrasts with the President's strongly stated position" in 1987 because this new policy "makes no explicit link between trade and human rights."

With membership would come desperately needed prestige and a network of financial contacts to tap into public and private credit sources. Currently, the Kremlin's central planners are on a borrowing binge, seeking low-cost loans, technology transfers, and subsidized food sales. Western banks are now providing Communist-bloc nations with over $1.5 billion each month in "untied loans" or funds not tied to any specific purchase or product. This capital infusion is in addition to the $2.5 billion the Soviet Union obtains monthly from weapons, gold, and oil sales. The latter revenues have traditionally been used by the Kremlin for purchases of food and technology, as well as debt servicing. . . .

A Change of Style

A regime with a reputation for gnawing the hands that feed it is an unlikely candidate for the loans, credit, and credibility Moscow desperately needs. But watch Western skepticism after talk of "democratizing" the Soviet state, floating pie-in-the-sky arms control balloons, and releasing a few dissidents.

Releasing dissidents has a wonderfully lulling effect. Remember, Nikita Khrushchev freed thousands of Stalin's political prisoners 30 years ago, then proceeded brutally to subjugate Hungary, to erect the Berlin Wall, and to build Communist-controlled Cuba into a major military installation 90 miles from our shores.

In the early 1970s, Leonid Brezhnev's seductive detente campaign and relaxed Jewish emigration policies netted the Communists a huge technology transfer—including having the West finance and build the world's largest truck factory on the Soviet Union's Kama River. By 1979, trucks from that facility were transporting Red Army combat troops into Afghanistan.

Yes, Gorbachev is different from Khrushchev or Brezhnev in *style*. But the *substance* of Communist policies has not changed. Consider:

THE LEFT HAND HAS NEVER BEEN RETRACTED

Jack Hamm. Reprinted with permission.

• The U.S. State Department's 1987 *Report To Congress On Forced Labor In The U.S.S.R.* documents more than 1,100 slave-labor camps with a combined population of about four million inmates.
• Former Gulag internee Mikhail Makarenko reports that some 150 concentration camps and prisons in the Soviet Union are reserved exclusively for children *under age two* and their mothers.
• In *The First Guidebook To Prisons And Concentration Camps Of The Soviet Union*, Russian refugee Avraham Shifrin estimates that

up to 40 percent of his native country's industry depends on slave labor. He was interned in a labor camp for more than 10 years himself.

Soviet Military Buildup Continues

Although the *perestroika/glasnost* campaigns have not really changed the Soviet system, and it appears to be just another part of the historic Communist cycle of growth and recovery, is there really anything to fear from the relaxation, albeit temporary, of East-West tensions?

Militarily, yes.

Congressman Jim Courter (R-NJ), a member of the House Armed Services Committee, has cautioned that in the wake of the Reagan era defense buildup and in the midst of a *perestroika,* "The United States still clearly lacks the capacity to defeat the Soviet Union if the U.S.S.R. should begin a war. Victory over the aggressor is not even a stated American objective. Our national objective, formally stated, is to terminate hostilities on favorable terms. Those are the U.S. Armed Forces orders. Whether we have given our forces the material resources to carry out those orders remains highly questionable."

While the strains of a continually failing socialist experiment have brought the Soviet empire to the brink of economic disaster, Moscow's military expenditures have not been reduced by a single ruble. After all, as Gorbachev himself has warned, the Reds "shall never turn off that road" to world domination. And that road has turned into a fast track. General John Gavin, U.S. Supreme Commander in Europe, revealed that since Gorbachev took power the Soviets have produced 700 combat aircraft per year and one nuclear submarine every 37 days. "Since Gorbachev took power," reported syndicated columnist Charley Reese, "the Soviets have built more new tanks than Great Britain and France have in their combined inventories." Gorbachev has pushed Soviet T-80 tank production to an estimated rate of one every three hours, 24 hours a day, 365 days a year.

NATO Military Inferiority

According to commentator George Will, even if all Communist tank production were to stop today, "and the tank production of all NATO [North Atlantic Treaty Organization] nations were tripled, it would take NATO 10 years to catch up."

As the *London Sunday Times* editorialized on October 23, 1988: "While Mr. Gorbachev has been preaching perestroika he has also presided over a massive modernization of the Soviet military. The Soviet navy has commissioned one Victor III nuclear submarine, one Sovremennyy, and two Udaloy missile destroyers; development of the new long-range supersonic Blackjack bomber has continued apace: ten have now been built and may already be operational; Soviet air defense troops have just received five hundred new SA-10 missiles, and the air force has replaced two hundred aging MiG-27's with two hundred SU-17's and one hundred fifty MiG-23's, and MiG-25's with the new MiG-29; most threatening of all for the West, Soviet ground forces on the border with West Germany have received three hundred new T-80 tanks, along with hundreds of new missiles, troop carriers, and mobile artillery."

A Potential Threat

For America and other free nations in this interdependent world, the major potential threat to our way of life will continue to be the Soviet Union. The basis of that threat is Soviet military power, whose forces and deployments have enabled Moscow to gain influence over other nations by its potential to dominate them militarily.

Frank C. Carlucci, *Defense 89*, January/February 1989.

Gorbachev's promise to cut his Eastern European troop strength by 50,000 – moving them 600 miles from the West German border to just inside the Soviet Union – and reduce his Warsaw Pact advantage in tank deployment from 3.1:1 to 2.5:1 must be viewed outside *perestroika.*

Will We Learn from History?

Fifty years after the Munich Pact with Hitler, the West seems hell-bent on embracing another policy of appeasement. This time the concessions are credit lines, not boundary lines. Just as ceding whole nations to the Nazis did not change the character of the regime, neither will unconditional credit lines, technology transfers, nor other concessions turn Mikhail Gorbachev off the road he's sworn to follow.

The slave-labor camps are running at capacity levels; Cuban mercenaries are creating mischief from Southern Africa to Central America; and Communist-supplied terrorist gangs are destabilizing whole nations from Pakistan to Peru to the Philippines.

The U.S. reaction to *perestroika* should be to push Gorbachev into making the choice between being a good Communist or a real peacemaker.

Some would say he has already chosen. Just ask Filipino families mourning relatives slaughtered by Communist-supplied insurgents; or orphaned Afghani children, maimed by Soviet booby-trapped toys; or any Vietnamese or other refugees who swam under the Bamboo Curtain or crawled over the Berlin Wall. They report that Communist actions say much more than all the glitter of *glasnost* and *perestroika* combined.

"Let us . . .go forward together to build that Europe we would like to see—a free, open, secure, and prosperous Europe; a whole Europe."

European Reunification Can Promote Peace

James A. Baker III

The author of the following viewpoint, James A. Baker III, calls for the reunification of Eastern and Western Europe. Baker argues that reunification of the two blocs, divided since 1949, would promote peace between the superpowers by eliminating a source of Cold-War confrontation. Baker is the Secretary of State for the Bush administration.

As you read, consider the following questions:

1. According to Baker, why should Eastern and Western Europe be reunified?
2. What conditions must be met for reunification to occur, according to the author?
3. How does arms control influence the European reunification process, according to Baker?

James A. Baker III, "New Horizons in Europe," *Current Policy No. 1154*, March 1989. Published by the United States Department of State, Bureau of Public Affairs.

After the Second World War, Europe and the world were confronted by two distinctly opposing views. The United States and its allies in Western Europe held the vision of free peoples, living under the rule of the law, their individual freedoms protected, and their democratic governments responsible to those people.

Natural Rights

We believed, and we continue to believe, that freedom of speech, and of religion, freedom from fear and freedom of opportunity, were and are the natural rights of free men everywhere. We were certain, and we continue to be certain, that free markets and individual initiatives are the surest routes to social and economic progress.

We sought, and we continue to seek, our security in a coalition of free nations drawn together by common values, not only mutual interests. And we envisioned then, as we envision now, a Europe at peace – its nations free to develop in diversity but united against war.

Our vision was not the only vision. There was another view opposed to the values most cherished by the West. And the competition between the two visions gave us the difficult legacy with which we live today: a Europe, forcibly divided against the will of its peoples; a Europe, the most heavily armed continent in the world.

New horizons are beckoning, horizons that offer us the opportunity to go beyond the conflicts of the past. The other vision is changing. It is changing because we in the West have been faithful to our own vision. And it is changing because realism has begun to triumph in the Soviet Union.

New Thinking

Perestroika, glasnost, and democratization are the slogans of the "new thinking." There are encouraging developments in human rights and in the emphasis upon the rule of law. Economies once rigidly fixed in the grip of centralized control are being loosened and a role for individual initiative has been decreed. [Soviet] General Secretary Gorbachev has declared, "World politics, too, should be guided by the primacy of universal human values." The rhetoric of Soviet foreign policy is being reshaped with less emphasis on the use of force. . . .

No one can foretell where this process will lead or even whether it will endure. Yet we cannot deny the reality of what is actually happening in Europe today. Dostoevsky, in his novel *The Possessed*, wrote that "The fire is in the minds of men, not in the roofs of buildings." The revolutionary changes in that part of Europe still behind a rusting Iron Curtain are changes above all in the minds of men, in their vision of the future. People want freedom:

221

freedom of the mind; freedom in the home; freedom in the workplace and free governments. And these freedoms will heal the wounds inflicted by stagnation and tyranny.

A Europe of Freedoms

I propose that we dedicate ourselves to creating a new Europe – a Europe based on these freedoms:
- The freedom of all Europeans to have a say in decisions which affect their lives, including freedom of the workplace. The legality of Solidarity, for example, should really be the norm and not the subject for negotiations.

A Larger Process

Negotiations are part of a larger process, one which must address the causes as well as the symptoms of the current divisions in Europe. Progress in the military field alone is not enough to bring enduring peace. What is needed is genuine reconciliation and an end to the division of Europe. True security cannot exist without guarantee of human rights and basic freedoms for all people.

George Bush, Statement made in Vienna, March 9, 1989.

- The freedom of all Europeans to express their political differences, when all ideas are welcome and human rights are truly inviolable. Monitors of the Helsinki agreements, for example, should be honored and not hunted by their governments.
- The freedom of all Europeans to exchange ideas and information and to exercise their right to freedom of movement. The researcher in Prague, for example, should be able to find the books he needs. Barbed wire should not separate cousins in Hamburg from cousins in Dresden. And a wall should not divide Berlin, continuing, as we've seen, to cost the lives of people seeking freedom.
- Finally, the freedom of all Europeans to be safe from military intimidation or attack. Those in the West should be free of the fear that the massive forces under Soviet command might invade them. Those in the East should be free of the fear that armed Soviet intervention, justified by the Brezhnev doctrine, would be used again to deny them choice.

"New thinking" and the Brezhnev doctrine are in fundamental conflict. We call today upon General Secretary Gorbachev to renounce the Brezhnev doctrine – beyond any shadow of a doubt. Let the "new thinking" sweep away this vestige from the era of stagnation.

These four freedoms are inseparable. They are the principles for the new Europe; they are the keys that open the door to the European house of the future. As the American President Abraham Lincoln said, "A house divided against itself cannot stand." A continent divided by a wall cannot be secure. A secure and prosperous Europe can never be built on the basis of artificial barriers, fear, and the denial of independence.

I am happy to report that we have made some progress toward realizing the new Europe of the freedoms – progress upon which we all can build. The Conference on Security and Cooperation in Europe – through the Helsinki, Madrid, Stockholm, and now the Vienna documents – has defined ever more precisely the obligations of states. We have emphasized a new freedom for individuals and the expanded concept of openness and confidence-building measures in the field of security. We support this process. The Helsinki Final Act embodies our vision of Europe. And NATO's [North Atlantic Treaty Organization] security dimension has always had the prevention of war as its only purpose.

Economic and Environmental Initiatives

Economic change is also a marked feature of the new Europe. The creation of a single market by 1992, looking outward to benefit all who wish to trade, would surely fulfill the hopes of those postwar visionaries who rightfully saw economic union as a buttress of peace and freedom. Centralized economies are slowly divesting the straitjacket of outmoded Marxist-Leninist theories. And the desire for increased commercial contact is strong and growing ever stronger. There is also a genuine possibility for all industrialized nations, both East and West, to work together on newly recognized transnational problems.

Dangers to our environment, for example, risk the most fundamental security of all the earth's citizens. To protect the globe's ozone layer, the European Community and the United States decided to end the use of all chlorofluorocarbons (CFCs) by the year 2000, assuming adequate substitutes can be found – as we believe they can. We hope the Soviet Union will consider joining us in the spirit of "new thinking."

Reducing Military Confrontation

This is progress. But while the old era apparently recedes before the horizons of the new Europe, those horizons are still too distant. The arms and the armies still face each other. An Iron Curtain still divides this continent. Too many governments have followed their solemn signature on human rights pledges with violent suppression of dissent.

And so, as we eye the horizon, important questions remain unanswered. Will the new rhetoric be translated into new actions or will we see a repetition of the past – of hopes disappointed once more?

Will East and West, together, be able to dismantle the barriers thrown up by the old era of competing visions? Will these barriers finally be removed; will the Berlin Wall and the barbed wire and the watch towers finally be relegated to history? Will the Soviet Union demilitarize its foreign policy in Europe; will it cease to threaten democracy's house with tens of thousands of tanks?

Far-Reaching Reductions

I was encouraged by what [Foreign] Minister Shevardnadze said as he spoke of far-reaching reductions. In recent years, we have seen reasons to be hopeful about the new Soviet thinking. But both realism and prudence require that we test the new thinking to make sure that it means new policy and, above all, changes in military deployments. We have sought to discover whether East and West could take steps together – irreversible steps – that lead toward the Europe of the freedoms. And we have also sought to reduce the level of military confrontation.

Beyond Containment

NATO is one of the great success stories, and it has guaranteed the peace in Europe, provided a shield for 40 years for freedom and prosperity. And now our Alliance faces new challenges at a time of historic transition as we seek to overcome the division of Europe. I call it "beyond containment." . . .

The results would dramatically increase stability on the continent and transform the military map of Europe. We can and must begin now to set out a new vision for Europe at the end of this century. This is a noble mission that I believe the Alliance should be ready to undertake. And I have no doubt that we are up to the task.

George Bush, Speech given at NATO Headquarters, May 29, 1989.

Here, too, there is progress to report. Responding to an American proposal, the Soviet Union joined the United States in achieving an Intermediate-Range Nuclear Forces Treaty that provides for the elimination of an entire class of nuclear-capable missiles. The treaty contains important precedents, especially in the areas of verification and asymmetrical reductions to equality. We have also made encouraging progress in the START [Strategic Arms Reduction Talks] toward reducing strategic forces. And we look forward, once our review is completed, to further steps on the road towards arms reduction and arms control. . . .

Progress on nuclear arms control, however, is not sufficient. We shall never be able to set East-West relations on an irreversible course toward enduring improvement unless we deal with the huge conventional military imbalances in Europe. We can define the issue simply: a vast force, spearheaded by heavily armored units and supported by massive fire power, has been fielded by the Soviet Union and its allies. That force points West.

We in the West have faced this threat since the dawn of the cold war. Today, Soviet and Warsaw Pact military forces go far beyond those conceivably needed for defense. Warsaw Pact tanks outnumber NATO tanks by over 3 to 1, Warsaw Pact artillery exceeds NATO's artillery by 3 to 1, and the Warsaw Pact holds more than a 2-to-1 advantage over NATO's armored troop carriers.

These ratios speak for themselves. And as NATO has pointed out, these are forces best suited to an invasion of Western Europe.

It is this array of Soviet armed might that divides Europe against its will and holds European hopes hostage to possibly hostile Soviet intentions.

Reasonable Sufficiency

Lately, we have heard that Soviet military doctrine is changing to meet a standard called "reasonable sufficiency." And in December 1988 at the United Nations, General Secretary Gorbachev declared the Soviet intention to withdraw 50,000 men, 5,000 tanks, and other selected equipment from certain areas of Eastern Europe. Several East European governments have also announced unilateral force reductions.

That's a start, a very good start. It's a very hopeful start, and, of course, we are watching to see the words become deeds. And equally clear is the necessity to go further. Even after these reductions, the Warsaw Pact would retain a 2-to-1 edge in tanks and artillery. The Warsaw Pact's conventional military preponderance, especially in the spearheads of attack, is, in fact, what makes an invasion possible.

These are hard facts. These are the facts that have to be changed if our negotiations are to be successful and if the foundations of a new Europe are to endure. The arms control process must now be focused strongly on this East-West imbalance.

The United States, together with the other Western participants in these talks, has developed serious proposals to end disparities in conventional ground forces and to introduce far-reaching confidence-building and stabilizing measures.

Achieving Reductions

Our approach focuses on the achievement of significant reductions in key military capabilities that are designed for invasion. For example, we propose an overall limit on the total armament in Europe and that no more than 40,000 tanks should be deployed by the 23 participationg states in the CFE [conventional armed forces in Europe] negotiations. In addition, Western participants are prepared to introduce new confidence-building measures in the near future, aimed at increasing transparency and reducing the possibility of surprise attack. Ultimately, of course, stability will be achieved when no country is able to dominate by force of arms.

Let me emphasize once more, however, that change in the military balance is only one part of the process. Only when the causes of the historic division of Europe have been removed, when we have achieved the free flow of people and information, when citizens everywhere enjoy free expression, only then will it be possible to eliminate totally the military confrontation. In other words, we cannot remove the symptoms, unless we deal fundamentally with the causes. I am encouraged that increasingly people from both East and West understand that relationship. We must all work to bring about far-reaching changes that end the division of this continent.

The United States is committed to working with reasonable men and women in all countries to achieve success. We approach the negotiations with a clear goal, solid principles, and well-defined objectives.

Our goal in these negotiations, as in all arms control negotiations, will be to prevent war—any war, nuclear or conventional—deter aggression, and increase stability at lower levels of armed forces. We shall judge every proposal not simply by the numbers of weapons reduced but by the impact on deterrence and stability.

Unity of Purpose

To achieve this goal, we reaffirm the unity of purpose between the United States and its European allies. We have long recognized, as NATO Secretary General Manfred Woerner said, that "Europe needs America as America needs Europe. . . . Separate, we would become victims of world historical development; together we can determine the course of world history for the better."

Our negotiating objectives are well defined.

First, as I mentioned earlier, the NATO allies have called for equal ceilings in key items of equipment at levels below current NATO forces. This would be the best step toward a secure Europe at lower levels of arms.

Second, no state should possess capabilities designed primarily for invasion.

Third, a regime of mutual openness and transparency about military matters should be expanded which can foster confidence, clarify intentions, and thereby strengthen stability.

In addition, we hope that all states will adopt doctrines and force structures which faithfully reflect defensive intentions.

As these negotiations unfold, we and our allies will explore every opportunity for progress. The current force levels and force structures in Europe are not engraved in stone. They are the product of history, the results of conflict. And they can be changed.

If the past is any guide, however, we can expect many proposals that promise the perfection of disarmament if we would only abandon the pragmatism of deterrence. To paraphrase Winston Churchill, the counsel of perfection is admirable in a clergyman but impractical in a statesman. The opportunities are too precious to be squandered in sweeping but impractical proposals. Instead, let us do the work of peace carefully, progressing step by step and verifying each step.

The Future of Europe

I have spoken of the new Europe, of the freedoms, of the new horizons beckoning to a continent divided 40 years ago because of a conflict of visions. As that conflict weakens, it may be possible to remove the old obstacles thrown up in Europe's path. That is our task. We must remove at last the conventional force imbalances and curtains of secrecy that have so long imperiled European security and, with it, world peace.

This essential step will not be easy. It will produce new challenges and perhaps some difficult moments. But we cannot desist from the task.

I have argued that a clearer understanding of the Europe of the future will ease the burden. Already, we can glimpse part of that horizon of a peaceful and prosperous Europe for which so many have sacrificed. Yet though it beckons, we know that nothing can be taken for granted. It falls to us to take the next step, if not the final one, on this journey.

Prophecy is God's gift to but a few, yet imagination is the birthright of every human being. We can but dimly see the future through the mists of change, yet we can all imagine the world we would like to see. That is the summons of our undertaking. Let us, therefore, go forward together to build that Europe we would like to see—a free, open, secure, and prosperous Europe; a whole Europe, ennobling by example all mankind.

"Genuine détente is possible only from below, through the growth of a world-wide revolution of grass-roots peace initiatives."

The Peace Movement Can Promote Peace

Joanne Landy

Joanne Landy is the director of the New York-based Campaign for Peace and Democracy/East and West, a network of activists committed to uniting peace and democratic movements in the West, East, and Third World. In the following viewpoint, Landy argues that the worldwide peace movement promotes peaceful relations between the US and the USSR.

As you read, consider the following questions:

1. According to the author, how has the peace movement contributed to improved superpower relations?
2. What fundamental goals do activists in the peace movement promote, according to Landy?
3. Given the improved superpower relationship, what should be the goal of the peace movement, according to the author?

Joanne Landy, "Can Summits Replace the Peace Movement?" *Tikkun*, November/December 1988. Reprinted with the author's permission.

We believe that only the efforts of an independent society, of the ordinary peoples of East and West, can guarantee the establishment of a climate of trust and a stable peace. Genuine d'etente is possible only from below, through the growth of a worldwide revolution of grassroots peace initiatives. . . .It is impossible to speak about peace without also discussing human rights. Peace in the world and peace in society depend on one another in the most intimate fashion.
—Moscow Group to Establish Trust Between East and West, Spring 1987.

The last years have seen a series of common initiatives by East-bloc activists. The first of these was a joint statement issued in October 1986 on the thirtieth anniversary of the Hungarian Revolution. On February 1, 1988, protests against repression in Rumania were launched in four Eastern European countries. Later the same month hundreds of people from Hungary, Poland, Czechoslovakia, Yugoslavia, and the Soviet Union issued a common declaration in defense of East German activists who were being harassed, imprisoned, and forced to emigrate. And in March of 1988 over four hundred peace and human right activists from the USSR and Eastern Europe, including Andrei Sakharov, signed an appeal calling on all countries that signed the Helsinki Accords to recognize the rights of conscientious objection and alternative service.

Cooperation among East-bloc activists began long before Gorbachev, but the current relaxation has made communication and mutual support across the invisible iron curtains between East-bloc countries somewhat easier. The Czechoslovakian playwright and Charter 77 member Vaclav Havel underscored the significance of this network of solidarity when he said in an interview: "A liberation movement in the Soviet bloc will succeed only if it goes beyond the borders of any single country. This is why all the campaigns in the past were suppressed."

Out of an urgent need to invigorate a stagnating system, Gorbachev has encouraged a more liberal climate not only in the USSR but throughout the Warsaw Pact countries. Both at home and abroad, he has taken the gamble that the Communist parties will be able to maintain control over the processes of reform they have started from above. The extraordinary citizens' initiatives in the USSR and Eastern Europe suggest he may well be riding a tiger.

The American Peace Movement

In the early 1980s the American peace movement had a great deal of influence. Today, despite its lasting effect on public consciousness in this country, the movement is far weaker and is searching for a way to recapture its former power. Pam Solo, a leader of the Freeze, has explained the movement's current state in terms that are worth bearing in mind, given the fact that both the Republican and Democratic parties have declared their commitment to a "strong defense." At a speech given at Hofstra University in December 1987, Solo said:

> Perhaps the most important reason for [the] success [of the Freeze movement] was that we were, in the early years, defining the terms of the debate.... We have to acknowledge, though, that at some point we lost the political initiative. The reasons for this loss are complex. These are a few of the highlights that we need to think about. The first is the cooptation by the Democrats. We allowed the constraints of our Congressional allies to become our own. There were times when, because of our grass-roots support, we had the power to push the politicians further, to demand more, but instead we took our signal from our allies on the hill, who, in fact, did not always share our political goals. We compromised at times when we should have confronted our allies.

In fact, it is not at all surprising that the once-powerful Freeze movement found itself lost in the halls of Congress. From the beginning, immediate legislative success rather than a long-term commitment to building an independent grass-roots movement was central to the Freeze strategy.

Military Forces

The huge standing conventional forces and huge nuclear warfighting forces, supported by military budgets that total $800 billion a year, still exist and get larger; but they cannot be used for anything other than marginal purposes—like the invasion of Afghanistan. We haven't really come to grips with this reality either in the United States or in Europe and the Pacific....

The peace movement has to do the creative thinking on these issues. It's up to the peace movement to first construct and then endeavor to implement alternative ways of resolving conflict that do not involve military force.

Randall Forsberg and Peter Hayes, *Defense and Disarmament News,* March/April 1987.

Fortunately, many activists have moved beyond the narrow limitations of the Freeze approach of focusing the goal of victory on a single legislative measure. For example, people opposing the arms buildup today generally link their position to the issue of the military budget. They stress the catastrophic effects of arms spending on the American economy far more than they did in the past, and they argue for the need to reallocate military funds to social services and genuine productive growth at home as well as to development in the Third World. Another example of the current more comprehensive approach is that activists now often bring up the "deadly connection" between interventionism and nuclear weapons. They point out that one of the most likely scenarios of nuclear confrontation is the escalation of a regional conflict between the superpowers. Moreover, many activists now believe it is important to oppose U.S. interventionism not only because it could lead to nuclear war, but because the peace movement should stand for an alternative U.S. foreign policy with respect to the rights of weaker nations.

Third World Issues

By broadening the agenda to include Third World issues, activists have also begun to sense the need for a radical restructuring of the relationship of the United States and other advanced Western countries to the rest of the world. With a 1987 Third World debt of $1.2 trillion and a net resource transfer of $29 billion that resulted from the debt service the Third World paid to Western creditors, the dimensions of the problem are enormous. Increasing numbers of movement activists are convinced of the importance of explaining to the American people that they have no stake in the IMF-[International Monetary Fund] World Bank austerity program for the people of the Third World—low wages abroad pull down wages at home–and that instead ordinary Americans have common interests with popular struggles for democracy and social justice in Asia, Africa, and Latin America.

This alternative, anticorporate foreign policy is still in its embryonic stages. In his campaign for the Democratic nomination Jesse Jackson began to suggest what such a foreign policy would look like–ending military interventionism and beginning to support the struggles of trade unions in developing countries, for example. Nevertheless, such a foreign policy still needs to be spelled out, and elaborating it will necessarily involve envisioning the possibility of cooperative economic relations among people from different countries, relations that go against the basic logic of the capitalist system.

An alternative foreign policy also has to be expanded to address the issues raised by the emerging movements for democratic rights in the Eastern bloc. It is necessary to demonstrate that over the years the cold war has enabled each side to use the other's militaristic and repressive actions to justify its own, and that a democratic and peaceful foreign policy on the part of the United States would help human rights everywhere by breaking this cycle of mutual justification. For too long, American peace activists have been unwilling to address this issue, out of a mistaken fear that doing so would give ammunition to the cold warriors. In truth, failure to address this issue has had the opposite effect. By ignoring or soft-pedaling human rights issues in the Soviet Union and the Eastern bloc, the movement has robbed itself of the ability to expose the American government for its hypocrisy in using a standard of judgment that varies depending on whether a particular government is friendly or hostile to the United States.

Disarmament Proposals

A key question for opponents of American militarism concerns their response to the USSR's recent foreign policy actions and proposals. In a desperate effort to rescue the Soviet economy, Gorbachev has advanced a broad range of initiatives with the goal of lowering tensions with the United States and reducing the Soviet military budget. These include offers for asymmetrical cuts in conventional forces in Europe, proposals for nuclear weapons-free zones in various parts of the world, cuts in strategic weapons, and an end to the arms race in space. With regard to regional conflicts, the Soviets have withdrawn from Afghanistan (not on principle – they still defend the legitimacy of their original intervention – but because, like the U.S. in Vietnam, they were defeated). They seem interested in encouraging the Cubans to withdraw from Angola,

"Oh, sure, you'll always have your fringe element."

From the May 5, 1987 *People's Daily World*.

232

and the Vietnamese from Cambodia. And they may be prepared to sharply reduce their support for Nicaragua in order to achieve détente with the United States.

For the most part, the American government has been reluctant to respond positively to these Soviet actions and initiatives, invoking either human rights considerations or arguments that the Soviet proposals leave the USSR with a military advantage. But, in fact, moves toward disarmament strengthen the hand of human rights activists by depriving states of one of their key alibis for repression. As for maintaining the military "balance of power," it is precisely the superpowers' quest for superiority or an elusive parity that has produced a perpetual and highly dangerous arms race. . . .

Such a new way of thinking means starting with an alternative vision of a bloc-free world and a democratic peace in which the terms "superpower" and "spheres of influence" —the very words describe the rule of strong countries over weak—would no longer be relevant. Such a vision has been put forward both by East-bloc human rights activists and by some currents in the nonaligned Western European peace movement. In fact, it has actually emerged out of a dialogue between members of these two movements, and was expressed eloquently by Czechoslovakia's Charter 77 movement, which declared:

> Peace is threatened everywhere, when the voice of the critically thinking citizen has been silenced. It is therefore foolish to think that peace efforts [can] be limited only to military-technical aspects of disarmament and that the problem of human rights and freedom can be left to organizations such as Amnesty International. . . . Real peace does not mean only the removal of despotism from relations among states, but also from relations between state power and a human being. . . .

If a revitalized peace movement adopts the goal of a democratic peace, and understands the symbiotic nature of the conflict between the superpower systems, it will be able to advance political strategies aimed at building effective transnational pressure and power from below. The United States should be called upon, for example, to take up Gorbachev's peace initiatives without hesitation because they offer a good starting point for de-escalating the arms race and because a positive response is the best way to challenge the Soviet Union's continuing imperial role in Eastern Europe and elsewhere. As long as the U.S. continues menacing the world with its own military interventionism and massive nuclear and conventional arsenals, it undercuts pressure on the Soviets to end theirs.

Gorbachev's Proposals

But peace activists should demand that the U.S. go beyond simply accepting Gorbachev's proposals. If this country took dramatic and unmistakable unilateral initiatives toward disarmament, such as withdrawing U.S. troops from Western Europe – the central theater of the U.S.-Soviet confrontation – it could break the vicious circle of the cold war. The Soviets have always claimed that the American threat necessitates their presence in Eastern European countries, and such a move on the part of the U.S. would offer invaluable political assistance to East-bloc activists demanding the removal of Soviet troops. Similarly, if the Soviets were unilaterally to initiate a consistent and thoroughgoing peaceful foreign policy, including withdrawal from Eastern Europe, such a policy would undercut the ability of cold warriors in the West to find acceptance for their policies. . . .

A Peace Millennium

The goals of abolishing nuclear weapons and building common security are visionary, but not utopian. We must take full advantage of growing chances to end the arms race and to chart a new way to live on this planet. We must establish clear direction and great unity among those in the United States and around the world who desire peace and justice. Let us join together in the closing years of this century to usher in a peace millennium—to make the year 2000 a turning point toward a peaceful, secure, humane world.

Disarmament 2000/Common Security Working Group, *Political Affairs,* November 1988.

Some people might argue that there is no need to call for such risky unilateral steps since the superpowers have already negotiated an INF [Intermediate-Range Nuclear Forces] Treaty, are having regular summit meetings, and seem to be working out agreements on strategic weapons and several regional conflicts. A cautionary note is in order here. While of course one should support agreements that reduce the levels of armaments and disengage the superpowers from other countries, we must keep in mind that the history of U.S.-Soviet relations has been marked by periods of alternating détente and confrontation. Moreover, past arms agreements have always been the starting point for continuing the arms race, albeit under new rules. Aside from any question of cheating, both sides build weapons systems permitted by the agreements signed. As mentioned before, such weapons-building is taking place right now with regard to the INF accord. And in an article for the Spring 1988 issue of *Dissent* magazine, military analyst Gordon Adams warns that the START [Strategic Arms Reduction Talks] treaty currently under negotiation may simply result in both superpowers possessing a meaner, leaner array of strategic nuclear weapons. . . .

While the START agreement could in theory be the beginning

of a process under which the United States and the Soviet Union gradually get rid of their nuclear and conventional arsenals and work out a lasting basis for peace, it would be a mistake to count on it. After all, the East-West conflict has been about something more fundamental than simple national competition: It is at root a conflict of rival socioeconomic systems in which "offensive" and "defensive" aims are inextricably intertwined. As long as the systems are in place, with the superpowers at their core, there is an inherent conflict of interest between the two countries, and consequently military competition could revive, whatever the current intentions of their leaders.

It is difficult to imagine regions of crucial imperial interest such as the Middle East, the Pacific, and Eastern Europe ceasing permanently to be areas of conflict. Both in regional conflicts and in the field of weaponry each side will find it difficult to resist the opportunities for substantial advantage, and when such opportunities arise the opposing side will feel "forced" to reciprocate because neither contender in this kind of contest can afford to lose too much to its rival. It is obvious that such sentiments motivate the U.S., and they probably shape Soviet policy as well. So, while the Soviet Union today clearly needs to de-escalate the arms race, and is prepared to make significant concessions in order to reduce tensions, it has not given up its claim as a global power. Moreover, the Soviet leadership is committed to maintaining its domination over Eastern Europe because of its deep fear of the contagion of democratic social developments if it loses control.

There are sections of the U.S. elite which, like the Soviets, urgently hope to reduce the costs of the arms race and seek a lowering of tensions. While neither U.S. nor Soviet foreign policy "moderates" are willing to jettison the interests of their respective capitalist or communist systems, their moves to avoid confrontation and reduce the level of armaments should be supported. But peace activists' basic commitment should be to social movements (in both blocs) which can offer a democratic resolution of the East-West conflict.

"Shared analysis of global trends provides the basis for a U.S.-Soviet agenda designed to build the foundations of a more cooperative relationship."

Cooperation Can Promote Peace

Richard H. Solomon

In the following viewpoint, Richard H. Solomon asserts that the US and the Soviet Union must cooperate to attain a peaceful relationship. He argues that collaboration on human rights issues, economics, and technology, will bring the superpowers together and will promote a lasting peace between the two countries. Solomon is the director of the US government's policy planning staff. This viewpoint is an excerpt from a speech he gave to the Soviet Ministry of Foreign Affairs in Moscow.

As you read, consider the following questions:

1. Why does Solomon argue that cooperation will promote peace between the US and the USSR?
2. According to Solomon, what are the global trends that necessitate a new relationship with the USSR?
3. What changes does Solomon recommend in US policy?

Richard H. Solomon, "An Agenda for US-Soviet Cooperation," *Current Policy No. 1129*, November 1988. Published by the United States Department of State, Bureau of Public Affairs.

One of our concerns, as we look toward the future, is the "new political thinking" put forward by President Gorbachev and Foreign Minister Shevardnadze. Their bold and farsighted program of reform for the Soviet Union, and the dramatic ferment it has unleashed in your country, have captured the interest and the hopes of many Americans. What kind of change will *perestroika, glasnost,* and *demokratizatsia* bring to your country? What does it mean for the United States when we are told that Soviet foreign policy is no longer governed by the theory of "class struggle?" And do the concepts of "reasonable sufficiency" and "nonoffensive defense" offer real prospects for diminishing the military confrontation that has burdened our relationship for the past 40 years? The form and substance you give to such concepts will have an important impact on our own approach to arms control, and to the evolution of our relations. . . .

Based on the substantial progress made in U.S.-Soviet relations in recent years, we are now able to explore the following question: In what ways can our two countries cooperate so as to move us beyond the confrontations of the cold war era?

Our "dialogue of planners" is designed to help answer this question. "New thinking" is required on our side as well as yours. We cannot allow rigid policy guidelines, outdated concepts, or stereotypes to prevent us from developing new ways of meeting the profound changes that are taking place in the world. We cannot afford to be prisoners of doctrines developed generations ago in very different times and circumstances. Yet, we must also be realists. It will take time and mutual efforts to unburden ourselves of the legacy of decades of confrontation.

I would like to share with you two future-oriented aspects of our dialogue: first, our assessment of the global trends that require us all to adjust to a new future; and second, the kind of agenda for U.S.-Soviet relations that could move us away from confrontation and toward increasing cooperation.

New Global Trends

Secretary of State Shultz, in a series of speeches, explored the transformation of our economies from the agrarian era to the industrial age to what is now emerging as an era of information technologies. As policy planners, what is particularly interesting about today's "information revolution" is its profound impact on global economic, political, and security trends.

I might summarize the most evident of these trends as follows.

• Scientific and economic power is dispersing widely around the world. Countries such as China, India, and Israel are getting into the space launch business. South Korea, Brazil, and Singapore are major producers of electronic products. At the same time, the gap between the advanced countries and the less developed, between those participating in the information revolution and those that are not, continues to widen. Even as China and India become self-sufficient in grain production and develop high-technology industries, a major portion of the African Continent is increasingly burdened with the threat of famine, and many of its people live generations away from the world of computers, industrial robots, and satellite communications.

More US-Soviet Cooperation

Even during the frosty years of the Cold War, the United States and the Soviet Union continued to pursue a variety of unpublicized cooperative efforts.

Now, as the current thaw proceeds, these measures have been reaffirmed, and agreements have been signed in the areas of transportation, navigation, space, fishing, nuclear reactor safety, environment and global climate, Arctic research, and drug trafficking. President Reagan's National Security Advisor, Colin Powell, has described these projects as "a very important aspect of building a lasting peace with the Soviet Union."

Friends Committee on National Legislation, *FCNL Washington Newsletter,* January 1989.

• This dispersion of power is eroding the bipolar world of the 1950s and 1960s. China is now moving to a position of greater equidistance in its relations between the United States and the U.S.S.R. New coalitions of states are forming, especially on a regional basis, to deal with problems of economic growth and security. I have in mind such groupings as ASEAN [Association of South East Asian Nations] in Southeast Asia and the Gulf Cooperation Council in Southwest Asia. And new international institutions are being created – or old ones are being strengthened – to deal with the challenges of this emerging era.

Interdependence

• There is a clear trend toward interdependence and integration on a global scale. Satellite communications and modern transportation now make possible a worldwide financial market, the cross-national production and marketing of industrial products, and instantaneous global transmission of news broadcasts. Yet, perhaps in reaction to these trends, we also see tendencies toward economic protectionism and isolationism – even in as internationalized a country as the United States.

• The character of the nation-state is being transformed. Countries are being "pulled apart" by the opposing forces of national integration into the global economic and political order and by the concurrent trend toward decentralization of domestic economic management and political democratization. Yet, the concept of state sovereignty endures, even as national governments are increasingly unable to control currency values or the information that crosses sovereign borders through electronic means, and as they find that problems of security or ecology can be dealt with only through cooperative measures with other states.

• This trend toward global interdependence is also producing a worldwide culture of common information and material products, shared music, and common cuisine. At the same time, we also see parochial trends of language, nationalism, and religious fundamentalism that, while giving people a sense of identity in this era of rapid change, also help to fuel unresolved ethnic conflicts and regional disputes.

Political Decentralization

• We see a worldwide trend toward political decentralization and a stress on human rights. Military regimes and highly centralized governments are finding that they cannot deal with the challenges and opportunities of this emerging new era without major political and economic reforms. From Argentina to El Salvador, from the Philippines to South Korea, there is a continuing, if unstable, pattern of democratization. And in the communist world – in China and the Soviet Union in particular – we find concurrent efforts to adapt Marxist-Leninist political institutions to this new era.

• And finally, despite the advances in material well-being offered by this era of spreading high-technology capabilities, there are also sources of greater insecurity: the proliferation of highly destructive weaponry – aircraft, missiles, chemical weapons – and the emergence of new threats to personal security – the international drug trade, terrorism, and ecological damage.

Ambassador Mendelevich and I, in our productive exchanges, largely agree on this assessment of global trends. Yet we have significant differences in our policy perspectives on dealing with these challenges. Our contrasting views could be described as the difference between a "top down" approach to problem-solving and one "from the bottom up." It is the difference between a "comprehensive system of international security" and day-by-day cooperation to combat terrorism or to constrain the international arms trade.

Despite these differences, our shared analysis of global trends provides the basis for a U.S.-Soviet agenda designed to build the foundations of a more cooperative relationship. Let me describe how I see this agenda.

The changes now underway in Soviet foreign and domestic policies have dramatically expanded the working agenda for U.S.-Soviet relations adopted at the Geneva summit in 1985. Our dialogue in the four areas of human rights and humanitarian affairs, arms control, regional problems, and bilateral issues is now intensive and increasingly focused on practical achievements.

And what is just as important as the practical issues we are working on is that we are gradually and carefully eroding the mistrust of the past and laying a foundation of mutual confidence. Over time, this will help us expand our agenda of cooperation. If we learned anything from the experience of detente in the 1970s, it was that trust cannot be manufactured simply through vague "agreements in principle" or by high-sounding exchanges between leaders. It must be built from the bottom up, issue by issue, and it must be fortified by continuing efforts to solve concrete problems. This is not to slight the importance of broad concepts which can guide us toward the future in a time of great change; yet, the most durable foundation of mutual confidence will be built by more agreements of the sort now helping to avoid incidents at sea and more treaties of the INF [Intermediate-Range Nuclear Forces] variety, not by new "codes of conduct" or abstract commitments to "peaceful coexistence."

Development of Cooperation

It is important to refrain from steps that could complicate the negotiating process and give a fresh impetus to the arms race, also under the pretext of modernization.

The all-around development of cooperation in other areas of international relations would also promote the growth of confidence among states and the enhancement of their mutual security. The creation of favorable conditions for the development of cooperation in the areas of economy, trade, science and technology, ecological safety, as well as in the area of human rights, human dimension with respect for the sovereignty of states, and noninterference in their internal affairs, would be to the benefit not only of Europe, but also of the whole world.

Warsaw Treaty Countries, *News and Views from the USSR*, May 23, 1989.

In assessing prospects for new forms of U.S.-Soviet cooperation, we must recognize that we are dealing with a process, one that will be prudent, practical, and evolutionary. We are not heading for utopia. The fundamental differences that have divided us in the past are not going to disappear as if by magic. Our two nations will continue to be competitors and to have conflicting interests; and our peoples will continue to have differing values and outlooks. Yet, to the extent that we succeed in identifying common interests and creating practical solutions to concrete problems, we can build a foundation of public support for cooperative efforts. And hopes are high in many circles that this is the new direction in which our relations are headed.

Let me develop this perspective in more detail, in terms of the four-part agenda.

The US-Soviet Agenda

First, human rights – Human rights is always high on our agenda, because the values we associate with the term are essential to a just and peaceful world, and because the American people give great weight to human rights concerns in our dealings with other countries. Public support for cooperative activities that our two governments might undertake rests on concrete progress in the human dimension of our relationship.

As we look at the recent pattern of Soviet human rights performance, we see a moving, shifting picture, not the grim, frozen image which was so long in our mind's eye. This is a vital area which you are now addressing in the context of your own political and legal reforms. We welcome this process, and anticipate further progress.

In this area, as in others, the United States favors a realistic, problem-solving approach. Our starting point is the plight of the individual – divided spouses, the refusenik, the religious believer, the dissident in a psychiatric hospital, and the imprisoned human rights activist. Our interest then extends to the larger legislative, administrative, and juridical framework in which the fundamental rights of the individual can be protected and their exercise given positive encouragement.

We have engaged in a practical, official dialogue on human rights and humanitarian affairs with you since 1987. This is a remarkable development in comparison with past practice, and the dialogue is now expanding beyond governmental channels to involve parliamentarians, lawyers, psychiatrists, and other interested private citizens. Our dialogue gives real meaning to *glasnost* and will facilitate the expansion of your external relations.

There is still great room for further developments both in your reforms and in our discussions. Your efforts will be an important source of the trust and confidence we hope to build into the relationship in the coming years.

Next, security and arms control, a major area of cooperation and progress in our relations –The recent achievement of the INF Treaty affirms the value of a concrete, practical approach to problem-solving. Unfortunately, some Soviet arms control proposals have been substantially less practical. One example is the notion of creating a non-nuclear world by the year 2000. We, too, look forward to a future free of the threat of nuclear annihilation. President Reagan and General Secretary Gorbachev agreed that "a nuclear war cannot be won and must never be fought." Yet, while we share this lofty goal, the United States and its allies are not about to cast aside – even rhetorically – the system of nuclear deterrence that, like it or not, has kept the peace for more than 40 years.

A More Secure World

We seek a safer, more secure world. Yet, history would not look kindly on us if, in the interest of eliminating nuclear weapons, we only made the world safer for conventional warfare. We want not only major reductions in nuclear arms but also a more stable balance in conventional arms at the lowest possible levels. We want reductions that are verifiable as well as stabilizing. This is not to say we can be complacent about the risks of nuclear weapons. Since the 1960s, the United States has unilaterally reduced its stockpile of nuclear weapons by 33% and our total megatonnage by 75%.

In the period ahead, we should complete the negotiations on 50% reductions in strategic offensive forces. And it is now time to give serious thought to where the broad range of arms control discussions—on strategic arms, defenses, testing, conventional weapons, chemical arms, and missile proliferation—is taking us. We have a unique opportunity to give concrete meaning to the goal of "strategic stability"—in part by considering whether strategic defenses can in time be used to enhance stability.

A Cooperative Model

A cooperative model of relations is needed to ensure the mutual security of the USSR and the United States. Such a model does not need a common enemy like traditional military and political alliances. The purpose of Soviet-American cooperation should be mutual survival on the basis of an enduring and positive balance of interests.

Sergey M. Rogov, *Foreign Policy,* Spring 1989.

We are learning from the experience of INF verification that the process of building trust is dynamic and evolutionary. Patterns of openness and cooperation on sensitive military matters are growing as we implement the treaty. Direct contacts between our military officials . . . can have a profound effect in building confidence and making possible further efforts to solve practical problems. . . .

Which brings me to the third element of our cooperative agenda: regional conflicts – Since 1987 we have achieved levels of mutual understanding that were quite unimaginable at the time we decided in Geneva in 1985 to embark on regional experts consultations. And we have made significant progress on some of the conflicts that have long engendered distrust in our relations – most notably Afghanistan and southern Africa. . . .

As *perestroika* advances, we are finding new areas of common interest for practical cooperation. Cultural and scientific exchanges have expanded dramatically since 1986. And our bilateral trade and economic relations are also likely to expand as the Soviet economy shifts toward a market orientation.

We must recognize, however, that economic success in today's world does not come with membership in this or that international organization. It is based on being competitive in a rapidly changing global marketplace; it comes with producing goods and services that are world class in quality. Achieving these objectives will depend largely on the progress of your reforms. Many nations before you have discovered that there are no easy solutions to such fundamental problems as price reform or currency convertibility; yet they are the basis of your integration into the international economy.

In conclusion, Americans draw great hope from the remarkable progress made in U.S.-Soviet relations since the Geneva summit of 1985. We now have before us new opportunities to resolve a broad range of problems that have long troubled our relationship, and to build new patterns of cooperation. . . .

US-Soviet Cooperation

Some countries may not always react positively to new forms of U.S.-Soviet cooperation. Some may exaggerate in their own minds the extent of U.S.-Soviet "collusion," and they may seek to resist our cooperative efforts. Should these concerns arise, they must be addressed. Our task will be to reassure allies and friends that improvements in U.S.-Soviet relations will not come at the expense of older and deeper friendships and alliance commitments.

And, as Ambassador Mendelevich suggested to [the State Department's] "Open Forum" audience, our two countries have a special responsibility to manage our differences so that we compete without becoming hostile adversaries, and we must seek new opportunities to transform our relationship from that of opponents to partners. . . .

We must strive—as Ambassador Mendelevich has suggested—to make the process of improving Soviet-American relations irreversible this time. Our common goal must be to attempt to redirect our competition into areas that are less threatening to our mutual security and to find cooperative ways to build the better world we each seek.

"Our goal is disarmament and the non-violent settlement of international conflicts."

Citizen Diplomacy Can Promote Peace

Galina Sidorova

The author of the following viewpoint, Galina Sidorova, participated in the Soviet-American Peace March during the summer of 1988 from Washington, DC to California. Sidorova writes that events like the Peace March deepen the relationship between ordinary citizens of the US and the USSR. She asserts that such citizen action can provide a base for a more peaceful relationship between the United States and the Soviet Union. Sidorova is a special correspondent for *New Times*, a Soviet weekly newsmagazine.

As you read, consider the following questions:

1. According to the author, what were some of the goals of the Peace March?
2. How were the Soviet members of the Peace March treated in the US, according to Sidorova?
3. What cultural differences did Sidorova and other marchers note between the US and the USSR?

Galina Sidorova, "Travellers on the Road," *New Times*, No. 26, July 1988.

We are on the move. Our feet leave imprints in the rubbery asphalt. Our clothing sticks to us. The humid 40-degree air is motionless. It begins to seem as if the inventive American civilization has faded away. To onlookers, we probably look like the first colonists who advanced to conquer new lands. But we differ from those who crossed the Atlantic at the dawn of the American state in certain achievements of scientific and technical progress: trailers carry our tents and sleeping bags, there are mobile toilets, and a bus to pick up those who have reached the limits of their endurance. But few people avail themselves of its services. Most persist in walking on their own two feet, despite the warnings of some of the people looking on that it is impossible to walk in such a heat.

We continue to march. Cars and faces pass us by. From time to time we hear the question: what are you marching for?

The Great Peace March

I, too, asked myself that question back in 1986 during the Soviet-American Mississippi cruise when, in the town of Davenport (Iowa), we met with participants in the Great Peace March. A week before I left for the United States this time I received a letter from Anne Macfarlane, a New Zealander, one of the few foreigners who took part in that march. Our paths had crossed in Davenport. She sent me her book "Feet Across America." Reading the details of that nine-month epic of Americans and like-minded foreigners, I again stopped to think: what had prompted them to go through such hardships and privations, to be drenched by the rain, covered with snow, cross the desert and fall ill? To attract attention to their aims and convictions? Yes, that, I would say, was the reason. Incidentally, in the United States marches are a traditional way of expressing one's views. It was, in 1986, that the American organization International Peace Walk (IPW) came into being and together with the Soviet Peace Committee sponsored the Leningrad-Moscow March in 1987 and now the march across the United States.

"If we have enough honesty and courage we can inspire others," Allan Affeldt, former psychology lecturer at a California college and now international Peace Walk President, remarked to me. "Our goal" he added, "is disarmament and the non-violent settlement of international conflicts. The most serious confrontations are those that could arise between the U.S.S.R. and the U.S.A. That is why today we are searching for ways to combat the causes that could give rise to them."

"We" means the 200 Soviet and about 100 American participants ranging in age from 8 to 70 who are taking part in the peace march. We have to walk across the United States from Washington to San Francisco in 32 days. Some sections of the route will be covered by bus or plane – since the territory of the country is so vast. Each day we walk about 12-15 miles.

How do we live?

We get up at 6.30 a.m., crawl out of our sleeping bags and tents, and rush to the water cisterns with toothbrushes and shaving equipment. Then we hurry to collapsible tables where a light breakfast and a packed lunch of sandwiches and vegetables await us. After that we pack the heavier equipment onto the trailer and set off. Some of the marchers make their ways to different local organizations – factories, schools, colleges, firms, farms and the church, while the majority march on to the next stopover.

Soviet-American Relations

There is an old tale about a teacher who summoned a pupil, drew a straight line on the sand and said: "Destroy it without moving the sand and without erasing the line." The pupil thought and drew another, longer line parallel to the first one.

In Soviet-American relations one can already discern the line drawn by new thinking, the recent meetings and agreements that have given a boost to citizen diplomacy. This line is now more pronounced, but the line left by the cold war and stagnation in international relations also makes itself felt. What will the relationship between these lines be by the beginning of the new year and the next decade? One hopes that the old line will be shorter than the new one.

Irina Lagunina, *New Times,* no. 48, November 1988.

During the 45-minute lunch break on the grass we more or less recover. We joyfully sluice ourselves down with water and drink without end: Americans believe that this is essential during a march in hot humid weather. Then we start off again. But with greater enthusiasm to the next place where we strike camp.

Each day we become more expert in putting up our tents.

Round about five o'clock, somewhere in the vicinity of our next camp, the shower rented by the organizers of the march starts functioning – that is the happiest moment of the day for everyone.

By the time we have had our showers, people from the neighbouring towns have gathered at the camp, attracted simply by curiosity or a sincere desire to learn more about our cause. Sometimes there are more, sometimes fewer. As a rule, there are more when we stop in middle-class prosperous places, and fewer where people have enough problems of their own.

Some of them take us to their homes, some to pot-luck meals in the local churches – a uniquely American arrangement, when parishioners bring some of their own cooking or baking to feed the whole company. At the camp there is a constant stream of people coming and going. We talk, talk, talk until late at night, and as the final act of each day we pump up our mattresses, and lie down on the moist warm American soil that smells so much like that of Central Russia. At night the police watch over us, especially when we stop over in areas closest to the poorest quarters, like in Fairmount Park, Philadelphia. In that backwoods, my colleagues from the daily papers had to walk a long way to the nearest telephone in the police precinct. A rare situation for America, where telephones exist in every house.

A Symbol

So what after all is our march?

Of course, it is a symbol of sorts. Its beginning at the steps of the Capitol was symbolic with the blessing of Senator Tom Harkin. It was he who in 1987 came out in the Senate in support of the Soviet-American march. Equally symbolic was the fact that the Senator quoted Abraham Lincoln's words about two ways of getting rid of an enemy: either destroying him physically, or making a friend of him.

Symbolic too were the proclamations adopted by the mayors of most of the towns along our route, starting with that of Mayor Marion Barry of the District of Columbia. He proclaimed the day we spent in the town as Soviet-American Peace March Day and called on the people to support it. In the town of Tacoma Park (Maryland) after making his proclamation, Mayor Stephen J. Del Giudice told us that recently the town's authorities had decided not to buy goods from companies that produced nuclear armaments. That too is symbolic, isn't it?

Equally symbolic was the candlelight concert in Willington given by Soviet and American artists taking part in the march. It took place on June 22, 1988 and attracted an audience of about fifteen hundred. Also symbolic that evening was the sermon in memory of those killed in the second world war preached by an Orthodox priest taking part in the march.

Symbolic too was the indifference to our march that we noticed passing through Washington and certain other towns, as well as the hospitality of those who offered us supper at our camps or to put us up in their homes.

The history of Soviet-American relations in recent years is in many respects made up of symbols. They are like beacons marking the way. They create the atmosphere without which concrete political decisions are impossible.

But of course the march was far from being just a symbol. Travellers met on a single road leading to a common goal – we want to build new mutual relations. Our small march community is a sort of model of such relations, with all the difficulties and

advantages of them. Pluses and minuses. A fairly motley community. How not to become just fellow travellers, sharing a tent, but
also friends. It turned out that learning to share the hardships and
discomforts of life on the march is easier than learning to understand one another. Especially since the Americans sought in every
way to make things easier for us and took over many of the camp
duties.

Why the difficulties?

One evening we discussed that with 27-year-old Marie Connor.
She is planning to teach in college or work in a Catholic church.
In general, mixing with people, helping them with advice and
bringing them reassurance is her goal in life.

Building Trust

Even if the U.S.A. and the U.S.S.R. destroy all nuclear weapons,
we would still be able to find many other ways of killing one
another. That's why I find it so important to . . . build up trust.

Personally I learned a lot when I was in Vietnam: people are the
same everywhere. The same problems. The same hurts.

Al LaGrange, *New Times*, no. 32, August 1988.

"My parents don't understand me," she said, "I left home and
live with strangers. But they have become closer to me than my
own family. I saw war and death when I traveled in Latin America.
And I'm no idealist, like many of my compatriots taking part in
this march."

"What do you mean by idealism?"

"Some Americans taking part in the anti-war movement come
from well-off families with few troubles. What they are doing is
done with sincerity. It comes from their hearts, but they don't
always see things realistically. They think that because we are walking across America together, because we have a common goal, we
are changing the world. I don't believe it is as simple as that. That
is only a beginning. And as in every new thing – I have in mind
the establishment of more normal relations between our countries
and individual citizens – lots of problems arise. In day-to-day relations between Soviet people and Americans, in the little things,
meetings and at times clashes of culture arise. Many expected that
here in our small community we would be able to create an ideal
world in which everyone would feel happy. It's as if we expect
perfection from others. But ideal relations have not developed. We
are not perfect, and that bothers some people. I think some of the
Americans would have dropped out of the march already if the
knowledge of the 2,500 dollars paid for it did not stop them, and

if so much effort had not been made to get you to come. But I think that by the end of the march many of those who would now like to drop out will be glad they didn't. Today we speak too often about how similar we are, shutting our eyes to the differences, but that too is wrong. Because it is through understanding the differences that the way to mutual understanding lies."

The Main Difference

"And what do you see as the main difference?"

"Well, culture and tradition, and our perception of certain problems. For instance, the Soviet leadership of the march seeks to overorganize everything down to the last detail, to programme it. Americans are inclined to let some things slide, which of course causes a degree of chaos, but we are used to it. And another thing that I believe to be very important – the horrors of war are in the Soviet people's blood. For Americans it is something more distant and abstract."

"So you're more of a pessimist than an optimist?"

"No, I'm not a pessimist. What gives me hope is people's reaction to the march. When we visit people in their homes, when we are greeted en route, when people express support through a joke or a kind word, then I feel they are beginning to see themselves in you. And then I feel both proud and happy that we are together."

We were joined by Ron Herson, now retired, but who in the past worked as a radiologist in California. Together with his wife Pat he took part in the Leningrad March, and in general has travelled half the world on foot. He's been to China, to the Himalayas.

The Peace Walk

The couple are enthusiastic supporters of the Soviet-American peace walk. But Ron and "Granny" Pat have their own ideas about the difficulties.

"You are far too secretive," he said, "You don't like to speak about your mistakes, as if they will disappear if you don't talk about them. We Americans shout at every corner about our mistakes. It's a good thing that you yourselves are beginning to view many things differently. And we look at ourselves more critically. During the march I took a fresh look at myself, at us Americans."

Listening to Marie and Ron I thought about us marchers, travellers on a road leading to a better world. We are both like and unlike those first American colonists. We are opening up "new territories" in ourselves, in our consciousness, education and culture. We are slowly and with difficulty ousting from these "territories" prejudice and mutual mistrust. We are rediscovering America. And it is discovering us. More about these discoveries in my next report. Meanwhile dawn is breaking and we are preparing to move on.

We are on the march. . . .

Understanding Words in Context

Readers occasionally come across words which they do not recognize. And frequently, because they do not know a word or words, they will not fully understand the passage being read. Obviously, the reader can look up an unfamiliar word in a dictionary. However, by carefully examining the word in the context in which it is used, the word's meaning can often be determined. A careful reader may find clues to the meaning of the word in surrounding words, ideas, and attitudes.

Below are sentences adapted from the viewpoints in this chapter. In each excerpt, one of the words is printed in italics. Try to determine the meaning of each word by reading the excerpt. Under each excerpt you will find four definitions for the italicized word. Choose the one that is closest to your understanding of the word.

Finally, use a dictionary to see how well you have understood the words in context. It will be helpful to discuss with others the clues which helped you decide on each word's meaning.

1. US dominance over the rest of the world after World War II was a *TRANSIENT* situation. It is now a thing of the past.

   TRANSIENT means:
   a) permanent   c) temporary
   b) bad   d) common

2. Throughout history successful dictatorships kept their captive peoples just hungry enough to *FORESTALL* revolt. With the growing discontent in Poland, Estonia, and Armenia, that careful balance is endangered.

   FORESTALL means:
   a) cause   c) crush
   b) prevent   d) preach

3. There are two opposing trends in today's world. One is a trend towards a worldwide culture of common information and consumer products. At the same time, we also see *PAROCHIAL* trends of maintaining ethnic identity and language. This divides the world and causes disputes.

PAROCHIAL means:
a) private
b) localized
c) universal
d) commercialized

4. The reunification of Europe will not be easy. But for the sake of peace, we cannot DESIST from the task.

DESIST means:
a) give up
b) succeed
c) try again
d) rise

5. People serving in government are often more cautious than those outside it. One reason the US peace movement has lost steam is that it allowed the *CONSTRAINTS* of politicians in Congress to become its own.

CONSTRAINTS means:
a) supporters
b) opponents
c) treaties
d) limits

6. The chance of improving Soviet-American relations is too precious to *SQUANDER* by making sweeping but impractical proposals. Instead, let us proceed carefully step by step so this opportunity is not lost.

SQUANDER means:
a) save
b) want
c) waste
d) grow

7. Recent changes in the Soviet Union are shaking the foundations of the Cold War, which were built on the image of the USSR as an *IMPLACABLE* and terrible enemy.

IMPLACABLE means:
a) large
b) unforgiving
c) approachable
d) insignificant

251

Periodical Bibliography

The following articles have been selected to supplement the diverse views presented in this chapter.

Wim Bartels
"Without a Polemic Itch," *New Times*, no. 28, July 20, 1987.

Janos Berecz
"From Big Brother to Big Mac," *New Perspectives Quarterly*, Winter 1988/1989.

Corneliu Bogdan
"Crossing the European Divide," *Foreign Policy*, Summer 1989.

Craig Comstock
"How the US Surprises the Russians," *World Monitor: The Christian Science Monitor Monthly*, July 1989.

Henry Kissinger
"Untangling Alliances," *Los Angeles Times*, April 16, 1989.

Michael Klamer, interviewed by John Galvin
"Keep the Powder Dry," *Time*, May 29, 1989.

The Nation
"By the Numbers," June 19, 1989.

William Pfaff
"The West Must Decide if It Would Feel Secure with an Independent Eastern Europe," *Los Angeles Times*, April 3, 1989.

Hella Pick
"Can Europe Be Separate but Equal?" *World Press Review*, December 1988.

Alexander Pumpyansky
"No Longer Unconcerned," *New Times*, no. 32, August 17, 1987.

Sergey M. Rogov
"Detente Is Not Enough," *Foreign Policy*, Spring 1989.

Galina Sidorova
"Accord Projected into the Future," *New Times*, no. 5, January 31/February 6, 1989.

Michel Tatu
"Bush Is Right About Moscow," *The New York Times*, May 30, 1989.

Alan Tonelson and Christopher Layne
"Divorce, Alliance Style," *The New Republic*, June 12, 1989.

James J. Townsend
"Moscow's Peace Offensive," *The World & I*, April 1989.

Organizations To Contact

The editors have compiled the following list of organizations which are concerned with the issues debated in this book. All of them have publications or information available for interested readers. The descriptions are derived from materials provided by the organizations. This list was compiled upon the date of publication. Names and phone numbers of organizations are subject to change.

American Committee on US-Soviet Relations
109 11th St. SE
Washington, DC 20003
(202) 546-1700

The committee includes members of the academic and business communities, former ambassadors, labor leaders, and public interest spokespersons. It believes tensions between East and West can be reduced by strategic arms agreements, trade, and scientific and cultural exchanges. The Committee publishes *Soviet Outlook*, as well as books and occasional papers, including, "Abstract, Stability, and Change in International Relations," "Gorbachev and the Ghost of Stalin: History and the Politics of Reform," and "The Nineteenth Conference of the CPSU: Politics and Policy."

American Enterprise Institute for Public Policy Research (AEI)
1150 17th St. NW
Washington, DC 20036
(202) 862-5800

AEI is a conservative research and education organization which aims to provide an analysis of national and international issues. It promotes the spread of democracy and a strong military to protect against the spread of communism and totalitarianism. It publishes the monthly *AEI Economist*, the bimonthly *Public Opinion*, and the book, *Taking Glasnost Seriously: Toward an Open Soviet Union*.

American Security Council
499 S. Capitol St., Suite 500
Washington, DC 20003
(202) 484-1676

The Council sponsors the Coalition for Peace Through Strength, an alliance of organizations, pro-defense lawmakers, and US citizens. It supports a strong defense policy and resisting Soviet influence around the world. The Council recently published the booklet *A Strategy for Peace Through Strength*, and publishes the monthly *National Security Report*.

The Brookings Institution
1175 Massachusetts Ave. NW
Washington, DC 20036
(202) 797-6000

The Institution, founded in 1927, is a liberal think tank that conducts research and education in economics, government, and foreign policy. It publishes the quarterly *Brookings Review*, the biannual *Brookings Papers on Economic Activity*, and the book, *The Struggle for the Third World*.

Cardinal Mindszenty Foundation
PO Box 11321
St. Louis, MO 63105
(314) 991-9490

This anti-communist organization was founded in 1958 to conduct educational and research activities concerning communist objectives, tactics, and propaganda. The Foundation publishes the monthly *Mindszenty Report*.

Cato Institute
224 Second St. SE
Washington, DC 20003
(202) 546-0200

The Institute is a conservative public policy research foundation dedicated to increasing foreign policy debate. Several of its publications have addressed superpower relations and the Cold War. It publishes the bimonthly *Policy Report*, the triennial *Cato Journal*, and the book, *Collective Defense or Strategic Independence?*

CAUSA USA
One Pen Plaza, Suite 100
New York, NY 10119
(202) 529-7700

CAUSA is an educational organization working to promote democracy. It opposes the influence and expansion of communism. CAUSA publishes the monthly *CAUSA USA Report*.

Christian Anti-Communism Crusade, Inc. (CACC)
PO Box 890
Long Beach, CA 90801
(213) 437-0941

The Crusade, founded in 1953, sponsors anti-subversive seminars "to inform Americans of the philosophy, morality, organization, techniques, and strategy of communism and associated forces." CACC publishes a free, semi-monthly newsletter called the *Christian Anti-Communism Crusade Newsletter* and the brochure, "Why I Am Against Communism." Its books include *You Can't Trust the Communists*, *Why Communism Kills*, and *What Is Communism?*

Citizen Diplomacy (CD)
PO Box 9077
La Jolla, CA 92038
(619) 456-8049

Citizen Diplomacy believes citizen exchanges can promote and improve US-Soviet relations. CD publishes *Citizen Diplomat* bimonthly.

Citizen Exchange Council (CEC)
12 W. 31st St.
New York, NY 10001-4415
(212) 643-1985

CEC seeks to promote mutual understanding between American and Soviet citizens. The Council organizes cultural, educational, and professional travel programs for Americans in the USSR and provides programs and hospitality for Soviet visitors in the US. It publishes pamphlets on its high school, college, religious, and arts groups, and the quarterly *Communique*.

Committee on the Present Danger
905 16th St. NW, Suite 207
Washington, DC 20006
(202) 628-2409

The Committee contends that the Soviet Union's advantage in military forces threatens US national security. Its occasional paper "Can America Catch Up: The US-Soviet Military Balance," addresses this issue. The Committee also collected several of its papers on US security policy in the book, *Alerting America*.

Communist Party of the United States of America
235 W. 23rd St., 7th Floor
New York, NY 10011
(212) 989-4994

The Communist Party works to create a socialist society. It believes Soviet policies support peace and it works for improved relations between the US and the USSR. It publishes the *People's Daily World* newspaper and the monthly *Political Affairs* magazine.

Council for the Defense of Freedom
1275 K St., Suite 1160
Washington, DC 20005
(202) 789-4294

The Council for the Defense of Freedom argues that the US must act to stop communist aggression. Its weekly paper, *The Washington Inquirer*, covers the arms race and Soviet intervention in other countries. It also publishes a monthly *Bulletin* and monographs.

Department of Defense
Public Correspondence Division
Defense Information Services
Office of Assistant Secretary of Defense (Public Affairs)
The Pentagon
Washington, DC 20301-1400
(202) 697-5737

The Department is responsible for providing the military forces needed to deter war and protect the security of the US. It also plans policy on strategic international security matters. Write for a list of books and materials on foreign policy and an order form.

Department of State
Office of Public Communication
Public Information Service
Bureau of Public Affairs, Room 4827A
Washington, DC 20520
(202) 647-6575

The Department of State determines US foreign policy. It publishes speeches and testimonies by government officials concerning US-Soviet relations and arms control. Write or call the State Department for a list of publications.

Educators for Social Responsibility (ESR)
23 Garden St.
Cambridge, MA 02138
(617) 492-1764

ESR believes US suspicion toward the Soviet Union is unjustified and prevents good relations between the two countries. It promotes peace by educating students to understand the Soviet people. ESR publishes the quarterly newsletter, *Forum*, and books, including *The Other Side: How Soviets and Americans Perceive Each Other*, *Getting Acquainted: Thinking About the Soviet Union*, and *Comprehensive Peace Education*.

Fellowship of Reconciliation (FOR)
Box 271
Nyack, NY 10960
(914) 358-4601

The Fellowship, founded in 1915, is a non-denominational pacifist organization. It "attempts, through education and action, to substitute nonviolence and reconciliation for violence in international relations." FOR publishes the pamphlets, "Grassroots Diplomacy: Reconciling the Superpowers," "Linking Bush and Gorbachev to the Love of God: A Faithful Response to Gorbachev's Reforms," and "Overcoming Obsessive Anti-Communism," among others. It publishes books, including *Making Friends with Enemies*, and *Pilgrim to the Russian Church*, as well as the monthly magazine, *Fellowship*, which covers nonviolence and disarmament issues.

Institute for Soviet-American Relations (ISAR)
1608 New Hampshire Ave. NW
Washington, DC 20009
(202) 387-3034

The Institute works to maintain and improve Soviet-American relations by encouraging exchanges between Soviet and American groups and individuals. ISAR encourages legislation to reinstate lapsed governmental exchange agreements and to increase federal support for other exchange programs. ISAR publishes the quarterly journal *Surviving Together*.

Liberty Lobby
300 Independence Ave. SE
Washington, DC 20003
(202) 546-5611

The Lobby, founded in 1955, is a group of "nationalists and populists interested in political action." It contends that the USSR continues to threaten US national security and that the US should not trust the Soviet Union. It publishes the weekly *Spotlight*, the *Congressional Handbook*, and *Liberty Ledger*.

National Council of American-Soviet Friendship (NCASF)
85 E. Fourth St.
New York, NY 10003
(212) 254-6606

The Council was established in 1943 to encourage better relations between the US and the Soviet Union so that the two powers can work together to bring about world peace. NCASF promotes good business relations as a basis for peaceful coexistence. It works to promote a US foreign policy of cooperation with the USSR and works for disarmament. It publishes the *Friendship News* quarterly.

Soviet Embassy
Information Department
1706 18th St. NW
Washington, DC 20009
(202) 232-6020

The Soviet Embassy distributes speeches by Mikhail Gorbachev and other Soviet leaders on topics including disarmament, Soviet reforms, and the development of the Soviet economy. Among the publications available are *Yearbook USSR*, an annual review of events; *Soviet Life*, a monthly photo feature newsmagazine; *USSR, 100 Questions and Answers*; and *News and Views from the Soviet Union*, its series of press releases.

United States Defense Committee (USDC)
450 Maple Ave. E., Suite 201
Vienna, VA 22180
(703) 281-5517

The Committee promotes a strong foreign policy and national defense. It lobbies Congress on defense issues. It publishes the bimonthly *Defense Watch* as well as letters and defense bills.

United States Institute of Peace
1550 M St. NW, Suite 700
Washington, DC 20005-1708
(202) 457-1700

The United States Institute of Peace is a federal institution created and wholly funded by Congress. The Institute seeks to limit international violence, achieve a just peace based on freedom and human dignity, and educate the public about peacemaking. It publishes the bimonthly *The United States Peace Institute Journal*.

Women's International League for Peace and Freedom, US Section (WILPF-US)
1213 Race St.
Philadelphia, PA 19107
(215) 563-7110

The League is a group of women who support nonviolence and disarmament and work to eliminate US economic and military intervention abroad. The League publishes the magazine, *Peace and Freedom*, the *Program and Action Newsletter*, and a bimonthly *Legislative Bulletin*, as well as pamphlets and leaflets.

World Policy Institute (WPI)
777 United Nations Plaza
New York, NY 10017
(212) 490-0010

Founded in 1948, the Institute formulates alternatives to war, social injustice, and ecological damage. WPI publishes *Alternatives: A Journal of World Policy*, the quarterly *Bulletin of Peace Proposals*, and *World Policy Journal*, as well as books and papers.

Forum for US-Soviet Dialogue
c/o Paul Stephen
School of Law
University of Virginia
Charlottesville, VA 22901
(804) 924-7098

The Forum is a cultural and educational exchange organization interested in improving communication between the US and the USSR. It sponsors an annual week-long conference of American and Soviet delegates to discuss US-Soviet relations, arms control, and trade relations. It publishes an annual newsletter, *The Forum*.

Fund for Peace
823 United Nations Plaza, Suite 8110
New York, NY 10017
(212) 661-5900

The Fund seeks ways to improve understanding between the US and the USSR. Its three monthly publications are *The Defense Monitor, First Principles,* and *In the Public Interest.* Its book is *Working for Peace.*

The Heritage Foundation
214 Massachusetts Ave. NE
Washington, DC 20002
(202) 546-4400

The Heritage Foundation is a conservative think tank that examines the Soviet challenge to Western nations and encourages the West to resist this challenge. The Foundation publishes the quarterly *Policy Review.* Its *Backgrounder* series of occasional papers and its *Lectures* series of speeches often cover superpower issues.

Institute for Policy Studies (IPS)
1601 Connecticut Ave. NW
Washington, DC 20009
(202) 234-9382

The Institute's program on national security analyzes and critiques foreign and military policy. It believes the Cold War is unnecessary and must be ended. IPS has a joint exchange with the Institute for the Study of the USA at the USSR Academy of Sciences. The Institute publishes several books, including *The Rise and Fall of the Soviet Threat* and *Soviet Policy in the Arc of Crisis.*

Bibliography of Books

Abel Aganbegyan	*Perestroika 1989*. New York: Charles Scribner's Sons, 1989.
Graham T. Allison and William I. Ury with Bruce J. Allyn, eds.	*From Cold War to Peaceful Competition in U.S.-Soviet Relations*. Cambridge, MA: Ballinger Publishing Co., 1989.
Annelise Anderson and Dennis L. Bark	*Thinking About America*. Stanford, CA: Hoover Institution Press, 1988.
Seweryn Bialer and Michael Mandelbaum	*Gorbachev's Russia and American Foreign Policy*. Boulder, CO: Westview Press, 1989.
Oleg Bogomolov	*Is There a Future for the Warsaw Pact?* London: Hutchinson, 1989.
Mike Bowker and Phil Williams	*Superpower Detente: A Reappraisal*. Beverly Hills, CA: Sage Publications, Inc., 1988.
Zbigniew Brzezinski	*The Grand Failure: The Birth and Death of Communism in the Twentieth Century*. New York: Charles Scribner's Sons, 1989.
Padma Desai	*Perestroika in Perspective*. Princeton, NJ: Princeton University Press, 1989.
Paul Dibb	*The Soviet Union: The Incomplete Superpower*. Champaign, IL: University of Illinois Press, 1988.
Boris Dimitriev	*A Policy Keeping the World on Edge*. Moscow: Progress Publishers, 1987.
Joseph D. Douglass, ed.	*Why the Soviets Violate Arms Control Treaties*. Maclean, VA: Pergamon-Brassey's, 1988.
Nicholas Eberstadt	*The Poverty of Communism*. New Brunswick, NJ: Transaction Books, 1987.
Jeffrey C. Goldfarb	*Beyond Glasnost: The Post Totalitarian Mind*. Chicago: The University of Chicago Press, 1989.
Mikhail Gorbachev	*Perestroika: New Thinking for Our Country and the World*. New York: Harper & Row, 1987.
Mikhail Gorbachev	*Socialism, Peace, and Democracy: Writings, Speeches, and Reports*. London: Zwan Press, 1987.
Mikhail Gorbachev	*Speeches and Writings, Volume Two*. Oxford: Pergamon Press, 1987.
Colin Gray	*The Geopolitics of Superpower*. Lawrence, KS: The University Press of Kansas, 1988.
Ed A. Hewett	*Reforming the Soviet Economy*. Washington, DC: The Brookings Institution, 1988.
Arnold L. Horelick	*U.S.-Soviet Relations*. Ithaca, NY: Cornell University Press, 1988.
Basile Kerblay	*Gorbachev's Russia*. New York: Pantheon Books, 1988.
William Kintner	*Soviet Global Strategy*. Fairfax, VA: Hero Books, 1987.

Richard J. Krickus *The Superpowers in Crisis.* Maclean, VA: Pergamon-Brassey's, 1987.

Walter Laqueur *The Long Road to Freedom: Russia and Glasnost.* New York: Charles Scribner's Sons, 1989.

Robert Legvold *Gorbachev's Foreign Policy: How Should the United States Respond?* New York: Foreign Policy Association, 1989.

Lawrence W. Lerner and Donald W. Treadgold *Gorbachev and the Soviet Future.* Boulder, CO: Westview Press, 1989.

Susan J. Linz and William Moskoff *Reorganization and Reform in the Soviet Economy.* New York: M.E. Sharpe, Inc., 1988.

Vladimir Lopatov *The Soviet Union and Africa.* Moscow: Progress Publishers, 1987.

Michael MccGwire *Perestroika and Soviet National Security.* Washington, DC: The Brookings Institution, 1989.

V. Mezhenkov and E. Skelly *Perestroika in Action.* Wellingborough, UK: Collets, 1988.

Richard Lawrence Miller *Heritage of Fear: Illusion and Reality in the Cold War.* New York: Walker and Co., 1988.

Michael Parenti *The Sword and the Dollar.* New York: St. Martin's Press, 1989.

Arch Puddington *Failed Utopias: Methods of Coercion in Communist Regimes.* San Francisco: Institute for Contemporary Studies Press, 1989.

Peter Savigear *Cold War or Detente in the 1980s?* Brighton, UK: Wheatsheaf Books, Ltd., 1987.

Brent Scowcroft, R. James Woolsey, and Thomas H. Etzold, eds. *Defending Peace and Freedom: Toward Strategic Stability in the Year 2000.* Lanham, MD: University Press of America, 1988.

Judy Shelton *The Coming Soviet Crash: Gorbachev's Desperate Pursuit of Credit in Western Financial Markets.* New York: Free Press, 1989.

Alan B. Sherr *The Other Side of Arms Control.* Boston: Unwin Hyman, 1988.

Alexander Shtromas and Morton A. Kaplan *The Soviet Union and the Challenge of the Future.* Vol. I, *The Soviet System: Stasis and Change.* New York: Paragon House, 1988.

Stewart Smith *Arms and Dollars: Roots of US Foreign Policy.* Moscow: Progress Publishers, 1987.

Jane Shapiro Zacek *The Gorbachev Generation: Issues in Soviet Foreign Policy.* New York: Paragon House, 1988.

Tatiana Zaslavskaya *The Social Dimension of Perestroika.* London: Hutchinson, 1989.

260

Index

263

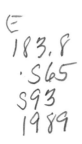